Speech Production and Second Language Acquisition

Speech Production and Second Language Acquisition

Judit Kormos

Eötvös Loránd University of Sciences, Budapest, Hungary

CSSLA
Cognitive Sciences and
Second Language Acquisition

LAWRENCE ERLBAUM ASSOCIATES, PUBLISHERS

2006   Mahwah, New Jersey   London

Lawrence Erlbaum Associates, Inc., Publishers
10 Industrial Avenue
Mahwah, New Jersey 07430
www.erlbaum.com

Cover design by Tomai Maridou

Library of Congress Cataloging-in-Publication Data

Kormos, Judit
Speech production and second language acquisition / Judit Kormos
        p. cm.
Includes bibliographical references and index.
ISBN 0-8058-5657-9 (cloth : alk. paper)
ISBN 0-8058-5658-7 (pbk. : alk. paper)
1. Second language acquisition. 2. Speech. I. Title
P118.2.K65 2006
418—dc22   2005052184
                                                          CIP

Printed in the United States of America
10 9 8 7 6 5 4 3 2 1

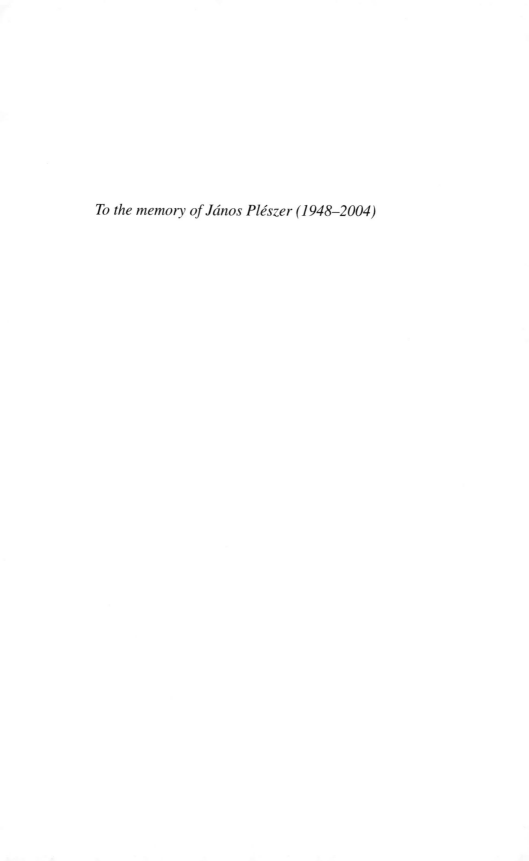

To the memory of János Plészer (1948–2004)

Contents

Series Editor's Preface   xiii

Acknowledgments   xv

Introduction: Issues in L2 Speech   xvii
Production Research
Overview of Issues in L1 Speech Production Research   xviii

Issues at the Major Stages of L2 Speech Production   xx

General Issues in Speech Production   xxiv

Summary   xxvi

PART I

1   *An Overview of Theories of First Language*   3
      Speech Production
Spreading Activation Theory   3

Levelt's Modular Model of Speech Production   7

Summary   11

2   *Issues in First Language Speech Production Research*   12

Research Methods Used in Studying Language Production   12

Conceptualization and Speech Planning   15

Lexical Encoding   19

Syntactic Processing   23

Phonological Encoding   27

Monitoring   **29**

Neurological Studies of Language Production   **33**

Summary   **35**

3 ***Theories of Automaticity and Their Relation to Speech***   **38**
   Production Models
Definitions and Characteristics of Automaticity   **39**

Theories of Automaticity   **40**

The Role of Theories of Automaticity in L1 Learning   **44**
   and Speech Production
Summary   **48**

Recommended Readings   **49**

PART II

4 ***Lexical Encoding and the Bilingual Lexicon***   **55**

Lexical Activation and Selection in L2   **56**

Control in Lexical Encoding   **64**

Conceptual and Lexical Representation in Bilingual Memory   **68**

Models of the Organization of the Bilingual Lexicon   **71**

Code-Switching and Lexical Processing   **82**

The Influence of L1 on Lexical Encoding   **84**

The Acquisition of L2 Lexical Knowledge   **86**

Summary   **90**

5 ***Syntactic and Phonological Encoding***   **91**

A General Overview of Syntactic Encoding Processes   **91**

Diacritic Features: The Encoding of Grammatical Gender   **93**

Accessing Grammatical Morphemes   **97**

The Activation of Syntactic Building Procedures   **99**

Transfer and the Acquisition of L2 Syntactic Knowledge   **100**

Code-Switching and Syntactic Encoding   **107**

Summary of Grammatical Encoding Processes   **108**

General Overview of Phonological Encoding Processes   **109**

The Activation of the Phonological Form of Lexical Items   **111**

Shared Versus Separate Phonological and Phonetic Systems   **112**

The Role of L1 in Phonological and Phonetic Encoding   **116**
   and the Acquisition of L2 Phonology
Summary of Phonological Encoding Processes   **120**

6   *Monitoring*   **122**

Monitoring Processes in L2   **123**

The Role of Attention in Monitoring L2 Speech   **130**

Monitoring and SLA   **132**

Summary   **135**

7   *Problem-Solving Mechanisms in L2 Speech*   **137**

Review of Definitions and Characteristics of Communication   **138**
   Strategies
Lexical Problem-Solving Mechanisms   **140**

Grammatical Problem-Solving Mechanisms   **146**

Phonological Problem-Solving Mechanisms   **147**

Time Pressure–Related Problem-Solving Mechanisms   **150**

Communication Strategies and Language Learning   **152**

Summary   **153**

Ackowledgments   153

8   Fluency and Automaticity in L2 Speech Production   154

Definitions of Fluency   154

Theories of Automaticity and the Development of L2 Fluency   156

Measures of L2 Fluency   162

Summary   165

9   Conclusion: Toward an Integrated Model of L2 Speech   166
      Production
      The General Characteristics of the Bilingual Speech   166
      Production Model
      Encoding Mechanisms and the Structure of Knowledge   169
      Stores in L2 Speech Production
      Transfer, Code-Switching, and Communication Strategies   174
      in the Bilingual Speech Production Model
      Development of L2 Competence in the Bilingual Model   176

Summary   178

Recommended Readings   179

Glossary   183

References   187

Author Index   211

Subject Index   217

CSSLA
Cognitive Sciences and
Second Language Acquisition

Series Advisory Committee Members

Series Editor's Preface

The Cognitive Science and Second Language Acquisition (CSSLA) series is designed to provide accessible and comprehensive coverage of the links between basic concepts and findings in cognitive science (CS) and second language acquisition (SLA) in a systematic way. Taken together, books in the series should combine to provide a comprehensive overview of the conceptual and methodological intersects between these two fields. This means the books in the series can be read alone, or (more profitably) in combination. The field of SLA is related to, but distinct from, linguistics, applied linguistics, cognitive psychology, and education. However, although a great many published book series address the link between SLA and educational concerns, SLA and linguistics, and SLA and applied linguistics, currently no series exists that explores the relationship between SLA and cognitive science. Research findings and theoretical constructs from cognitive science have become increasingly influential on SLA research in recent years. Consequently, there is great reason to think that future SLA research, and research into its educational applications, will be increasingly influenced by concerns addressed in CS and its subdisciplines. The books in the CSSLA series are intended to facilitate this interdisciplinary understanding, and are grouped into four domains: (1) Knowledge Representation, (2) Cognitive Processing, (3) Language Development, and (4) Individual Differences. Each book in the series is composed of two sections. In the first section authors attempt to make conceptual and operational issues in each area clear, and then summarize existing research findings. In the second section, authors point to potential future research concerning them of relevance to studies of SLA. Each section concludes with an annotated bibliography of important references, intended to orient interested readers to primary sources in the areas covered.

Judit Kormos fulfills these series goals admirably in the present book, *Speech Production and Second Language Acquisition,* which falls within the second domain of cognitive science just described, *Cognitive Processing.* Chapter 1 presents an overview of the issues to be addressed, and following that, chapters address competing theories of speech production processes, research findings concerning them, and issues in the study of skill learning and automaticity as it relates to the notion of fluency in L2 production. The chapters in the second section address important issues of specific concern to SLA theory and SL pedagogy. These include the organization of the bilingual lexicon; grammatical and phonological encoding in the L2; and the conscious processes involved in monitoring speech production, and in successfully deploying communication strategies.

Throughout her book, Judit Kormos relates the research she reviews to issues of current importance in SLA theory and pedagogy, such as the cognitive processes implicated in *pushed output;* the role of attention to and awareness of (i.e., *noticing*) grammatical and phonological form while monitoring one's own, and an interlocutor's production; the nature of encoding and retrieval processes in the bilingual lexicon; and the cognitive factors contributing to variation in the accuracy, complexity, and fluency of speech production as it takes place in instructed L2 settings. Researchers, teachers, and students interested in these areas will find Judit Kormos' book an extremely valuable and up-to-date guide to the relevant basic concepts in the broad field of cognitive science, as well as to research and findings concerning them arising within the more specialized domain of second language acquisition.

—Peter Robinson
Series Editor

Acknowledgments

First and foremost I thank my mother for taking over many of my responsibilities at home and making it possible for me to write this book. I am very grateful for my husband's patience and help while I was writing this book. Thanks are also due to Peter Robinson and the anonymous reviewer for their invaluable comments on the manuscript, and to Zoltán Dörnyei, who has helped me all through my professional career even from thousands of miles away. I thank my colleagues at Eötvös Loránd University: Pál Heltai, Kata Csizér, Anna Csíky, Brigitta Dóczi, Gábor Kovács, Tibor Prievara, and Gergő Tamási for reading parts of the manuscript. Finally, I thank my editor, Cathleen Petree, for her unwavering support of this book. The writing of this book has been supported by the Békésy György Postdoctoral Research Grant.

—*Judit Kormos*

Introduction: Issues in L2
Speech Production Research

Today there are more bilinguals than monolingual speakers in the world (Crystal, 1987). Many children acquire two languages simultaneously, and an ever increasing number of teenage and adult students learn a second or foreign language (L2) in a school setting or in a naturalistic environment due to migration from one country to another. Conversation is one of the most frequent and fundamental means of communication, and its primary and overriding function is the maintenance and establishment of social relationships. No wonder that when learning a second language, one of the most frequent aims is being able to speak the language, and the acquisition of other skills such as reading or writing is often seen to be secondary to speaking. Thus understanding how one produces speech in an L2 is highly important in order to aid the teaching of this skill. By being familiar with the mental processes involved in producing L2 speech, teachers can understand the problems their learners have to face when learning to speak, course book writers can produce more efficient teaching materials, and language testers can develop instruments that can measure oral language competence in a more valid way. The aim of this book is to acquaint readers with the most important theories and findings on speech production in general cognitive science, and show how these theories and empirical studies can be related to second language acquisition (SLA) research. It is hoped that this book helps practitioners (teachers, testers, curriculum and material designers), students, and researchers in the field of SLA and psychology to have a better understanding of how L2 speech is produced and learned.

Giving a systematic account of L2 speech production, however, is not an easy enterprise. Even though there are well-established theories of first language (L1) production, there remain more unanswered questions than there are conclusive answers. If one adds an L2 component to these models, a host of new issues arise that need to be considered when drawing up a comprehensive model of L2 speech. As we see in this chapter and throughout this book, there are two major approaches to L2 speech production research. The primarily cognitive psychological line of research is often done by the same researchers who investigate L1 production. These studies mainly address the question of how the problems that appear in L1 research apply to L2 speakers. Researchers in this field generally use sophisticated experimental techniques, and investigate speech production processes elicited under laboratory conditions. The other line of research, which can be called the applied linguistic approach, is mainly done by SLA researchers, who often have solid background knowledge in psychology. In this approach, the questions that are asked about L2 speech production frequently derive from issues of L2 learning and are investigated by both experimental and observational methods. Whereas early applied linguistic research of L2 speech production was largely ignorant of the field of cognitive psychology, in the past 20 years information gained from this field is made extensive use of in this approach. Naturally, there is some overlap between the two approaches and some researchers belong to both groups, but the difference is apparent even in the fact that studies in the cognitive psychological line of research of L2 production are almost exclusively published in journals of psychology, whereas applied linguistic studies mainly appear in SLA journals.

In this introductory chapter, I outline the main questions in L2 speech production research that have received attention in the past 20 years. In order to help readers understand these issues, I start with a brief introduction to theories and issues in monolingual speech production research. Next, I follow the steps of speech production, and discuss the questions that arise at the particular stages. Following this, I present the questions that are specific to L2 production and cannot be tied to a particular stage of speech processing or occur at every phase, such as the issue of automaticity, transfer, code-switching, and the use of communication strategies. The various answers to the questions I raise in this introduction can be found in the subsequent chapters of the book, and in the concluding chapter I give a coherent account of L2 speech processing in the form of a new L2 speech production model, which incorporates the recent psycholinguistic theories of speech production and fits most of the empirical data in this field.

OVERVIEW OF ISSUES IN L1
SPEECH PRODUCTION RESEARCH

Speech production researchers all agree that language production has four important components: (a) *conceptualization,* that is, planning what one wants to say; (b) *formulation,* which includes the grammatical, lexical, and phonological encoding of the message; (c) *articulation,* in other words, the production of speech sounds; and (d) *self-monitoring,* which involves checking the correctness and appropriateness of the produced output. There is also agreement on the questions that conceptualization, formulation, and articulation follow each other in this order, and that in L1 production planning the message requires attention, whereas formulation and articulation are automatic, and therefore processing mechanisms can work in parallel, which makes L1 speech generally smooth and fast. Researchers also share the view that one of the basic mechanisms involved in producing speech is *activation spreading*. Activation spreading is a metaphor adapted from brain research, which is based on the finding of neurological studies that neural networks consist of interconnected cells (neurons) that exchange simple signals called activations via the connections they have with each other (Hebb, 1949). The speech-processing system is assumed to consist of hierarchical levels (conceptualization, formulation, articulation), among which information is transmitted in terms of activation spreading, and of knowledge stores such as the lexicon and conceptual memory store, within which activation can also spread from one item to related items. Decisions are made on the basis of the activation levels of the so-called *nodes* that represent various units such as concepts, word forms, phonemes, and so on.

There exist two major theories of L1 speech production: *spreading activation* (the latter name is somewhat misleading because, as just mentioned, both models assume that the way information is transmitted in the speech-processing system is activation spreading) (e.g., Dell, 1986; Dell & O'Seaghda, 1991; Stemberger, 1985) and *modular theories* (e.g., Fry, 1969; Garret, 1976; Laver, 1980; Levelt, 1989, 1993; Levelt, Roelofs, & Meyer, 1999; Nooteboom, 1980), and there are two major differences between them. The first main difference is whether they allow for feedback between the various levels of encoding. Spreading activation models allow for the backward flow of activation from a subordinate level to the superordinate level, whereas in modular theories activation can only spread forward. This means that in spreading activation theory, if an error occurs in one specific process, a warning signal is immediately issued, and activation flows upward to the superordinate level. Processing starts again from this superordinate level. In modular models, the error is not noticed at the level it is made, but only once the erroneous fragment of speech has been phonologically encoded or later when it is articulated. Therefore in this view, bits of message that contain an error need to be encoded again from the level of conceptualization. Researchers working with modular theories argue that the processing components in the speech production system are autonomous, that is, have their own characteristic input, and they process this input independently of other components. Hence the name modular theory of speech production. The second major difference between these theories concerns syntactic and phonological encoding. In spreading activation theories, it is assumed that speakers first construct frames for sentences and for phonetic representations and then select the appropriate words or phonetic features for the slots in the frame. Modular models are *lexically driven,* which means that words activate syntactic building procedures, and they postulate that lexical encoding precedes syntactic encoding and that phonological encoding can start only when lexico-syntactic processes are ready.

A major shortcoming of the models just described is that they consider speech production a creative process, in the course of which utterances are constructed word by word using rules of syntax and phonology. Pawley and Syder (1983) were one of the first researchers to point out that most of the language one produces is not creatively constructed but consists of sequences of words or phrases retrieved from memory as one unit. Recent corpus-based research on the frequency of these memorized sequences, which are traditionally referred to as *formulaic language,* has also confirmed the importance of Pawley and Syder's assumptions (Altenberg, 1998; Eeg-Olofsson & Altenberg, 1994; Moon, 1998). Neither the spreading activation nor the modular models of speech production discuss the role of formulaic language in language processing. Levelt (1989), in his book on speaking, mentioned that idioms and phrases might be stored in the lexicon in the same way as single words—that is, they might also have their own lexical representations—but he did not discuss how these units of language can be retrieved. In chapter 3 of this book, I make an attempt to place formulaic language in models of speech production.

ISSUES AT THE MAJOR STAGES OF L2 SPEECH PRODUCTION

In modular models, planning the message takes place in the conceptualization phase. The output of the conceptualization process is the *preverbal plan,* which contains the conceptual specifications for the message to be conveyed. At this stage speakers have access to declarative memory that contains information about the communicative situation and rules of discourse. Because this is the only place where conscious decisions about the content and form of the message can be made, the language of communication has to be selected at this phase. Language selection is constrained by sociolinguistic (e.g., the prestige of the languages, social position of the interlocutors) and individual factors (e.g., L2 speaker's anxiety, self-confidence, proficiency). The question that arises at this stage is whether speakers formulate *parallel speech plans*—a plan for L1 and another one for L2—or a single speech plan in which each concept is labeled with a language tag. The idea of parallel speech plans was very short-lived; it was formulated by de Bot in 1992, but in an article with Schreuder published a year later it was already abandoned (de Bot &

Schreuder, 1993). Since then, the well-received view about language selection is that it is done in the form of adding a language cue to the preverbal plan.

The other question that is relevant for both conceptualization and the organization of the mental lexicon is whether the words stored in the lexicon, which are called lemmas, contain semantic information. An important part of planning the message in the conceptualization phase is choosing the concepts one wants to express. Concepts can be both lexical and nonlexical. Lexical concepts can be expressed by one word (e.g., TEACHER–teacher), whereas nonlexical concepts have no direct correspondence to a given word and can only be expressed by phrases, clauses, or sentences (e.g., in Russian there is no one word for the concept of PRIVACY). In recent modular models of speech production, lemmas do not contain semantic information, only syntactic features (e.g., Levelt et al., 1999; Roelofs, 1992). Conceptual and semantic information are seen to be inseparable and are believed to be stored together in long-term memory based on the assumptions of memory research that both word meanings and other experience (sensual, emotional, etc.) one has with a lexical item form a network of interrelated memory traces. In L2 production, however, there is considerable disagreement concerning whether there are separate semantic and conceptual levels of representation (for a review, see Pavlenko, 1999).

In lexical encoding, the first question that needs to be addressed is whether the conceptual specifications contained by the preverbal plan activate only L2 items in the lexicon, or whether L1 and L2 words both receive activation. Research evidence from observations of slips of the tongue and experimental studies of picture naming suggests that L1 words are also activated to some degree (e.g., Costa, Caramazza, & Sebastian-Gallés, 2000; Hermans, Bongaerts, de Bot, & Schreuder, 1998; Poulisse, 1999; Poulisse & Bongaerts, 1994). The next issue is whether the fact that both L1 and L2 words are activated also means that these words are both candidates for lexical encoding. One possibility is that even though L1 words also receive activation, they are not considered for selection, and they are ignored. The other option is that both L1 and L2 words compete for selection. The majority of the studies suggest that the latter is the case (Costa, Colomé, Gómez, & Sebastian-Gallés, 2003; Hermans et al., 1998; Lee & Williams, 2001), whereas a few researchers using one specific picture naming task (Costa & Caramazza, 1999; Costa, Miozzo, & Caramazza, 1999; Hermans, 2000) found that L1 words do not enter into competition with L2 words. The third question that we need to answer in the process of lexical encoding is how lexical selection is controlled, in other words, how a speaker can ensure that words in the intended language are chosen for further processing. The most economical and logical solution to this problem seems to be that the information including semantics, style, register, and the language to be used is specified during conceptualization in the preverbal plan, and selection is simply based on finding the lexical entry that matches all the conceptual specifications.

As regards the bilingual lexicon, one of the first issues in bilingualism research was whether L1 and L2 words are organized in the same lexicon. By now it is a well-received view that L1 and L2 words are stored in a common lexicon, which is conceptualized as an interconnected network (for a recent review, see Kroll & Tokowitz, 2005). In other questions concerning the bilingual lexical storage system, however, there is great disagreement and theoretical confusion in this field. The problem starts with the question of what information the lexicon contains. As mentioned previously, there is an ongoing debate as to whether semantic information is also stored in the mental lexicon or whether only word forms (called lexemes) and syntactic and phonological information about lexical items can be found there. The second issue concerns the organization of the bilingual conceptual/semantic system, more precisely the extent to which conceptual representations for L1 and L2 words are shared (e.g., de Groot's, 1992, *conceptual feature model*). A few recent studies have also been concerned with the associations and connections that exist between words in the bilingual lexicon (e.g., Wilks & Meara, 2002; Wolter, 2001).

Syntactic encoding is a less frequently researched area of L2 speech production than lexical encoding. The majority of the studies have been carried out by cognitive psychologists, who are primarily experts in L1 speech production and have investigated questions of to what extent the encoding mechanisms of the syntactic information stored together with a lexical item (e.g., gender) and the activation of syntactic building procedures in L1 and L2 are different. In terms of gender (and other diacritic values such the countability status of nouns and the transitivity of verbs), there are two important issues: (a) whether the syntactic information related to L1 and L2 words can be shared across languages if the two languages have similar syntactic information structure (e.g., gender systems) and (b) whether grammatical features are accessed automatically every time a word is retrieved or features are selected based on the activation level of the syntactic feature nodes (Costa, Kovacic, Franck, & Caramazza, 2003). In other words, the second question is concerned with whether gender selection takes place automatically and as such is independent of the activation level of gender feature nodes, or gender selection is an activation-based process that is influenced by factors such as the gender of the previously used word. As regards the activation of syntactic building procedures, only one study to date has investigated what happens if L1 and L2 syntactic building procedures for specific structures are the same in both languages. Meijer and Fox Tree (2003) found that syntactic rules shared by both languages are not labeled for language and as such are stored together. The third question in the field of syntactic encoding in L2 has been addressed by primarily SLA researchers and is concerned with how grammatical morphemes are accessed. Research findings and theoretical considerations suggest that grammatical morphemes can be activated in two different ways: conceptually (i.e., based on the specifications of the preverbal plan for example in the case of tense of verbs) and by syntactic encoding procedures (e.g., case assignment in German) (Myers-Scotton & Jake, 2000; Pienemann, 1998).

Similarly to syntactic encoding, phonological encoding is an underresearched area of L2 speech production. One of the most important questions at this stage is whether the phonological form of nonselected but nonetheless activated words also receives activation, that is, whether activation can cascade from the lemma to lexeme (phonological word form) level (Colomé, 2001; Costa et al., 2000; Hermans, 2000; Kroll, Dijkstra, Janssen, & Schriefers, 2000). To illustrate this, when a German-English bilingual speaker wants to name a dog, the concept of DOG will spread activation to both the English lemma "dog" and the German "hund."[1] If the intended language is English, the lexical entry "dog" will be selected because it is the most highly activated one. As a next step, activation will flow to the phonological form of the lexical entry "dog," and it will be phonologically encoded. As regards the cascading of activation, the question is whether the German lemma "hund" also spreads activation to its phonological form even if it is not selected for further processing. Results of most of the studies in this field suggest that cascading of activation takes place between the lexical and phonological levels in L2 production (Colomé, 2001; Costa et al., 2000; Hermans, 2000; Kroll et al., 2000). The other question that has recently been tested by means of experimental techniques is whether representations of phonemes are shared or separate in L1 and L2 (Poulisse, 1999; Roelofs, 2003b). To this question the most probable answer is that L1 and L2 phonemes are stored together, and identical phonemes in L1 and L2 (e.g., English and Dutch [t]) have a joint memory representation (Roelofs, 2003b). The third question in the field of phonological encoding is whether L2-processing mechanisms at this level work in a similar way as in L1 speech production. Roelofs' findings indicate that phonological encoding in L2 proceeds in a similar way as in L2. As regards articulation, in

---

[1]In this book, concepts are printed in capital letters, and lemmas and lexical items are included in quotation marks.

L1 production it is assumed that syllables are the basic unit of articulatory execution and that articulatory programs are stored as chunks in the memory store called the syllabary (Levelt, 1989). De Bot (1992) claimed that beginning L2 speakers rely heavily on L1 syllable programs, whereas advanced L2 speakers usually succeed in creating separate chunks for L2 syllables.

Both L1- and L2-monitoring research has been primarily concerned with testing the modular and spreading activation models empirically, because by uncovering how monitoring works a major issue in the field of speech production, namely the direction of the flow of activation, can be solved. Few comprehensive studies on the self-correction behavior of L2 speakers have been conducted to date that have attempted to answer the question of which theory can best account for monitoring in L2 speech (but see Kormos, 2000b; van Hest, 1996). In a number of respects, monitoring in L2 has been found to be different from L1, and the most important reason for this difference derives from the fact that monitoring requires attention. Attentional resources are limited, and because L2 speech processing frequently needs attention at the level of lexical, syntactic, and phonological processing (unlike in L1), L2 speakers have little attention available for monitoring. The role of attention in monitoring has been investigated by a number of studies, which suggest that attentional resources for monitoring are constrained by the level of proficiency and the task learners have to perform (for a review, see Kormos, 1999).

GENERAL ISSUES IN SPEECH PRODUCTION

One of the most important differences between L1 and L2 production is that L2 learners' knowledge of the target language is rarely complete, as they often lack the language competence necessary to express their intended message in the form originally planned. Therefore L2 speakers frequently have to make conscious efforts to overcome problems in communication, which efforts have traditionally been called communication strategies (Færch & Kasper, 1983; Tarone, 1977). Dörnyei and Scott (1997) distinguished four main problem sources in L2 communication: (a) resource deficits, (b) processing time pressure, (c) perceived deficiencies in one's own language output, and (d) perceived deficiencies in decoding the interlocutor's message (this fourth problem source is not discussed in this book as this concerns speech comprehension rather than production). Resource deficit might be associated with three stages of speech processing: lexical, grammatical, and phonological encoding (Dörnyei & Kormos, 1998; Poulisse, 1993). In addition to the lack of knowledge of L2 lexis, syntax, and phonology, L2 speakers often have to face the problem that due to limited attentional resources they cannot process their message within the time constraints of real-life communication. L2 speakers might also experience problems deciding on whether their message has been accurate, appropriate, and understandable to the interlocutor, which problems arise in the phase of monitoring.

The other major source of difference between monolingual and bilingual speech processing is that in bilingual speech production the effect of the other language, which is generally the influence of L1 on the L2, cannot be eliminated. The findings of L2 speech production research suggest that knowledge stores such as conceptual memory, the lexicon, the syllabary, and the store of phonemes are shared in L1 and L2, and therefore L1 and L2 items compete for selection (La Heij, 2005; Poulisse, 1999; Poulisse & Bongaerts, 1994). One of the consequences of this competition is that it can happen that linguistic units in the nonintended language are selected, which are generally called unintentional code-switches. Code-switching can also happen intentionally either due to lack of competence or because the speaker thinks that the word, phrase, or expression in the other language matches his or her communicative intentions better in the other language (Myers-Scotton, 1993). Although in the last 10 years there seems to be hardly any disagreement among researchers concerning lexical code-switching, the syntactic structure of code-switched utterances has been the subject of an intensive debate. From the perspective of speech production, the question is how it is decided which language is going to dominate syntactic encoding, and how it is possible that even though elements from both languages co-occur in code-switched utterances, they still follow certain rules of well-formedness (MacSwan, 2000, 2003; Myers-Scotton, 1993; Woolford, 1983).

The L1 can also have other types of influence on L2 production, which most frequently manifests itself in the conscious and unconscious transfer of L1 production procedures. Conscious transfer is a subtype of communication strategies that is applied to compensate for lack of knowledge in the L2, whereas unconscious transfer is the effect of L1 on L2 of which is the speaker is not, or only partially aware. Transfer can take place in lexical encoding by means of conceptual, syntactic, and phonological transfer. Transfer is a more complicated issue in syntactic and phonological processing than in lexical encoding. In the case of syntactic encoding, the question is whether there are any constraints on transfer from L1, in other words, whether any type of production procedure is transferable from L1 at any level of language competence (for a recent review, see Pienemann, Di Biase, Kawaguchi, & Håkansson, 2005). The role of L1 is also central in L2 phonological processing because there is accumulating evidence that L2 learners frequently substitute L1 phonemes for similar but nonidentical L2 sounds, and that they often use L1 rules when phonologically encoding words or phrases (for a review, see Leather, 1999). Moreover, series of articulatory movements used to produce the syllables of a given language (called *gestural scores*) are automatized for pronouncing L1 phonemes to such an extent that even advanced speakers find it difficult to acquire new gestural scores for L2 phonemes.

Besides the incomplete knowledge of the target language and the effect of L1 on L2, the third important difference between L1 and L2 production is the speed with which L2 speakers talk. The considerably slower nature of L2 production can be explained with reference to the fact that whereas L1 speech processing is largely automatic in both the formulator and the articulator, and can, as a result, run in parallel, L2 speech processing requires attention in both the grammatical and phonological encoding phases, and as a consequence, part of the output can only be processed serially. In other words, whereas lexical, syntactic, morphological, and phonological encoding is mostly automatic in L1 production, these mechanisms are only partially automatic even in the case of advanced L2 learners. Therefore the question of what role automaticity plays in L2 production and how it develops in the course of L2 learning is of great significance in SLA research. Even though most L2 learners' ultimate aim is to attain a high level of fluency, that is, to learn how to produce speech smoothly, efficiently, and within the time constraints of real-life communication, the question of automaticity has long been a neglected one in the field of L2 speech production. The main reason for this probably is that although theories of speech production and general models of learning are highly developed, there is little interface between them. In the field of L1 speech production, no attempts have been made to account for how the various speech-processing mechanisms proposed by the modular and spreading activation models are acquired; this question has only recently been raised by a few SLA researchers. In chapters 3 and 8 of this book, I argue that automatization takes place in three different areas of speech production: rule-based syntactic and phonological encoding mechanisms, lexical retrieval processes, and the creation of memorized units of language.

SUMMARY

The aim of this chapter was to introduce readers to the most important issues of L1 and L2 speech production research, which is discussed in more depth in the remaining seven chapters of this book. Chapter 1 provides an overview of the basic theoretical claims made by the two most important theories of speech processing: the modular and the spreading activation models. Chapter 2 further explores the differences between the two theories by considering the questions that arise at each phase of speech production and the studies that have been conducted in order to find answers to these questions. Chapter 3 describes the basic cognitive theories of learning and automatization and makes an attempt to relate models of skill acquisition to theories of speech production. The second part of the book presents a detailed overview of L2 speech production research. The chapters discuss every phase of speech production in detail: Chapter 4 is concerned with lexical encoding and the bilingual lexicon, chapter 5 with grammatical and phonological encoding, and chapter 6 with monitoring L2 speech. In each of these chapters, first basic speech production processes are elaborated, which are always followed by the discussion of the relevant issues of code-switching, transfer, and acquisition. Chapter 7 is devoted to communication strategies, the functions of which are explained within the framework of modular models of speech production. Chapter 8 acquaints the readers with fluency and automaticity in L2 speech and relates theories of learning to acquisition of L2 speech production procedures. In the conclusion of the book, a new comprehensive bilingual speech production model is presented, which summarizes what is currently known about L2 production to date and incorporates recent advances in the field of psycholinguistics.

1   An Overview of Theories of First Language Speech Production

Interest in the psycholinguistic processes involved in producing L1 speech dates back to as early as the beginning of the 20th century, when Meringer (1908) first published his systematic collection of slips of the tongue made by German native speakers. Nevertheless, the first comprehensive theories of L1 production were not constructed until the 1970s. In the 35 years that have passed since then, the research into oral L1 production has grown into an autonomous discipline within the field of cognitive psychology. Although many questions concerning how we produce language have remained unanswered, with the help of the modern methods of experimental psychology and the recently available neuroimaging techniques, we now have a good understanding of a number of speech processes. The aim of this chapter is to acquaint the reader with the most influential theories of L1 production. Most theories of monolingual and bilingual speech production follow two main trends: the *spreading activation theory* (e.g., Dell, 1986; Dell & O'Seaghda, 1991; Stemberger, 1985) and the *modular theory of speech processing* (e.g., Fry, 1969; Garret, 1976; Laver, 1980; Levelt, 1989, 1993; Levelt et al., 1999; Nooteboom, 1980). Researchers working in the spreading activation paradigm assume that speech processing is executed in an interactive network of units and rules, in which decisions are made on the basis of the activation levels of the so-called *nodes* that represent these units and rules. Traditional modular theories, on the other hand, postulate that the speech-encoding system consists of separate modules, in which only one way connections between levels are allowed.

SPREADING ACTIVATION THEORY

The spreading activation theory of speech production has not been adopted as widely as Levelt's (1989, 1993) modular model, which is the most frequently cited theory in L2 speech production research. Nevertheless assumptions of the spreading activation models have influenced most of the research carried out on the slips of the tongue (e.g., Poulisse, 1993, 1999), unintentional code-switching (e.g., Poulisse & Bongaerts, 1994), and the organization of the bilingual lexicon (e.g., Colomé, 2001; Costa et al., 1999; Hermans et al., 1998; van Hell & de Groot, 1998).

3

Stemberger (1985) and Dell (1986) devised the first comprehensive model of interactive activation spreading in speech production. Because Stemberger's model differs from that of Dell only in some details used in describing the grammatical encoding procedures, here only Dell's model is discussed. Like in modular models of speech production (e.g., Fry, 1969; Garrett, 1976; Levelt, 1989), in Dell's spreading activation theory it is also assumed that there are four levels of knowledge involved in producing L1 speech: semantic (i.e., word meaning), syntactic (e.g., phrase building and word order rules),), morphological (e.g., the morphological make up of words and rules of affixation), and phonological levels (e.g., phonemes and phonological rules). Adopting the tenets of generative grammar (Chomsky, 1965), and those of the so-called frame-slot models of production (for more detail, see the section Syntactic Processing in chap. 2), Dell postulated that the generative rules on a given level build a frame with slots to be filled in by insertion rules. For example, on the syntactic level the rules in English create a position for the subject of the sentence, another one for the verb phrase and, if needed, slots for prepositional phrases. As a next step, words or phrases to fill in these slots are selected. At the morphological level there are slots for stems and affixes, and at the phonological level slots are assumed to exist for onsets and rimes as well as for phonemes. To illustrate this process, let us take Dell's own example, the sentence "This cow eats grass." In this sentence there is a slot for the determiner "this," the noun "cow," the present-tense verb "eats," and the noun "grass." In the case of the word "eats," a slot is created at the morphological level for the stem "eat" and another one for the affix "s." In the process of phonological encoding, there is an onset slot for [k] and a rime slot for [au] at the syllable level, and a consonant slot for [k] and a vowel slot for [au] at the phoneme level.

In Dell's (1986) spreading activation model, the lexicon is considered a network of interconnected items and "contains nodes for linguistic units such as concepts, words, morphemes, phonemes, and phonemic features, such as syllables and syllabic constituents as well" (p. 286). In the lexicon, conceptual nodes are assumed to be connected to word nodes that define words, and word nodes are conjoined with morpheme nodes, which again represent specific morphemes. Next, there is a connection between morpheme and phoneme nodes specifying phonemes, and finally phoneme nodes are linked to phonological feature nodes such as labial, nasal, voiced, and so on. In order for the words to be able to be selected for specific slots in the sentence, each word is labeled for the syntactic category it belongs to (e.g., in our example sentence "cow" is labeled as noun). Similarly, morphemes and phonemes are also marked for the class they are the members of (e.g., "eat" as stem, "s" as affix) (see Fig. 1.1 for the illustration of how encoding works in spreading activation models).

The mechanism responsible for sentence production is the process of spreading activation. In error-free processing, the node of the required category that has the highest level of activation is accessed. Immediately after this node is selected, it spreads its activation further to the lower level nodes. As an illustration, in the case of the word node "construct," activation is forwarded to the constituent syllable nodes: "con" and "struct." First, "con" is more highly activated than "struct"; otherwise one might say "structcon" instead of "construct." Next, activation will be passed on to the phonological segment nodes [k], [o], and [n]. Once the encoding of the syllable "con" is finished, the level of activation of this syllable node decreases so that it would not be selected repeatedly. Following this, the encoding of the next syllable "struct" can start. In

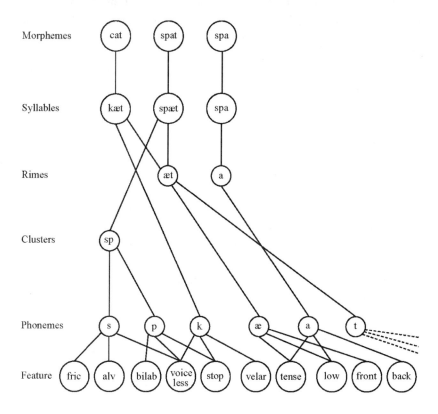

FIG. 1.1.   An illustration of the spreading activation model of speech production. Based on Dell (1986). Copyright 1986 by Gary Dell. Adapted by permission.

Dell's (1986) model selected nodes are tagged, and their tags specify the order in which they need to be encoded. Activation spreads not only from one level to the other, but also across levels. For example, at the lexical level, semantically and phonologically related items in the lexicon also receive some activation (e.g., if "dog" is the target word, "hog" and "cat" are also activated to some degree). This explains the occurrence of lexical substitutions and phonologically related lexical errors such as saying "cat" instead of "dog" or "hog" instead of "dog."

Dell (1986) also assumed that activation can spread bidirectionally, that is, top-down and bottom-up. In the case of sentence production, activation spreads downward from words to morphemes, from morphemes to syllable. On the other hand, speech perception is seen as the backward spreading of activation: when one perceives a sound, it sends activation to the syllable nodes, syllable nodes activate morphemes, and so on. To illustrate this, if one hears the phonemes [k] [æ] [t], they will activate the syllable node [kæt], which passes on activation to the word node "cat," which in turn selects the concept CAT. Because monitoring involves perceiving one's own speech, the existence of a separate monitor is not assumed, and monitoring is hypothesized to be done in the same way as understanding the interlocutor's speech. For example, in the case of the phonological substitution error of saying "hog" instead of "dog," once the speaker perceives the phoneme [h], activation will flow backward to the syllable node of [hog], and the encoding process will start again from the syllable level of [dog].

We have to note that although Levelt and his colleagues' work on speech production is called the modular model, Dell's theory is also modular in the sense that it supposes the existence of hierarchical networks of words, morphemes, syllables, phonemes, and phonological features. However, unlike in Levelt's model, where at least certain bits of the message need to be processed by the higher order module before lower order processing mechanisms can be initiated, traditional spreading activation models allow for parallel processing at the various levels.[1]

---

[1]By the end of the 1980s and the beginning of the 1990s, the modular and spreading activation approaches began to show increasing signs of convergence. The modular models adopted some of the tenets of the spreading activation models, especially as regards the organization of the lexicon and lexical access (e.g., Levelt, 1989, 1993, 1995; Levelt et al., 1991a, 1991b). In view of the results of Levelt et al.'s (1991b) experiments, Dell and O'Seaghda (1991) also modified their spreading activation model by assuming that the system of speech production is globally modular but locally interactive; in other words, backward spreading of activation is not possible between every adjacent level. In a later article, Dell, Juliano, and Govindje (1993) gave up the claim that activation can spread backward from the phonological to the lexical level, and they concluded that there is no need for the frame-slot mechanism and generative rules in syntactic and phonological encoding.

LEVELT'S MODULAR MODEL OF SPEECH PRODUCTION

Several attempts have been made in the literature to set up a comprehensive model of speech processing, but the most widely used theoretical framework in L2 language production research is Levelt's (1989, 1993, 1995, 1999a, 1999b) model originally developed for monolingual communication (for a schematic representation, see Fig. 1.2). Here we describe the newest version of the model (Levelt, 1999a). Levelt argued that speech production is modular; that is, it can be described through the functioning of a number of processing components that are relatively autonomous in the system. Two principal components are distinguished: the *rhetorical/semantic/syntactic system* and the *phonological/phonetic system*. The model supposes the existence of three knowledge stores: the *mental lexicon,* the *syllabary* (containing *gestural scores,* i.e., chunks of automatized movements used to produce the syllables of a given language), and the store containing the speaker's *knowledge of the external and internal world.* This last store comprises the *discourse model,* which is "a speaker's record of what he believes to be shared knowledge about the content of the discourse as it evolved" (Levelt, 1989, p. 114), *the model of the addressee* (the present context of interaction and the ongoing discourse), and *encyclopedic knowledge* (information about the world). The basic mechanisms of speech processing are conceptualized by Levelt in a fairly straightforward manner: People produce speech first by conceptualizing the message, then by formulating its language representation (i.e., encoding it), and finally by articulating it. With regard to speech perception, speech is first perceived by an *acoustic-phonetic processor*, then undergoes linguistic decoding in the speech comprehension system (i.e., the *parser*), and is finally interpreted by a conceptualizing module. The unique feature of the model is the integration of the processes of acoustic-phonetic encoding and sentence processing into one comprehensive system, and its richness in detail. For example, it precisely specifies the role of the lexicon and the procedures of monitoring in relation to the processing components and delineates explicit directional paths between the modules outlining their cooperation in producing their joint product, speech.

   In Levelt's model, the processing components are "specialists" in the particular functions they are to execute; that is, they do not share processing functions. A component will start processing if, and only if, it has received its characteristic input. This model assumes that processing is *incremental,* which means that as soon as part of the preverbal message is passed on to the formulator, the conceptualizer starts working on the next chunk regardless of the fact that the previous chunk is still being processed (Kempen & Hoenkamp, 1987). As a consequence, the articulation of a sentence can begin long before the speaker has completed the planning of the whole of the message. Thus, parallel processing is taking place as the different processing components work simultaneously. This is possible only because most of the actual production mechanisms, particularly in the encoding phase, are fully automatic. The incremental, parallel, and automatized nature of processing needs to be assumed in order to account for the great speed of language production.

Let us now look at the main processing components involved in generating speech as depicted in Fig. 1.2, which is the "blueprint" of the language user. In

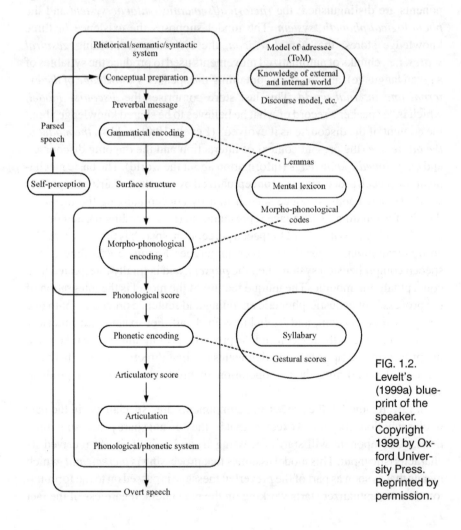

FIG. 1.2. Levelt's (1999a) blueprint of the speaker. Copyright 1999 by Oxford University Press. Reprinted by permission.

the first phase, called *conceptual preparation,* the message is generated through *macroplanning* and *microplanning.* Macroplanning involves the elaboration of the communicative intention. Communicative intentions are expressed by *speech acts,* which are actions one performs by speaking such as informing, directing, requesting, apologizing, and so on (Austin, 1962; Searle, 1969). In order to perform a speech act, one needs to select the information to be encoded and decide on the order in which this information will be conveyed. Once these decisions have been made, microplanning can start. In microplanning, speakers decide on the perspective that they need to take in conveying the message (e.g., whether he or she should say "The book is behind the vase" or "The vase is in front of the book"). The so-called "accessibility status" also needs to be determined. This means that one needs to consider whether an object, a person, a situation, and so forth have already been mentioned in previous discourse. This influences decisions such as whether a noun or phrase or pronoun (e.g., "the mother" or "she") should be used. Similar decisions concerning what constitutes new and old information also need to be made in the microplan. In addition, microplanning involves giving propositional content to the message, such as specifying the argument structure of the message, as well as assigning thematic roles (e.g., who is the experiencer or patient of actions), specifying the referents (i.e., quantifying and/or describing it), and determining the mood of the message (e.g., declarative, interrogative, imperative, etc.) (Levelt, 1999a). The microplan needs to contain language-specific information as well, for example, the selection of the appropriate tense and distal relations that are specified by the language one speaks. The outcome of macro- and microplanning is the *preverbal plan.* As the name suggests, this preverbal plan is not yet linguistic although it is linguistically accessible; that is, it is assumed to contain all the necessary information to convert meaning into language.

The preverbal plan is the input of the next processing phase, called *grammatical encoding,* in the course of which the selection of lexical units and syntactic encoding takes place. In grammatical encoding, information from the speaker's *mental lexicon* is retrieved, which in Levelt's (1989) model consists of *lexical entries,* each made up of (a) *lemmas* that contain syntactic information about the lexical entry and (b) *lexemes* that carry information about the morpho-phonological form of the lexical entry. In the recent version of the model (Levelt, 1999a, 1999b; Levelt et al., 1999) lemmas do not contain semantic information because a separate conceptual level is included in the lexicon where semantic specifications are stored. The primary procedure that takes place in grammatical encoding is *lemma activation;* the speaker will retrieve the lemma whose meaning best matches the semantic information carried by the corresponding chunk of the preverbal plan. Based on Bresnan's (1982) lexical theory of syntax, Levelt (1989) assumed that the selection of the lemma activates its syntax, which, in turn, triggers syntactic building procedures. For example, in the case of the verb "enter" the information concerning optional complements is activated, and a verb-phrase building procedure is initiated, which encodes the object such as "the room."

The output of grammatical encoding is the *surface structure,* which is "an ordered string of lemmas grouped into phrases and sub phrases" (Levelt, 1989, p.11). This is further processed in the course of *morpho-phonological encoding,* when the first step is the retrieval of the morpho-phonological information of the lexical item contained in the lexicon. This information specifies the morphological and metrical structure of the word as well as its segmental makeup. In phonological encoding, first the morphemes constituting the word are accessed. Next, the metrical and segmental features such as stress and pitch are set. This is followed by the selection of the phonemes of a morpheme. The final result of phonological encoding is the *phonological score* (or internal speech). In the next step, phonetic encoding draws on the repertoire of articulatory gestures stored in the syllabary and generates the *articulatory score* (for more detail on phonological and phonetic encoding, see the section Syntactic Processing in chap. 2). The last phase is articulation when the articulatory score is converted into overt speech.

Levelt's model also accounts for *monitoring* in speech production. The *monitor* is located in the conceptualizer but receives information from the separate *speech comprehension system* (or *parser*), which, in turn, is connected to the mental lexicon. In order to avoid the necessity of duplicating knowledge, Levelt assumed that the same lexicon is used for both production and perception, and the same speech comprehension system is used both for attending to one's own speech and for checking other speakers' utterances (via the acoustic-phonetic processing module). Furthermore, the interpretation of the perceived messages is carried out by the same conceptualizing module as the one in charge of generating one's own messages.

In Levelt's system of speech processing, there are three monitor loops (i.e., direct-feedback channels leading back to the monitor) for inspecting the outcome of the production processes. The first loop involves the comparison of the preverbal plan with the original intentions of the speaker before being sent to the formulator. In this phase, the preverbal plan might need modification because the speaker finds that the formulated message is not appropriate in terms of its information content or is not acceptable in the given communicative situation. The second loop concerns the monitoring of the phonetic plan (i.e., "internal speech") before articulation, which is also called "covert monitoring" (see also Postma & Kolk, 1992, 1993; Postma, Kolk & Povel, 1990; Wheeldon & Levelt, 1995). In simple terms, this means that in certain cases the speaker notices an encoding error such as an erroneously selected word before it is actually uttered. Finally, the generated utterance is also checked after articulation, which constitutes the final, external loop of monitoring, involving the acoustic-phonetic processor. Upon perceiving an error or inappropriacy in the output in any of these three loops of control, the monitor issues an alarm signal, which, in turn, triggers the production mechanism for a second time (for more detail on monitoring, see the section Phonological Encoding in chap. 2).

SUMMARY

In this chapter, the main theories of L1 speech production were reviewed. Two main models of monolingual speech processing were presented in detail: the spreading activation and the modular theories. It was pointed out that one of the main differences between these theories is whether they allow for feedback between the various levels of encoding. Spreading activation models allow for the backward flow of activation from a subordinate level to the superordinate level, whereas in modular theories activation can only spread forward. The two theories also view syntactic and phonological encoding differently. In spreading activation theories, it is assumed that speakers first construct frames for sentences and for phonetic representations and then select the appropriate words or phonetic features for the slots in the frame. Modular models are lexically driven, which means that words activate syntactic building procedures, and postulate that lexical encoding precedes syntactic encoding and that phonological encoding can start only once lexico-syntactic processes are ready. Despite a few shortcomings, which are discussed in the next chapter together with the empirical studies testing the two models, the modular theory of speech processing provides the most detailed and systematic account of the generation of verbal messages to date and has therefore been the most influential in the study of L2 speech. Spreading activation theories also have a lot to offer for the L2 field, especially in the area of the bilingual lexicon and lexical encoding. A detailed evaluation of the two models is given in the Summary section of chap. 2.

2   Issues in First Language Speech Production Research

In the previous chapter, we saw that there are two major theories of L1 speech production. As its name suggests, the modular model assumes that speech processing is carried out in a serial fashion by autonomous modules that are specialists in the particular phase of speech production. The modular theory also supposes that the basic process in speech production is activation spreading, but researchers subscribing to the modular view hold that activation can spread in only one direction, whereas scientists working in the spreading activation paradigm argue that activation can also flow backward from subordinate to superordinate levels of processing. Besides this major difference, there are a number of minor but important points in which the modular and spreading activation theories disagree. Because one of the main aims of L1 speech production research is to test the predictions of the two models and to build an empirically based and valid model of speech processing, these points of disagreement constitute the basic issues of L1 production research to date. This chapter starts with an overview of the research methods used in studying L1 speech production. Then I discuss the most important issues arising at each phase of speech production, the ways these issues are researched, and what conclusions can be drawn from the research findings. This is followed by an overview of the results of neuroimaging studies of speech production. The chapter ends with an evaluation of the current models of speech production.

RESEARCH METHODS USED IN STUDYING LANGUAGE PRODUCTION

In order to have a better understanding of L1 and L2 production research, it is important to be familiar with the basic techniques applied to study production mechanisms. The methods of language production research can be divided into three different groups: observational, experimental, and neuroimaging. Early psycholinguistic research dating back to the 1950s almost exclusively applied various techniques of speech observation, whereas experimental tasks started to be used in the 1970s. Neuroimaging techniques became available for speech production research at the end of 1980s and are now complementary to experimental research.

12

Observational methods involve the distributional analyses of spontaneous speech and the study of disfluencies and errors in spontaneous speech. Distributional analyses of naturally occurring speech have been concerned with how frequently various sentence types, prosodic markers, word forms, and syntactic structures occur in extensive databases of recorded speech, for example, oral corpora, and what they reveal about speech production processes. Disfluency research investigates the distribution of silent and filled pauses (e.g., um, er), false starts, repetitions, rephrasings, and self-corrections, whereas error research studies the frequency and types of errors. Both disfluency and error research aim to reveal what mechanisms underlie speech production by drawing inferences from instances when "things go wrong." The advantage of observational research is that it looks at speech processing under natural circumstances and can yield an insight into how speech production works as an integrated system. This method, however, has been plagued with the problem of classification and identification (Bock, 1996), which makes many of the findings of this field if not outright invalid, at least unreliable. Inconsistencies between raters trying to classify disfluencies and errors have been reported (for a review, see Bock, 1996), and until the use of computer technology became widespread in pausological research, transcribers were found to be inaccurate in recording the occurrence of pauses (see, e.g., Friedman & O'Connell, 1991; O'Connell, 1988).

Experimental methods used in the field of cognitive psychology to study speech production are numerous, and here we describe only the most frequently used techniques. Experimental methods might involve the elicitation of errors, most frequently slips of the tongue, and various units of production such as words, phrases, specific syntactic structures, and sentences. The majority of speech production experiments can be divided into two groups: *concurrent* and *successive stimulation paradigms*. In concurrent stimulation paradigms (also called interference) the processing of the distractor and the target word or structure overlap in time, whereas in successive stimulation paradigms (also called priming) participants are first presented with the stimulus (the prime), and only later do they produce the target. One of the most famous examples of a concurrent stimulation task in word elicitation research is the so-called *Stroop task*. In this task participants are shown a picture, which they have to name, but along with the picture a distractor word is also presented. The picture to be named in the original version of the task denotes a color, and the distractor word describes a different color, but Stroop tasks can also include pictures of objects and distractor words referring to objects (for an example, see Fig. 2.1). Distractor words are manipulated along the factor of semantic and phonological similarity to the target word. The time of the pre-

Lines with arrows indicate unidirectory connections and lines with double-headed arrows show bidirectional relatianships.

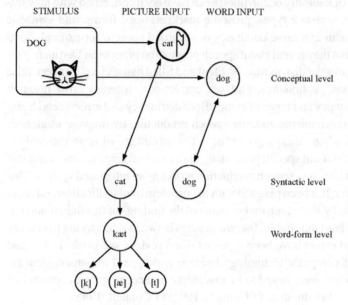

FIG. 2.1. Lexical selection using the binding by checking mechanism. Based on data from Roelofs (2003a).

sentation of the distractor item can also be varied. The measure used to make inferences about speech processing in this task is the naming latency, that is, the speed with which the respondent comes up with the picture name. A frequently used example for successive stimulation task is the structural priming experiment, in which participants first hear a prime sentence in which a particular syntactic structure is used (e.g., The boat carried five people.), then they see a picture denoting an event such as a boy being awakened by an alarm clock, which they have to describe in a sentence. Participants will use either the same structure as they heard in the prime sentence (e.g., The alarm clock awakened the boy.) or a different one (e.g., The boy was awakened by the alarm clock.). The variable measured in this task is the number of same syntactic structures used relative to the total number of trials. Although in these experiments many interfering variables can be controlled, and the scope of investigation can be clearly delineated, the disadvantage of these tasks is that they look at production processes in isolation and not as they occur in real-life communication (for a comprehensive review of experimental tasks used in language production research, see Bock, 1996).

Neuroimaging techniques used in investigating speech production can be divided into three groups: ERP (event-related brain potential), PET (positron emission tomography), and fMRI (functional magnetic resonance imaging) studies. ERPs are recorded with the help of EEG (electroencephalogram), which shows how the flow of electricity changes in the brain. ERPs are EEG changes that signal sensory, motor, or cognitive events registered in the brain. PET scans are made with a device called a PET scanner, which creates pictures of the physiological processes taking place in human brain with the help of radioactive substances called tracers. Increased level of activation in brain areas is characterized by higher blood flow, which the tracers indicate by emitting stronger signals. This enables researchers to localize various brain functions. The technique of fMRI is based on the fact that hemoglobin (the blood's oxygen carrier) emits different magnetic signals when it carries oxygen and when it does not. Increased brain activity is characterized by an augmented number of oxygen-carrying hemoglobin molecules, which can be recorded with the help of fMRI. Nowadays the preferred imaging technique is fMRI because it is cheaper, more widely available, noninvasive, and imposes fewer risks for the participants than PET (for a recent review of neuroimaging techniques in speech production, see Fiez, 2001).

CONCEPTUALIZATION AND SPEECH PLANNING

Research into speech planning and conceptualization is traditionally carried out not only in the field of psycholinguistics but also in fields such as sociolinguistics, pragmatics, and discourse analysis. This is mainly due to the fact that among other things, conceptualizing one's message involves the knowledge of the situation, power relations between speakers, norms of interaction in the given language, rules of politeness, and general knowledge of the world. If we compare the spreading activation and modular models, it also becomes apparent that because spreading activation theory has little to say about speech planning, there is no major theoretical disagreement between psycholinguists concerning this phase of speech production. Nevertheless, there are a few problematic issues in speech planning that psycholinguistic research has addressed. One of these concerns the unit of speech planning, and connected to this, the existence of temporal cycles in speech production. The other debated question is related to how concepts are encoded in the preverbal plan.

As regards the unit of speech planning, several building blocks were proposed such as clauses, ideas, information units, tone units, phrases, sentences, and so on (for a more comprehensive review, see Levelt, 1989). Levelt argued that "there is no single unit of talk" (p. 23), and therefore the whole debate concerning units of speech is pointless. He rightly claimed that each level of processing works with different units, for example, lexical encoding with lemmas, phonological encoding with phonemes. An issue that is related to units of speech planning is whether there are temporal cycles in speech production. In the classic study that marks the beginning of the psycholinguistic study of speech production, Henderson, Goldman-Eisler, and Skarbek (1966) observed that in spontaneous speech phases of low and high fluency alternate, and they named these alternations *temporal cycles*. They argued that producing speech involves planning and execution, and that during planning speech slows down, whereas in execution fluency increases. The existence of temporal cycles, however, has been debated by several researchers such as Jaffe, Feldstein, and Gertsman (1972), Warner (1979), and Beattie (1984). Roberts and Kirsner (2000) pointed out that previous studies had serious methodological flaws such as the inaccurate measurement of temporal parameters (e.g., pauses), subjective judgments involved in the analysis of cycles, and the use of inappropriate statistical procedures. Roberts and Kirsner's research attempted to overcome these problems and brought convincing results as regards the cyclical nature of speech production. They found that in spontaneous speech fluent and nonfluent phases indeed alternate, and that these cycles are regular and periodical. Another interesting result was that there was a strong and consistent relationship between topic structure and fluency. Fluency was found to decrease before a new topic, and production speeded up after the introduction of the topic. Roberts and Kirsner claimed that "macro-planning is a topic-driven form of planning" (p. 150). This study also indicates that speech planning requires attention because conscious decisions concerning the message need to be made; thus, it is a controlled process, which is generally slow, whereas speech processing in L1 is largely automatic and fast (Greene, 1984; Greene & Cappella, 1986; Levelt, 1989). This difference between automatic and controlled processing explains why fluent and nonfluent cycles alternate in speech production.

A different issue that arises in the phase of speech planning is the so-called *convergence problem*. This problem refers to the question of how it is possible that when searching for the appropriate lemma for the intended concept, the selection process almost always converges on the right word. This issue arises because there is no one-to-one correspondence between a number of concepts and lexical entries in the lexicon. It might be the case that a concept cannot be matched with a single lemma; for example, though we can express "female actor" by one word, "actress," there is no such word for "female teacher" in English. Another case is the synonymy problem, when seemingly the same concept such as RECEIVE can be expressed by two or more words such as "receive," "obtain," or "get." A subtype of the convergence problem is the so-called hypernym problem. Hypernyms are words the meaning of which entails the meaning of other words, such as the hypernym "animal," which includes dogs, cats, mice, and so forth. The problem is that conceptual specifications for a hypernym are to a great extent overlapping with the conceptual specifications of the list of words that can be classified under this hypernym. For example, animals as well as cats, dogs, and mice can be characterized as + ANIMATE, – HUMAN. How is it possible, then, that we hardly ever say "I am afraid of animals" rather than "I am afraid of dogs"; in other words, how is it that errors when hypernyms are accessed instead of the intended lemma hardly ever occur?

The convergence problem was a central issue in speech production when feature theories of word meaning dominated language production research (for an overview of this research, see Levelt, 1989). These theories assumed that concepts are made up of a list of semantic features—such as PUPPY is constituted of the features + ANIMATE, – HUMAN, + CANINE, + YOUNG—and that in lexical access these conceptual features are matched with the appropriate lemma (e.g., Bierwisch & Schreuder, 1992) (see Fig. 2.2). The major question for these theories was how the relevant conceptual features are established so that lexical retrieval can be successful. For example, how does an English speaker know what conceptual features should be specified in order to select the word "receive" instead of "obtain" and whether there is a corresponding lemma to FEMALE TEACHER? This question was very important because in modular speech production models the conceptualizer does not have access to the lexicon; therefore, it does not have information on which conceptual specifications are needed to render lexical access successful. In order to solve this question, Bierwisch and Schreuder proposed a separate module, the *verbalizer*, where the process of

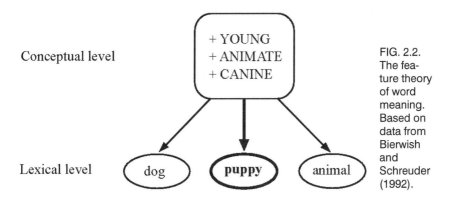

Conceptual level

+ YOUNG
+ ANIMATE
+ CANINE

Lexical level   dog   **puppy**   animal

FIG. 2.2. The feature theory of word meaning. Based on data from Bierwish and Schreuder (1992).

establishing lexically relevant conceptual features could take place, and which module would have access to the lexicon. The idea of the verbalizer module was not long lived because Levelt (1992), Levelt et al. (1999), and Roelofs (1997a) claimed to have solved the issue of lexically relevant conceptual features by arguing that concepts should rather be regarded as complete entities in themselves and not as a set of features. Roelofs (1992) proposed that there was a separate concept level, where the meaning of words is specified, and that concepts spread activation to lexical items (lemmas). Concepts are represented by nodes; for example, there is one node for YOUNG, another one for DOG, and a third one for PUPPY. If the preverbal message contains specifications for the concept PUPPY, the PUPPY node will receive the highest level of activation and will be selected; thus, the speaker will not say "young dog" instead of "puppy" (see Fig. 2.3).

Recently La Heij (2005) argued that the synonymy issue is not really relevant in speech production research because complete synonyms hardly ever exist; there is almost always a subtle pragmatic or affective difference in meaning between words. Consider for example the stylistic difference if a mother tells her child, "Look at that young dog" instead of saying "Look at that puppy." Therefore La Heij proposed that the preverbal message contains all the information that specifies a given word, and that this information includes not only the core meaning of a word but cues concerning how formal the selected word should be, whether to use euphemism, and whether to avoid taboo words and low-frequency technical terms. The list of cues can further be extended to dialect and register. The cues are set based on the knowledge of the communicative situation and the interlocutor. Figure 2.4 illustrates La Heij's proposal with the word "bloke," which contains semantic specifications for the concept

Lines with arrows indicate unidirectory connections and lines without double-headed arrows show bidirectional relationships.

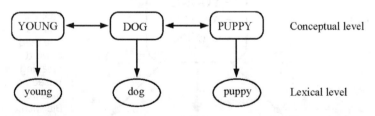

FIG. 2.3. The nondecompositional view of word meaning. Based on data from Roelofs (1992).

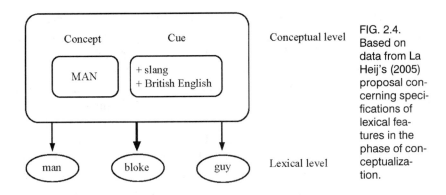

FIG. 2.4. Based on data from La Heij's (2005) proposal concerning specifications of lexical features in the phase of conceptualization.

MAN and cues specifying the style of communication as + informal and the dialect as + British English.

LEXICAL ENCODING

Although a number of different views exist as regards how lexical encoding takes place in L1, for certain questions there is remarkable agreement among researchers. First of all, it is generally accepted that three levels of processing are involved in generating a spoken word: conceptual planning, that is, deciding on the meaning one wants to convey; lexical encoding, which involves the selection of the lexical item that matches the concept one wants to communicate; and finally phonological encoding. Researchers also agree that all these processes are competition-based mechanisms; concepts, words, and phonemes compete for selection. Selection is made on the basis of the item's activation, which represents how available it is. The item that has the highest level of activation is the "winner" of the competition and is selected for further processing. The higher the difference in the level of activation between the intended item and related item, the easier and quicker selection is; the lower the difference, the more difficult it is to choose from the competitors.

It is also a generally accepted view that in speech planning not only the intended concept but other related concepts are activated. If, for example, one wants to name a table, concepts of other pieces of furniture will also become activated to some degree. This activation then spreads forward to the lexical level; thus, lexical items such as "bed" and "desk" will also compete for selection. Accordingly one of the basic questions for lexical encoding that becomes even more important in bilingual language production is how words are selected. If one is presented with the picture of a cat, generally no problem occurs because the concept of cat will receive the highest level of activation and will be selected for further processing. If, however, the task is to name a picture depicting a cat, and a word such as "dog" is also written in the picture (this is called the Stroop task, discussed earlier in the section Research Methods Used in Studying Language Production), how does the speaker select between the target concept and the written distractor? This question is very similar to the one we have to address in bilingual lexical selection, because there the L2 speaker is presented with the concept of the cat and has to select the word in the intended language. Two possible ways this process can take place are proposed in the literature. One possibility is to assume that there exists a so-called task activation, which in this case means that because the task is to name visually presented picture input, the task instructions activate visually recognized items to a higher degree than those perceived by reading (La Heij, 2005; Starreveld & La Heij, 1996). In this view, selection is based only on the level of activation of the lexical items (see Fig. 2.5). The second option is that some kind of checking process ensures that the appropriate word is selected. Roelofs (1992) proposed that both the target picture name and the written distractor word receive activation, and they also receive a tag. The picture name is marked with a picture tag, and the written distractor receives a word tag. Roelofs and later Levelt et al. (1999) presumed that the lexical selection mechanism will choose the lexical entry that has the tag determined by the task instructions, and a verification mechanism checks if the right word was selected (Levelt et al., 1999, called this mechanism binding by checking) (see Fig. 2.1). It is easy to see that the second option, tagging and checking, raises a number of problems.

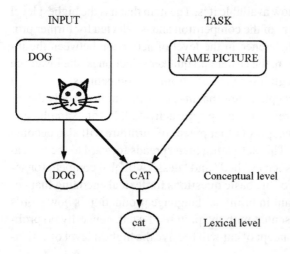

FIG. 2.5. Lexical selection based on task activation in picture word interference tasks. Based on data from La Heij, 2005.

La Heij (2005) pointed out that this model is too complex and involves unnecessary checking mechanisms; moreover, in more complex tasks it can lead to the proliferation of tags, which is highly uneconomical. He also argued that supposing the existence of checking mechanisms is against the principle of modularity that is at the core of Levelt's own model, because Levelt (1989, 1999a) assumed that one processing component works with only one kind of input and does not need to consult other processing modules. Starreveld and La Heij's (1996) and La Heij's (2005) solution to the problem is appealing because of its simplicity, and it seems to be supported by theories of attention that assume that channeling attention to particular aspects of production specified by task instructions will raise the activation level of the concepts relevant for the successful performance of the task (Phaf, van der Heijden, & Hudson, 1990).

The other major question in lexical encoding today is whether lexical access is a serial or so-called cascaded process. As I have pointed out previously, there seems to be a consensus among researchers that lexical access consists of two phases: the selection of the lemma, which contains syntactic information (e.g., for nouns' gender, countable vs. uncountable, plural form), and the activation of the lexeme, which is the phonological word form (e.g., [kæt] for "cat"). The question is what the relationship is between these processes. Jescheniak and Schriefers (1997) explained the difference between serial and cascaded processing in the following way:

> The discrete two-stage view assumes that *selection* of a single lemma takes place before phonological activation starts, only the phonological word form of the selected lemma (e.g., *cat*) will subsequently become active. The phonological forms of the semantic competitors remain completely inactive. By contrast, cascade models and spreading-activation models allow for phonological activation of the target and any activated semantic competitor, resulting in phonological co-activation. (p. 848)

Let us take another example to illustrate cascaded processing. If one wants to encode the concept TABLE, the lemma "table" will receive primary activation. Nevertheless, semantically related lemmas such as "desk" or "bed" might also receive some activation. Thus, it is possible that the lemma for "table" is selected, but the lemma of "desk" is also activated (see Fig. 2.6). Cascaded processing models (Jescheniak & Schriefers, 1997; Peterson & Savoy, 1998) assume that not only the phonological word [table], but also [desk] and [bed] will be activated; in other words, activation will cascade to the related lexemes. In cascaded models, it is also hypothesized that lexical selection is not always

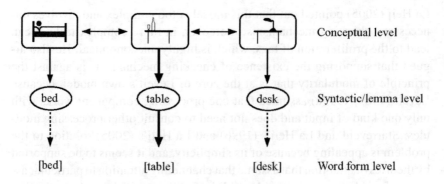

FIG. 2.6.   Lexical activation in speech production. Lines with arrows indicate unidirectory connections and lines with double-headed arrows show bidirectional relationships; ⤳ indicates possible cascading of activation.

finished before phonological word form activation starts; that is, lexical selection and phonological encoding can run partly parallel.

The most frequently cited counterevidence against cascaded processing comes from research using electrophysiological methods of brain activity measurement (ERP) (Jescheniak, Hahne, & Schriefers, 2003; van Turennout, Haggort, & Brown, 1997). Van Turennout et al.'s study is described here in some detail because of its groundbreaking and interesting research methodology. In this research, participants' brain activity was recorded while performing two types of decision tasks. The participants were presented with pictures and had to decide whether they saw animate or inanimate concepts and whether they started with a particular phoneme. In the first experiment, they had to respond with one hand if the picture showed an animate concept, and with the other if they saw an inanimate concept. Phonological information determined whether they should respond or not (so called go/no-go condition). In the other experiment, the beginning phoneme determined which hand should be selected, and decision to respond was made on animate status. The observations concerning the participants' brain activity showed that semantic information was available earlier than phonological information. This they took as a support for the assumption that lemma activation precedes phonological word form activation and as a further proof for the validity of the serial access models.

Rahman and Sommer (2003), who used a similar research design and obtained similar results, however, argued that the fact that semantic information is available earlier than phonological information does not necessarily support the serial view and does not mean that cascading of activation is not possible. Cascaded processing also supposes that lemmas become activated first, and the activation of phonological word forms takes place following it. What cascaded models say is that activation can flow downward to the phonological level before lexical selection is finished; that is, lexical and phonological encoding can run in parallel. Using electrophysiological research techniques, Rahman and Sommer found that "phonological encoding appears to start at the same time as semantic retrieval" (p. 380). In the cascaded-versus-serial-processing debate, it is worth considering that there is converging evidence that activation in L2 production can spread from the lemma in the nonintended language to its phonological form (see chap. 4), which indicates that in L2 production cascading is possible. It seems highly unlikely that cascading takes place only in an L2 and not in the L1.

SYNTACTIC PROCESSING

Spreading activation and modular models also disagree as regards the nature of syntactic processing. As mentioned in chapter 1, spreading activation models assume that in sentence production syntactic rules generate a frame for the sentence, which is then filled with words. On the other hand, in modular models the words' syntactic properties guide sentence production. The spreading activation models do not elaborate in great detail how syntactic processing is carried out. Modular models are much more detailed in this respect. Based on Kempen and Hoenkamp's (1987) Incremental Procedural Grammar, in these theories grammatical encoding is assumed to consist of six phases and involves a grammatical memory store, which is responsible for storing the intermediary processes of grammatical encoding. Let us take the example of the sentence "The child enters the room." As a first step, the lemma corresponding to the first conceptual element CHILD is retrieved. Next, the lemma's syntactic category initiates a categorial procedure in the course of which the phrasal category in which the lemma can be a head of the phrase is established. For the lemma "child," it is established that it is a noun, and that it can be the head of a noun phrase. Third, the message is inspected as regards what conceptual material can fill the obligatory and/or optional complements and specifiers of the lemma, and the diacritic parameters are set. To remain with our example of the lemma "child," it is established that it is singular and has the status + accessible, and therefore a determiner node will be attached to the NP (noun phrase) node and the lemma "the" will be activated. After this, the formulator can proceed with the next step of grammatical encoding, when the categorial procedure selects a grammatical function for the processed material, which means that it will decide whether the output will become a head or a complement of a higher order categorial procedure such as a noun or verb phrase or a sentence.

In this phase of processing, the noun phrase "the child" becomes the subject of the sentence. Next, the word order rules are activated, which specify that the subject should occupy the first position in our sentence. After this, if applicable, the subordinate clause procedure builds the subordinate clause attached to the phrase. Finally, the higher order categorial procedure described earlier will be activated, and it will start processing the relevant fragment of the message from either the phase of lemma retrieval or Stage 2. In our example, the lemma "enter" will be called on next, and in the phrase procedure the inflection "s" will be added based on the information retrieved from the grammatical memory store that the subject is singular.

One of the basic differences between spreading activation and modular models is the degree to which lexical selection mechanisms and syntactic building procedures interact. Strictly feed-forward theories (e.g., Levelt et al., 1999) assume that lexical selection precedes and governs the generation of syntactic frames, and the syntactic structures constructed in this way do not have an effect on the choice of successive lemmas. Interactive theories, on the other hand, propose that a syntactic frame might influence the lexical selection process by raising the activation level of the lexical entries that might be possible candidates for lexical choice (Dell, 1986; Stemberger, 1985). Support for the latter assumption mainly comes from speech error data. It was observed that word substitution errors such as "I switched on the *sun" instead of saying "I switched on the light" always involve the substitution of words belonging to the same grammatical class (Garrett, 1980) and often to the same gender (Berg, 1992). This suggests that the syntactic frame creates a bias for words belonging to one grammatical category. It is only in the past few years that researchers started to investigate this issue with the help of experimental techniques. Vigliocco, Lauer, Damian, and Levelt (2002) found no interaction between syntactic and semantic processes, which might be taken as a support for feed-forward models. In a more recent study, however, Vigliocco, Vinson, Indefrey, Levelt, and Hedwig (2004) experimentally induced substitution errors in various phrasal structures in German, which is a gender-marking language. They found that when the substituted nouns followed a determiner the form of which depends on the gender of the noun (i.e., der [masculine], die [feminine], das [neuter]), the erroneously encoded nouns tended to be of the same gender as the originally intended noun. The authors argued that this is possible only if in certain cases the syntactic frame becomes available earlier than the lemmas that should be inserted into the frame. This poses a problem for strictly modular models, which assume that syntactic encoding does not precede lemma retrieval. The increased interest in this issue in the past few years will probably spark off new studies that might bring more conclusive evidence concerning the existence of interaction between semantic and syntactic processes.

While the research concerning the interplay of syntax and semantics has been primarily concerned with phrasal structures, a number of studies have also been conducted on sentence construction. Sentence production is primarily researched with the help of the method called syntactic priming. In syntactic priming experiments, it was observed that the use of one syntactic structure in one sentence (called the prime) increased the likelihood of the use of the same structure in another sentence (so called priming effect) (Bock, 1986). For example, if participants were presented the sentence "The lightning struck the church," they were more likely to describe a picture showing a dog chasing cat by saying that "The dog chases the cat" than "The cat is chased by the dog." If, however, they saw or heard the sentence "The church was struck by the lightning," the more frequently produced sentence was "The cat is chased by the dog." These experiments also showed that it is only the similarity of syntactic structure that produces the priming effect, and that lexical, thematic, metrical, or phonological similarities between the prime and target do not result in priming (for a review, see Bock & Levelt, 1994; Levelt, 1989). This was an important finding because it indicated that one syntactic production rule activates another similar rule, and therefore the mechanisms of spreading activation are also at work in syntactic encoding. The question is how activation spreads in this system. Does it spread from one syntactic frame to the other as assumed by spreading activation theory, or does activation take place within the framework of lexically driven syntactic encoding as proposed by the modular theories? In extensions of the classical syntactic priming experiments, participants were asked to recall sentences that they were presented some time earlier. In these experiments (Potter & Lombardi, 1990; Tree & Mejer, 1999) it was found that people remember the gist of the sentence and use recently activated words to reconstruct the sentence. In Tree and Mejer's study, the participants were first presented with prime sentences containing various noun phrase constructions such as "The rich widow gave the university a million dollars." Following this, they heard a number of distractor words including a synonym for the verb "give" such as "donate." The results of the study showed that instead of using the verb and syntactic structure presented in the prime (e.g., give + NP + NP), participants tended to reformulate the sentence using the distractor verb and applying the syntactic structure called on by the distractor. In our example, they tended to recall the sentence as "The rich widow donated a million dollars to the university." This experiment provides strong support for the assumption that syntactic encoding is lexically driven, because instead of using recently activated syntactic structures, speakers tend to reconstruct a sentence by employing recently activated words and the syntactic structure these words point to.

The other much debated issue as regards syntactic encoding concerns the order of the availability of syntactic and phonological information. This debate is somewhat similar to the one on the sequence of lexical and phonological encoding (see the Lexical Encoding section), and research in this field usually examines the relationship of gender encoding and phonological processing in languages where nouns have a specific gender (e.g., German, Dutch, and Italian). Proponents of Levelt's model of speech production (e.g., Roelofs, Meyer, & Levelt, 1998; B. M. Schmitt, Meyer, & Levelt, 1999; Schriefers & Jescheniak, 1999) assume that grammatical gender is the lexico-syntactic property of nouns, which is looked up whenever a noun is produced. In other words, the gender of a word is not computed on the basis of morpho-phonological properties every time it is encoded (e.g., native speakers of Italian do not compute gender on the basis of what vowel the word ends in, but remember the gender of each and every word). All nouns of a given gender are connected to gender nodes that specify gender, which means that there is one abstract gender node for each gender. Let us take an example from German. The word "Übung" [practice] is a feminine noun, and it is assumed that native speakers of German do not establish the gender based on the word's ending "-ung," which is always associated with feminine gender, but look up the word's gender. "Übung" is therefore connected to the abstract feminine gender node, as are all the feminine words of the language, such as "Mutter" [mother].

The question is whether grammatical gender is always accessed or only when it is needed, and whether information concerning the gender of a given word is available earlier than information concerning the phonological form of the word. Bock and Levelt (1994) claimed that the phonological form of a word is selected only after the lexico-syntactic properties have been accessed. This proposition was interpreted by Caramazza (1997) as the *syntactic mediation hypothesis,* according to which the syntactic information of a word, such as gender, is always activated before phonological encoding. Bock and Levelt, however, did not claim that this information is always selected; there might be cases when gender information is not necessary. For example in the sentence "Was machen die Kinder?" [What are the children doing?] it is not necessary to retrieve the gender of the word "Kind" because the plural determiner in German is gender nonspecific. In a series of experiments, Caramazza and Miozzo (1997) demonstrated that in states of tip-of-the-tongue Italian speakers are able to correctly tell the gender and the first phoneme of a word even though they are not able to produce the word itself. Thus, they argued that conceptual representations can directly activate the phonological representation of a word, and the activation of lexico-syntactic information can proceed parallel with phonological encoding. Therefore, in their so-called independent network model there is no need for a separate lemma level. Roelofs et al. (1998) cited a number of pieces of research evidence that makes this theory highly problematic. The most convincing argument for the assumption that information concerning grammatical gender is available earlier than phonological information comes from van Turennout, Haggort, and Brown's (1999) electrophysiological study, which adopted a similar design to their research into the relationship of lexical and phonological encoding (van Turennout et al., 1997). In this study, the observations of participants' brain activity showed that grammatical gender of a given word is accessed earlier than its phonological form.

PHONOLOGICAL ENCODING

Phonological encoding is also perceived of differently in spreading activation and modular theories, although the most elaborate model of word form encoding, developed by Roelofs (1997b) and called WEAVER (Word form Encoding by Activation and VERification), combines the assumptions of both theories. In this section, I first describe the two conflicting views of phonological encoding—the so-called featural and segmental theories—and then present the WEAVER model, which is a computational model that has been found very successful in accounting for a number of empirical research findings.

Featural theories of phonological encoding assume that phonological segments are represented only by their features (e.g., the phoneme [b] is represented as [+ voiced] [+ labial] [– nasal]) and that in phonological processing morphemes are mapped onto features that make up the sounds of the morpheme. The featural view is usually associated with spreading activation theories (Dell & Juliano, 1996; Mowrey & MacKay, 1990). In the segmental view, which is held by researchers working within the modular theory, phonological segments have their own abstract representations in memory that are stored as a group of features (called chunks; Levelt, 1989; Roelofs, 1997b; Shattuck-Hufnagel, 1979). Roelofs (1999) conducted a number of experiments using a method called *implicit priming*[1] and also ran computer simulations. In the first phase of implicit priming experiments, which were first used

---

[1]The reviewer of this book rightly pointed out that this type of experiment should rather be called paired associate learning followed by cued recall because no prime is presented. I nevertheless use the term *implicit priming* because the authors of these studies themselves named these experiments in this way, and this terminology is frequently used in the study of phonological encoding processes.

by Meyer (1990, 1991), participants have to learn pairs of words. When the first word of a pair is presented visually, participants have to produce the second word. Two different sets of words are involved in these experiments: a homogenous set, when response words share part of their form, and a heterogeneous set, when there are no similarities between the forms of words. Researchers measure the response latency and establish whether similarities speed up the production of the response. In Roelofs' (1999) experiments, two different homogenous sets of words were used: words that shared their initial segment (e.g., table, tennis, token) and words that shared their initial segment except for one feature such as voicing (e.g., door, table). Roelofs found no facilitation effect for words that did not start with exactly the same segment, which seems to support the assumption that phonemes are stored and retrieved as chunks in speech production.

Roelofs' (1997b) WEAVER model is a comprehensive model of phonological encoding that combines elements of spreading activation and Levelt's (1992) assumptions concerning online syllabification. The model computes syllabifications instead of using stored syllable chunks, and the online syllabification process takes neighboring morphemes and words into consideration. For example, in the sentence "I've seen him," "I" and "have" are treated as one phonological word [aiv]. Phonological segments (i.e., phonemes) and metrical structure (e.g., stress placement) are the input to the syllabification process, which in this model is conceived of as weaving a fabric from first segment to second, from second to third, and so on. In other words, phonemes are activated in a serial fashion starting with the first phoneme of the word and ending with the last one. Positions for phonological segments are assigned following the syllabification rules of the language. "Essentially, each vowel and diphthong is assigned to a different syllable node and consonants are treated as onsets unless phonotactically illegal onset clusters arise" (Roelofs, 1997b, p. 259). If we take the word "tiger," [t] is assigned to the onset position of the first syllable, [ai] to the nucleus of the first syllable, [g] to the onset position of the second syllable, and [ə] to the nucleus of the second syllable. In phonetic encoding, metrical representations are used to set parameters for loudness, pitch, and duration, and the program is made available for the control of the articulatory movements. The model assumes incremental production, which means that a fragment of the input is enough to trigger production. Therefore syllabification can start on the initial segment of a word if the metrical structure is available, such as [tai] in the case of "tiger," and the interim results of the syllabification process can be buffered until further segments are ready (e.g., until the encoding of the syllable [gə] is finished]. In the articulation phase, motor programs are retrieved from a store of learned programs: the syllabary. Syllables are produced as packages of scores for the articulatory movements to be made, such as lip protrusion and lowering of the jaw. Scores also specify the gestures and their temporal relationships. Assimilation of sounds is assumed to be the result of the overlap of gestural scores. In the model, only forward spreading of activation is allowed, in the course of which each node sends a proportion of its activation to the neighboring nodes, and activation decays spontaneously (see Fig. 2.7).

MONITORING

As I mentioned in the introduction to this chapter, one of the major differences between spreading activation and modular models is how they view feedback

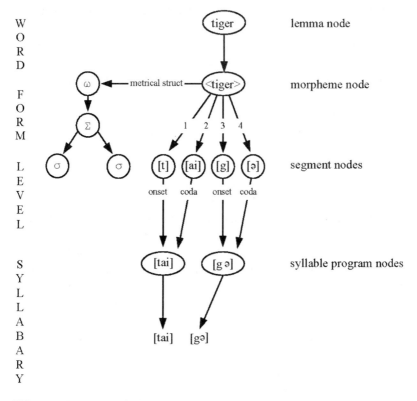

FIG. 2.7. Illustration of phonological encoding in Roelofs' (1997b) WEAVER model. Reprinted from *Cognition, 64*, A. Roelofs, The WEAVER Model of Word-Form encoding in speech production. Copyright © (1997), with permission from Elsevier.

and monitoring in speech production. Classic theories of spreading activation assume that speech perception proceeds through the bottom-up flow of activation, and this mechanism is also in operation when speakers monitor their own speech. Therefore, in this theory, monitoring is assumed to be an inherent feature of the perception and production processes, and the existence of a separate monitoring device is not postulated (Dell, 1986). This assumption has been criticized for a number of reasons. First of all, if errors were detected automatically, the monitor would perceive all the errors, which, in turn, would all be automatically corrected (Levelt, 1989). Empirical research, however, proves that speakers do not correct every mistake in their speech (Levelt, 1983). To address some of these problems, MacKay (1992) devised the *node structure theory* (NST), which was based on research carried out on awareness. MacKay claimed that if a node formed a new connection with another "uncommitted" node, prolonged activation could come about, and this would be capable of triggering awareness and, thus, contributing to the detection of the error. In response to the criticism that this model predicts that all the errors will be detected (Levelt, 1989), MacKay argued that although error detection is automatic, speakers make conscious decisions concerning whether or not to correct their errors. The factors affecting these decisions, however, have not been elaborated in detail.

The second group of theories of monitoring, called *editor* or *production theories of monitoring,* is not directly related to any of the major theories of speech production. As their name suggests, these theories presume the existence of an editor that sees to the vetoing and replacement of the incorrect output of the speech production processes. The main question is where the editor derives its processing power from, and where it is located in the system. One possibility is that the editor has its own system of rules against which the output is checked. Baars, Motley, and MacKay (1975) and Motley, Camden, and Baars (1982) proposed a model in which the prearticulatory editor tests the utterance before articulation using the criteria of lexical legitimacy, syntactic and semantic appropriacy, situational context, and social appropriateness. It is obvious, however, that if this mechanism worked perfectly, it would not allow for the occurrence of errors at all; thus, in order to match the theory with reality, it must be assumed that either the system of rules it uses is degenerate (e.g., Garnsey & Dell, 1984) or that the rules used at a given moment must vary (e.g., Motley et al., 1982). In the latter case, the application of a particular rule would depend, among other things, on the context and the available attention. The drawback of this type of model is that the editor can only inspect the outcome of the processes and is unable to intercept erroneous output at intermediary levels. In addition, the knowledge necessary for the decision about the appropriateness of the prearticulatory output needs to be reduplicated in the editor, which is highly uneconomical (Berg, 1986; Levelt, 1989).

In order to eliminate some of these problems, several researchers (e.g., Nooteboom, 1980; Norman, 1981; cf. Postma & Kolk, 1992) proposed that there should be a specialized monitor at each level of the processing system, which would see to the appropriateness of the outcome of each process. This version of the editor theory is called the *production theory of monitoring* (production-based monitoring or PBM) because the monitor has access to the different stages of production. Nevertheless, in this case again, the monitor would have to contain the same or almost the same knowledge as the processing component. In addition, it is unclear how this monitor would operate because if it halted the process of speech production at each level, it would considerably slow down the speed of processing (Berg, 1986; Blackmer & Mitton, 1991; Levelt, 1989).

Drawing on the main tenets of the theories of prearticulatory monitoring and spreading activation, Levelt (1983, 1989) devised his own model for intercepting erroneous output, which he called the *perceptual loop theory* (PLT). From the theory of prearticulatory editing, he adopted the assumption that prearticulatory output can be inspected. On the basis of spreading activation theory, he proposed that the same mechanism could be applied for checking one's own message as for the perception and checking of other speakers' utterances. In order to avoid the necessity for reduplication of knowledge, in Levelt's model the speech comprehension system is used for attending to one's own speech as well as to others'. As mentioned in the Research Methods Used in Studying Language Production section, in this model, there are three loops for inspecting the outcome of processes: (a) the conceptual loop, when the preverbal message is compared to the original intentions of the speaker, (b) the prearticulatory loop, when the outcome of the phonological processes is checked, and (c) the external loop of monitoring, when the articulated message is parsed. In the conceptual loop, it is generally the appropriacy of the message in the given communicative context that is checked, whereas in the prearticulatory loop, encoding errors are intercepted before articulation. In the external loop, the speaker inspects both communicative appropriacy and the linguistic form of the utterance.

Based on recent research on reaction times in self-monitoring, Wheeldon and Levelt (1995) further investigated what prearticulatory monitoring entails. Levelt (1989, 1993) assumed that phonological encoding consists of three phases: (a) the activation of phonological segments, (b) the production of the phonological word, and (c) the generation of the phonetic-articulatory plan. In order to find out at which of these stages "internal speech" is parsed, Wheeldon and Levelt conducted a series of experiments, which suggested that speakers could self-monitor without having access to the phonetic-articulatory plan. They also found that prearticulatory monitoring was sensitive to syllable structure, which becomes available in the second stage of phonological encoding, that is, upon the production of the phonological word. The results of Wheeldon and Levelt's study, therefore, indicate that speakers are able to monitor at the level of abstract phonological representation before the phonetic-articulatory plan is encoded.

Let me briefly summarize the major differences between the three theories of monitoring just outlined (for a comprehensive review, see also Postma, 2000; for a summary, see Table 2.1). The first of these concerns where the monitor can be found in this system. In the PLT, the monitor is centrally located; in PBM, it is distributed at various levels of processing; and in NST, it is assumed to be an inherent feature of the production processes. PLT and NST suppose that monitoring is a conscious activity, whereas in PBM it is auto-

TABLE 2.1

Overview of Differences Between Perception- and Production-Based Speech Monitors and the Node Structure Theory of Monitoring

	Perceptual Loop Theory (Levelt, 1989)	Production Theory of Monitoring (Noteboom, 1980; Norman, 1981)	Node Structure Theory (MacKay, 1992)
Location of the monitor	Central	Distributed	Inherent in the production system
Awareness	Conscious	Automatic	Awareness is a necessary condition for error correction
Monitoring levels	1. conceptual loop 2. prearticulatory loop 3. external loop	At each phase of speech production	As many as the number of the node levels
Speed of monitoring	Relatively slow	Fast	Fast
Repair mechanism	Elaborated revision	Simple retrace and restart	Not discussed
Relation to speech comprehension system	Monitoring is done with the help of the speech comprehension system	No relation	Node system is shared by production and perception

Note. Based on data from Postma, 2000.

matic. Furthermore, PLT presumes that the monitor is limited by attentional resources, whereas the other theories do not pose such limitations concerning capacity. Because in PLT monitoring is conscious and uses limited attentional resources, it is supposed to be a relatively slow process, whereas NST and PBM regard monitoring as fast.

The theory whose viability has been put to the test most frequently is the PLT. Its assumptions concerning prearticulatory monitoring have gained empirical support because a number of studies demonstrated that people are able to detect errors in their speech even if they do not hear what they say (e.g., Postma & Kolk, 1992; Postma & Noordanus, 1996). Research concerning the timing of self-corrections (Blackmer & Mitton, 1991; Oomen & Postma, 2001), however, has brought a number of problems to light concerning the theory. One of the most important issues is the existence of very short time periods between the interruption of speech flow upon error detection and the onset of the repair process. In Levelt's model (1989), the planning of the self-correction is supposed to take place in this interval, and it is also assumed that interruption and replanning are strictly serial. One possibility is that interruption and repair are "simultaneously starting parallel processes, beginning immediately upon error detection" (Hartsuiker & Kolk, 2001, p. 148). Hartsuiker and Kolk ran computer simulations using timing data collected by Oomen and Postma to test this hypothesis. Their research showed that the computer model could successfully reproduce the timing patterns if parallel interruption and planning were supposed. They concluded that with this modification the PLT seems to be a viable model of speech monitoring.

NEUROLOGICAL STUDIES OF LANGUAGE PRODUCTION

With the development of neuroimaging techniques, a number of studies have investigated the cerebral areas involved in speech production and comprehension. Indefrey and Levelt (2000, 2004) performed a meta-analysis of research in this field and summarized what parts of the brain have been found to be active at various stages of speech processing. Neurolinguistics is a rapidly developing discipline within cognitive psychology, which is indicated by the fact that whereas in 2000 Levelt and Indefrey found 58 studies that they could include in their analyses, by 2004 this number grew to 108. The higher number of investigations in 2004 also means that Indefrey and Levelt were able to identify new cerebral areas involved in speech processing.

Indefrey and Levelt (2000, 2004) found that one single region, the left middle temporal gyrus, was active in word generation and picture-naming tasks but not in word-reading tasks, which, as opposed to the other tasks, do not involve concept selection. This indicates that the left middle temporal gyrus is involved in conceptually driven lexical selection. Conceptualization of the message, however, is done in several distributed areas of the brain that are difficult to identify with these types of tasks. The retrieval of word forms is necessary in picture-naming, word generation, and word-reading tasks but not in pseudo-word-reading experiments. Therefore, cerebral regions active in the former three tasks but not in the latter task can be regarded as areas where word form retrieval takes place. Such areas are the right supplementary motor area, the left anterior insula, and the left posterior superior and middle temporal gyri (Wernicke area). The next step in word production is syllabification, which takes place both in overt and in silent word production tasks. In order to identify brain areas responsible for syllabification, Indefrey and Levelt (2000, 2004) argued that these areas should be active in all the production tasks and should not be sensitive to whether the task requires overt or covert production. In their study published in 2004, they found that it was only the Broca's area that met this requirement, and that the left mid superior temporal gyrus probably plays a less important role in syllabification than they assumed in their earlier meta-analysis. Regions responsible for phonetic encoding and articulation were identified based on three criteria: The given region should be found to be (a) active in at least twice as many studies using overt production tasks than in research applying silent production experiments, (b) active in more studies involving overt responses than in studies where visual processing takes place, and (c) not active in word perception. Indefrey and Levelt (2004) identified 17 regions that met these criteria, of which 12 are part of the central nervous motor system (bilateral ventral motor and sensory regions, right dorsal motor region, right supplementary motor area, left and medial right cerebellum, bilateral thalami, right midbrain) and that can be regarded as indeed responsible for phonetic and articulatory encoding. Indefrey and Levelt (2004) argued that the role of the other five regions in this phase of speech processing is questionable. Neuroimaging studies have provided proof for the assumption held by the PLT of monitoring that parsing one's own speech is done with the help of the same mechanisms as listening to other people talk. The bilateral superior temporal gyri with the exception of the right anterior section were found to be active both in word-listening tasks and in overt production experiments. This cerebral area is probably responsible for the external monitoring of speech. Indefrey and Levelt's (2000, 2004) meta-analysis could not reliably establish what brain regions are involved in internal monitoring.

A number of studies have investigated the involvement of various cerebral areas in L2 production. The problem with these studies, however, is that they mainly used single word processing tasks and that they often did not make an appropriate distinction between proficient and nonproficient speakers and students who use the L2 frequently and those who speak the L2 only rarely. Therefore, as Abutalebi, Cappa, and Perani (2001, 2005) pointed out, it is very difficult to draw conclusions from neuroimaging studies of L2 production. Nevertheless, Abutelabi et al. concluded that the pooled results of research in this field suggest that neither the extent of brain activation nor the regions involved in processing in L1 and L2 are different for bilinguals who learned the L2 early in their lives and for highly proficient speakers with extensive L2 exposure. Late bilinguals, especially those who are not proficient in the L2 and have had low exposure to the target language, activate larger cerebral areas when speaking in L2 than in L1 and activate different regions within the Broca area for L2 than for L1.

SUMMARY

In this chapter, the main issues arising at each phase of L1 speech production were reviewed. Let us now summarize what we seem to know about L1 speech production currently, and which model seems to be able to account for this knowledge better: the modular or the spreading activation theory. As regards the conceptualization of the message, we can conclude that there is no single unit of speech planning, although speech planning seems to be largely dependent on the topic structure of the utterance, which is manifested in the existence of temporal cycles of speech production. As far as conceptual activation is concerned, we can also reject the assumption that concepts are made up of lists of semantic features. In L1 speech production research, the most widely held view is that concepts are undivided wholes, which cannot be broken down into semantic components (Levelt, 1999b; Roelofs, 1992, 2003a). Furthermore, the most logical and economical position in the issue of conceptual specifications and the control of lexical selection seems to be that the preverbal plan should contain not only semantic information but also cues that specify the formality and register of the given word (La Heij, 2005).

In the field of lexical encoding, there seems to be an agreement that lemma selection takes place first, which is then followed by the activation of the phonological form of the lemma. Cascaded processing models assume that lemma selection and phonological activation can run partly in parallel, and that the phonological form of activated but nonselected lemmas can also receive activation. In my personal view, the experimental evidence against cascaded processing is not strong enough, and given the fact that ample support for the cascading of activation was found in L2 research, it is unlikely that the strictly serial view is tenable in L1 speech production research. It seems that the case is similar in syntactic encoding, where there is accumulating research evidence that to a certain extent syntactic information affects lexical selection. This again might mean that the serial nature of the model will need to be given up in the near future. The assumption of modular theories that syntactic encoding is lexically driven and that it precedes phonological encoding, however, seems to be supported by a number of studies. From the results of Roelofs' (1999) research, we can also conclude that in the process of phonological encoding, phonological segments are represented as chunks of features rather than as a series of individual features that are accessed separately in order to encode a phoneme. From monitoring research, it seems to be apparent that with minor modifications the PLT (Levelt, 1989) is a valid model of monitoring in L1 speech. Thus we can assume that there are three loops of monitoring at three different levels of speech production—the conceptual, prearticulatory, and post-articulatory levels—and that the speech comprehension system is used for checking the correctness and appropriacy of the utterance.

Having summarized what knowledge we seem to have about L1 production to date, let us see which of the two speech production theories seems to be more valid and what modifications are needed in the preferred model to make it fit the research findings. The obvious advantage of the modular model over spreading activation theory is that it is definitely more detailed at every level, which makes it easier to test and apply at every phase of speech processing. Nevertheless, I do not think that this is a sufficiently strong reason to give preference to the modular model. In order to decide on one model over the other, we need to consider the four major differences between the theories: featural versus segmental view in phonological encoding, frame-slot model versus lexically driven syntax, the direction of the flow of activation, and related to this, monitoring.

In my view, research findings concerning phonological encoding suggest more convincingly that phonological segments have their own abstract memory representations than that they are represented by their features. Moreover, evidence for lexically driven syntactic encoding also seems to be stronger than support for the assumption that syntactic frames activate words. Thus at this point, the modular theory looks more viable than the spreading activation model. As regards monitoring, the best account of how the checking of errors is done also seems to be provided by the modular model. The strongest evidence for modular monitoring comes from neuroimaging studies, which found that speech comprehension and speech production are not done exactly in the same regions of the brain, although there is a partial overlap and that it is possible to identify the brain region that is responsible for monitoring (see Indefrey & Levelt, 2000, 2004). Spreading activation theories assume that speech comprehension is the backward flow of activation in the speech production system, and if this was the case, identical brain regions would be activated in both speech production and speech comprehension, and no brain region responsible for monitoring could have been identified. In addition to the results of neuroimaging studies, in experimental psychology there also seems to be a lack of support for the assumption that the backward flow of activation takes place at all the levels of processing. Given all this, the modular model seems to be a more valid model of speech production than the spreading activation theory.

Nevertheless, there are two important issues that modular theories need to consider in the future. One of them is the inclusion of the possibility of cascading of activation in the model, and the other is the explanation of the effect of syntactic information on lexical encoding. These two issues are both related to how activation can flow in the system, and it seems that the strictly serial nature of the modular model needs to be revised. Though current evidence suggests that activation cannot flow backward indiscriminately at every level, between specific stages such as the lexical and syntactic encoding processes some kind of interaction needs to be assumed. It would also need to be accepted that the flow of activation of nonselected items does not stop at encoding-level boundaries but can cascade to the following encoding level. It is also worth considering research findings and theories of speech comprehension, because to date speech comprehension is seen to be an interactive and parallel process (for a review, see Harrington, 2001); therefore, it is highly unlikely that certain stages of production cannot run parallel and do not interact.

3 Theories of Automaticity and Their Relation to Speech Production Models

One of the most complex automatic human activities is linguistically encoding what one wants to say in his or her mother tongue. L1 speech is mostly effortless, fast, requires no attention on the part of the speaker, and can be done parallel with other activities such as driving, washing up, and listening to music. It is no wonder that the automaticity of this process takes years to develop and requires thousands of hours of practice. It is also understandable that research on the development of automaticity first started to explore the automatization of lower level skills such as letter recognition and simple arithmetic tasks and has only recently ventured into the territory of language production and comprehension. When investigating how automatic processing works in language production, one has to face several problems. The first of these is that researchers greatly disagree on what is meant by automaticity, and as a result, they often hold conflicting views of how it develops. Second, language production involves different types of encoding processes—using rules and retrieving memorized lexical units from memory—and therefore it is possible that for these two types of mechanisms different theories of automatization should be applied. Third, researchers in the field of L1 and L2 acquisition are also divided along the line of whether they regard language learning as being similar to acquiring any other type of skill or whether they believe that language acquisition is a unique cognitive process, which is not comparable to any other skill. Theories of automaticity, all of which consider language learning to be one type of the many cognitive processes that humans perform, though the most complex of these, have little to say to those researchers in the field of L1 and L2 learning who regard language a unique cognitive skill that is acquired with the help of innate capacities. The final problem in this field is that the investigation of speech production and automaticity are two separate fields of cognitive psychology with hardly any interface between them; therefore when one wants to explore automatization in oral language processing, one ventures into an uncharted territory.

In this chapter, I make an attempt to weave the lines of speech production and automaticity research together and discuss how the development of various types of speech-encoding mechanisms might be explained with the help of

38

different theories of automaticity. In the first section, definitions and characteristics of automaticity are reviewed. This is followed by the description of various theories of automaticity. Finally, I look at each process of speech production, including retrieving lexicalized units from memory, and apply theories of automaticity to these production mechanisms.

DEFINITIONS AND CHARACTERISTICS OF AUTOMATICITY

Though intuitively it is easy to tell what it is that someone does automatically and what processes are nonautomatic, there are numerous and often conflicting definitions of what automaticity means. DeKeyser (2001) collected 14 different criteria of automaticity proposed in the field of psychology between 1974 and 1993. These characteristics include the following: fast, parallel, effortless, capacity-free, unintentional, result of consistent practice, little interference from and with other processes, unconscious, always based on memory retrieval, does not benefit from further practice, error-free and flexible, strong production rule, no interference from working memory, and no correlation between the mean and standard deviation in performance measures. Looking at the definitions from a historical perspective, we can see that in the most influential view of the 1970s and 1980s (Schneider & Shiffrin, 1977; Shiffrin & Schneider, 1984) automatic processing and its counterpart, which was termed controlled processing, were regarded as dichotomies, that is, as two points at the end of a continuum. In this theory, it was claimed that automatic processing had the following characteristics: (a) it is fast and efficient, (b) it is not limited by the capacity of the short-term memory, (c) it does not require any effort on the speaker's part, (d) it cannot be controlled voluntarily, (e) its modification and inhibition is difficult, and (f) its processes are unavailable for introspection. On the other hand, controlled processing was seen as (a) slow and inefficient, (b) limited by the capacity of the short-term memory, (c) requiring effort on the speaker's part, (d) controllable by the speaker, (e) flexible, and (f) partly available for introspection. Schneider, Dumas, and Shiffrin (1984), however, pointed out that many of the criteria that they proposed in their earlier work were unnecessary, and that the two most important characteristics of automaticity are that it does not require processing capacity and attention. Kahnemann and Treisman (1984) were the first to argue that automatic and controlled processing are not dichotomous because automaticity can have different degrees. Since the middle of the 1980s one can see two different types of views of automaticity emerging, and these views are divided along the line whether they are held by researchers who consider automaticity to be the conversion of *declarative* (factual) *knowledge* into *procedural* rules (the *rule-based approach*) or a single-step access of a memorized item (*item-based approach*). Whereas for rule-based theories the most important criteria are related to the degree of attention paid to the process, in item-based theories memory-based retrieval plays the central role.

In his review of the characteristics of automaticity, N. Segalowitz (2003) listed the following features that have been investigated by empirical research in the past 30 years: fast, ballistic (unstoppable), load-independent (independent of the amount of information to be processed), effortless, and unconscious. Research evidence seems to suggest that although it is generally true that automatic processing is faster than controlled processing, the development of automaticity is not only a quantitative change as proposed by Shiffrin and Schneider (1977). Nor was sufficient support gained for the assumption that automatic processing is always load-independent (Schneider & Shiffrin, 1977; Shiffrin & Schneider, 1977). Studies conducted in the field of automaticity, however, seem to indicate that automatic mental processes are ballistic (Neely, 1977), effortless (Posner & Boies, 1971), and unconscious (Jacoby, 1991). Neely's research showed that automatic processes such as word recognition are ballistic, in other words, unstoppable, as his participants were unable to avoid the processing of the meaning of presented words. Posner and Boies demonstrated that automatic tasks do not require effort and attention, and therefore they do not slow down performance on an other task. Jacoby devised an ingenious set of experiments with the help of which he was able to find empirical support for the unconscious nature of automatic processes.

THEORIES OF AUTOMATICITY

As mentioned earlier, two main groups of theories of automaticity exist: rule-based and item-based approaches. Rule-based approaches to automaticity view the development of automaticity as the transformation of factual knowledge into production rules, which are called *procedural knowledge*. To take an example from the field of L2 learning, when an L2 speaker is taught the distinction between the articles "a" and "an," namely that one is used before nouns starting with a consonant and the other before nouns the first sound of which is a vowel, he or she will first store it as factual or *declarative knowledge*. With practice, this knowledge will be transformed into a production rule: such as, if I see a noun starting with a vowel, I say "an." Finally, this rule will be applied automatically, that is, without conscious attention. Rule-based approaches to automaticity attempt to account for how this conversion takes place.

Anderson's (1983) ACT* (adaptive control of thought) and ACT–R theory (adaptive control of thought–revised) (1995) proposed that the development of automatic processes involves not only a quantitative change, that is, speeding-up, but also qualitative modifications in the nature of processing. Anderson argued that five learning mechanisms contribute to the development of automatic performance: *composition, proceduralization, generalization, discrimination,* and *strengthening.* Composition and proceduralization constitute the subprocesses of knowledge compilation, in which the former involves the creation of "macro-productions" from the smaller units of processing and the latter the removal of declarative knowledge, which results in the retrieval of the production as a whole. In other words, the creation of macroproductions is called chunking, which refers to the psychological process of transforming items into larger units in order to help processing in the working memory. The simplest example for this is remembering telephone numbers. Due to the fact that the working memory can hold between five and seven items at a time, when trying to remember a phone number, which is a long list of unrelated one-digit numbers, people tend to chunk this list into larger units in order to help keeping it in working memory (e.g., 2 4 6 1 9 2 2 3 6 gets chunked as 246-19-22-36). The process of proceduralization has the potential to explain that once a production has become automatic, the initial declarative knowledge underlying it is often not retrievable anymore. For example, L2 learners who were once taught explicitly in which situations to use the present-perfect tense in English might not remember the exact rules after the application of these rules becomes automatic. Qualitative changes in procedural knowledge can come about with the help of three *tuning processes.* The first of these, generalization, widens the scope of the application of the declarative knowledge necessary for production and ensures that production rules are applied in all the contexts where they are appropriate, whereas the second process, discrimination, narrows the scope of application and sees to the application of rules only in the appropriate context. Finally, the tuning process of strengthening is responsible for the weakening of poorer rules and the strengthening of better rules. Strengthening in this model does not mean the establishment of connective links between elements of a response or a procedure, but the increased likelihood with which a particular production procedure is selected.

Cheng's (1985) model of restructuring addressed the issue of qualitative processes involved in automatization. She proposed that improvement in executing a certain task can be due to the "restructuring of the task's components so that they are co-ordinated, integrated, or reorganized into new perceptual, cognitive, or motor units" (p. 414). Thus, the rapidity of the performance is not only caused by the speeding up of the processes, but by the creation of completely new mechanisms. N. Segalowitz and S. Segalowitz (1993) and S. Segalowitz, N. Segalowitz, and Wood (1998) also argued that the development of automaticity is not only a simple speed-up process, but a qualitative change that takes place in task components. They supported this claim by examining the change in the variability of performance as a result of practice. They found that at the beginning of the practice session, learners' performance was characterized by high variability and low efficiency, whereas with the development of the given skill processing became more efficient and less prone to errors, and variability of performance decreased.

In the theory of *competitive chunking,* Servan-Schreiber and Anderson (1990) further refined the concept of composition in Anderson's (1983) ACT* model and assumed that new productions are built from old ones by collapsing units of the old mechanisms if they follow each other and if the goals of the productions are similar. In the framework of chunking theory, Newell (1990) was the first one to argue that it is sufficient to postulate a single set of mechanisms that underlies human cognition including learning, production, and comprehension, and this process is chunking. He claimed that "a chunk is a unit of memory organization formed by bringing together a set of already formed chunks in memory and welding them into a larger unit. Chunking implies the ability to build up such structures recursively, thus leading to the hierarchical organization of memory" (p. 7). Newell (1990) and Newell and Rosenbloom (1981) assumed that three basic processes are involved in building chunks:

1. People chunk at a constant rate, and with experience they build additional chunks.
2. Task performance speeds up as more relevant chunks are built.
3. Due to the fact that higher level chunks occur more rarely than lower level ones (e.g., compare the frequency of "You should go to bed now" to "to bed"), they become less useful, and learning slows down.

Logan's (1988) instance theory was the first model that addressed the issue that not all learning involves the conversion from declarative to procedural learning. Logan assumed that automatic processing equals memory retrieval; that is, the use of an algorithm is substituted by a single-step retrieval of the solution from memory. Thus, in this theory no change is supposed to take place in the workings of the algorithm, but it is presumed that if a problem is solved repeatedly, the solution becomes stored as one unit and is called upon when encountering the problem again. With practice, associations between problems and the memory traces of their solutions become stronger, and consequently retrieval speeds up. Logan also argued that there is a competition between rule-based processing and memory retrieval, and the speed of the two different processes determines which one will be applied. Logan's theory makes three important assumptions about how a memory trace for a particular solution is established:

1. Encoding in memory is an obligatory and unavoidable consequence of attention; in other words, people only encode what they pay attention to.
2. Retrieval from memory is also an obligatory and unavoidable consequence of attention.
3. Each encounter with a stimulus is encoded, stored, and retrieved separately.

Logan's instance theory is best illustrated with mathematical operations: When one first learns doing multiplications such 6×3, he or she will use the algorithm $6 + 6 + 6$. With practice, one will sooner or later remember the solution (18), and instead of applying the algorithm, will retrieve the solution from memory. Memory retrieval will take place when its speed exceeds that of the algorithm.

Apart from Logan's (1988) instance theory, there are other theories of learning that attribute the development of automaticity to memory. One of these is strength theory (e.g., MacKay, 1982), which assumes that connections between the response and stimulus become stronger as a result of practice. MacKay argued that automatic processes can be flexible, and with practice automatized solutions of lower level tasks can be transferred to higher level ones as well. Thus, the practice of lower level examples is necessary for a higher level automatic skill to develop.

Although all the aforementioned models can account for the *power law of practice* observed in skilled performance, they are obviously applicable in different types of learning situations. The power law of practice says that initial practice speeds up performance to a considerable extent; but after a certain stage, practice has diminishing effect on reaction times, finally the human limits of performance are reached, and practice does not influence performance at all. Both rule- and item-based approaches correctly predict this curve of learning (for a review, see DeKeyser, 2001). Nevertheless, the scope of instance theory is rather limited as it assumes that only identical stimuli can trigger memory-based retrieval processes, and this model is silent on what happens with similar stimuli; in other words, this model is not able to generalize a solution for a novel situation. On the other hand, traditional rule-based approaches fail to consider the fact that in certain situations solutions might be memorized and production rules might be replaced by direct retrieval from memory. Palmeri's (1997) and Nosofsky and Palmeri's (1997) *exemplar-based random walk model* is primarily an item-based model, in which a central role is attributed to memory processes, but it includes the comparison of the incoming stimulus to stimuli in other categories, and the assumption that responses from the target category and other categories compete with each other. The exemplar-based random walk model departs from traditional item-based theories and marks a step in the direction of rule-based models. Anderson, Fincham, and Douglass' (1997) work also indicates a mode of convergence as in certain situations they allow for the use of memory-based solutions.

THE ROLE OF THEORIES OF AUTOMATICITY IN L1 LEARNING AND SPEECH PRODUCTION

In L1 speech production research, no attempt has been made to relate theories of automaticity to models of speech production. The only work that has considered how theories of general skill learning might find their place in models of speech production was written by Towell, Hawkins, and Bazergui (1996) in the field of SLA. Based on the quantitative and qualitative investigation of the development of fluency of advanced learners of French, they argued that proceduralization in the sense proposed by Anderson (1983, 1995) takes place in the formulator module of Levelt's model, because this is the place where production rules concerning syntax, morphology, and phonology are applied, and where conversion from consciously used declarative knowledge to automatic rule application can come about. When discussing the role of automaticity in speech production, one needs to consider several issues, namely whether language learning is a rule- or item-based process and whether language production is mainly creative or memory based. Pawley and Syder (1983) convincingly argued that most of the utterances that one produces are not composed of sentences constructed word by word with the help of syntactic rules, but of sequences of words or phrases retrieved from memory as one unit, called formulaic language. This would mean that language production, especially speaking that is done under time pressure, is primarily a memory-based process. The problem is that models of speech production proposed in the psycholinguistic literature only account for creative language processing and do not discuss how formulaic language is stored and retrieved. In what follows, I show how theories of automaticity can account for learning formulas and for the acquisition of language production processes such as lexical access and syntactic and phonological encoding.

Whatever model of speech production we consider, the only place where formulaic knowledge can be stored is the lexicon. Without going into the debate on what a formulaic phrase is (for a recent review, see Wray, 2002), we consider formulas units of language that are stored and retrieved as one single unit. From a psycholinguistic point of view, we need to account for two aspects of formulaic language use: how formulas are retrieved and what role they play in the syntactic encoding of the message. Formulas can be of different types, of which idioms, multiword phrases, and collocations probably function as other lexical items in the mental lexicon. Therefore, whatever theories of speech production assume about how words are accessed also applies to these types of formulas. As regards retrieval, the problem is with longer variable and invariable structures that generally express one pragmatic function such as apologizing, requesting, and so on.[1] In other words, the question is how we can account for the fact that a native speaker will retrieve the phrase "I regret to tell you" as one unit from the lexicon, rather than accessing the words that constitute the phrase and create an utterance based on the syntactic rules of the language. In any model of speech production, concepts activate lexical items; therefore, we have to assume that chunking or the creation of larger units of meaning takes place at the conceptual level. Adopting La Heij's (2005) view of complex selection and simple access, it can be hypothesized that most pragmatic functions are probably conceptualized as one unit and include specifications concerning the level of formality, style, and so forth, and that these conceptual units send activation to preassembled lexical units (for a similar line of argumentation, see also Kasper, 1995). As regards the syntax of formulaic language, in modular models of speech production (Levelt, 1989, 1993; Levelt et al., 1999) formulas can also point to various types of syntactic information just as other lexical items can, and this information is used in syntactic encoding.

The acquisition of formulas can be explained both by chunking theories of automaticity and by Logan's (1988) instance theory. There is an abundance of research that views both L1 and L2 vocabulary and idiom acquisition as chunking (for a review, see N. Ellis, 2001, 2003). The law of contiguity proposed by James in 1890 claims that "objects once experienced together tend to become associated in the imagination, so that when any of them is thought of,

---

[1]Research in the field of formulaic language use suggests that formulas generally have pragmatic functions; moreover, many researchers consider pragmatic function as a defining criterion for formulaic status (for a review, see Wray, 2002).

others are likely to be thought of also, in the same order or existence as before" (quoted by N. Ellis, 2001, p. 42.). In the terms of modern cognitive psychology, this means that "nodes which are simultaneously or contiguously attended in working memory tend to become associated in the long term" (N. Ellis, 2001, p. 42). In other words, lexical items that often occur together tend to form chunks (higher order phrases or clauses), and when the conceptual specifications call on them, they are retrieved as one unit. In terms of Logan's instance theory, the acquisition of formulaic phrases can be seen as a competition between the encoding procedures that assemble larger linguistic units with the application of syntactic rules and the retrieval of memorized units. In this view, at the beginning of the language-learning process the application of rules is faster because linguistic units are not yet sufficiently encoded in memory. With experience and practice, the speed of memory retrieval exceeds that of rule-based processing, and formulaic expressions are accessed in memory as one unit. It has to be noted that because instance theory assumes that memorized solutions can be triggered by exactly the same stimuli, it seems to lack the flexibility necessary for language production, in the course of which identical stimuli rarely occur. The recent version of the theory, the exemplar-based random-walk model (Nosofsky & Palmeri, 1997; Palmeri, 1997), however, allows for memory retrieval in the case of similar and not necessarily identical stimuli; therefore it seems to be more applicable to language learning than is traditional instance theory.

Research carried out concerning how children acquire formulaic language suggests that both chunking and instance theories can be regarded as viable accounts of how formulas become memorized. Peters' (1977) in her groundbreaking study, the basic assumptions of which have been supported by numerous later investigations (for a review, see Wray, 2002), found that children tend to adopt a mixture of two different strategies to L1 learning: Holistic or gestalt L1 learners tend to use unanalyzed sequences at the beginning of the acquisition process and abstract linguistic rules from chunks at later stages, whereas analytic learners tend to construct utterances from single words and attempt to apply simple rules of language already at the start of learning. Children can be placed on a continuum between being completely analytic and completely holistic. Peters' finding that children differ as regards how they approach L1 learning might suggest that formulas might be acquired both as unanalyzed chunks and as phrases that are first assembled with the help of rules and are only later memorized as one unit.

Having placed formulaic language in models of speech production and discussed how it might be acquired, I elaborate on the automatization of lexical, syntactic, and phonological encoding processes. The primary procedure in lexical encoding is accessing lexical items stored in the mental lexicon. In order to efficiently retrieve words, strong links between concepts and words need to be established and search mechanisms need to be replaced by direct, one-step retrieval. Automatization in this field of speech production can be best explained by memory strength theories, including connectionism. These theories, specifically MacKay's (1982) work, propose that practice strengthens the links between nodes in hierarchical networks such as language, in this case, between concepts and lexical items. In this view, automaticity means that once a particular node in the network is activated, it will automatically send further activation to nodes connected to it. As regards the development of automaticity in lexical access, lexical retrieval can be considered as fully automatized if the concept that is activated by visual or other types of input will automatically pass on the highest level of activation to the corresponding lexical node.

Accounting for the development of automaticity in syntactic and phonological encoding is more complicated than explaining automatic access of lexical entries. In discussing automaticity in syntactic and phonological processing, we need to distinguish mechanisms that are based on the application of rules such as phrase- or clause-building procedures and the activation of syntactic and phonological information of lexical entries. Selection of syntactic and phonological information related to items in the lexicon is similar to lexical access; therefore, the assumptions concerning the development of automaticity in lexical retrieval outlined previously can be applied to these processes. As proposed by strength theory (MacKay, 1982) connections between lemmas and relevant syntactic information such as gender, countability status, and so on, as well as between lemmas and their phonological forms can be considered automatic if the appropriate links become so strong that there is no need for a searching mechanism. We can approach automatization of syntactic and phonological rules from the perspective of both rule- and item-based theories of automaticity. Among the rule-based models, Anderson's (1983, 1995) ACT* and ACT–R theory have been tested on L1 acquisition, and evidence was found that automatic application of syntactic rules is the result of proceduralization (for a recent study in this field, see Matessa & Anderson, 2000), that is, the conversion of consciously acquired syntactic knowledge into automatic production rules. No studies have been conducted on automatization in the field of phonological rules, but findings concerning syntax might be transferable to this field. In ACT–R theory, proceduralization is seen not only as the speed-up of encoding processes, but qualitative changes in the application of the processes such as generalization, discrimination, and strengthening are also assumed to take place (see also the Definitions and Characteristics of Automaticity section). On the other hand, chunking and connectionist theories argue that rules of syntax are not learned through proceduralization but by acquiring a high number of exemplars (i.e., unanalyzed chunks) first, and by abstracting linguistic rules from these items. The most often cited support for this view comes from computer simulations of grammar acquisition, which showed that associative learning programs that were exposed to a large amount of language input were able to abstract rules of syntax and phonology simply based on the analysis of probability with which items tend to co-occur (for a review, see N. Ellis, 2001).

SUMMARY

In this chapter, I first reviewed various definitions of automaticity and concluded that the interpretation of this term is largely dependent on how one sees the process of automatization. In theories where the development of automaticity is primarily regarded as a rule-based process, the lack of attention is one of the basic defining criteria, whereas in item-based theories single-step memory retrieval is the most important characteristic of automaticity. Next, I presented various theories of learning such as Anderson's (1985, 1993) model of proceduralization, chunking, instance and strength theory, as well as recent views that combine rule- and item-based approaches. The rest of the chapter was devoted to the discussion of how processes of speech production can be related to theories of automaticity. It was pointed out that in order to understand the development of automaticity in speech production, we first need to place formulaic phrases that are retrieved as one unit from memory in models of speech processing. I argued that formulas are stored in the mental lexicon and are accessed by single-step memory retrieval based on the conceptual specifications included in the preverbal plan. This entails that conceptual chunks corresponding to lexical units are established in the conceptualizer. I also showed how both chunking theories and instance theory can account for the acquisition of formulas. Strength theories were found to be the suited best for explaining automaticity in lexical retrieval, whereas to rule-based syntactic and phonological encoding mechanisms both Anderson's (1983, 1995) theories of proceduralization and chunking theories can be applied. In the lack of empirical research that investigates development of automaticity beyond the level of word recognition, the ideas I outlined concerning the automatization of speech production processes are highly speculative. Both laboratory research and longitudinal observational studies with special focus on automaticity would be needed to put these assumptions to test.

RECOMMENDED READINGS

1. Levelt, W. J. M. (1989). *Speaking: From intention to articulation.* Cambridge, MA: MIT Press. This book is the most detailed discussion of monolingual speech production ever published in the field of psycholinguistics. Levelt first elaborates how communicative intentions are cast into linguistic plans and how these plans take sociolinguistic, pragmatic, and contextual factors into consideration. Next follows a detailed description of lexical, grammatical, and phonological encoding, articulation, and monitoring. Levelt draws up a comprehensive theory of speech production, which belongs to modular models of production, and considers how the model can accommodate findings of research on monolingual speech production. Although spreading activation theories of speech processing are not elaborated in great detail, the results of studies conducted in this paradigm are discussed in chapters on lexical, grammatical, phonological encoding, and monitoring.

2. Levelt, W. J. M. (1999). Language production: a blueprint of the speaker. In C. Brown & P. Hagoort (Eds.), *Neurocognition of language* (pp. 83–122). Oxford, England: Oxford University Press. This book chapter contains the most up-to-date and easily accessible summary of Levelt's modular model of speech production. It starts with the review of the evolutionary development of the speech production system, and then Levelt goes on to discuss various steps of speech processing incorporating the most recent theories of speech encoding and findings of empirical research. The two major changes in comparison with his 1989 theory are the inclusion of Roelofs' (1997b) WEAVER model of word form encoding and the assumption that lemmas do not contain semantic information. Because considerable modifications have been made in the original model since 1989, it is highly recommended that researchers and students in the field of SLA also become familiar with this recent version of the theory.

3. Dell, G. S. (1986). A spreading activation theory of retrieval in sentence production. *Psychological Review, 93,* 283–321. This classic article contains the basic tenets of the spreading activation theory of speech production. Dell starts with the linguistic assumptions underlying his theory, namely that the lexicon contains nonproductive stored knowledge of words and that linguistic rules create frames into which words are inserted. He also describes the hierarchical structure of his model consisting of interconnected concepts, words, morphemes, phonemes, phonemic features, syllables, and syllabic constitu-

ents. This is followed by a discussion of the processing assumptions of the theory, the most important of which is that activation can spread in two directions. The rest of the article is an attempt to accommodate speech error data within the model, and a computer simulation experiment of the model is also presented.

4. Meijer, P. J. A., & Fox Tee, J. E. (2003). Building syntactic structures in speaking: A bilingual exploration. *Experimental Psychology, 50,* 184–195. This article presents recent findings concerning syntactic encoding in speech production and contains an excellent summary of previous research on syntactic processing. Participants in this study performed a revised version of the classic syntactic priming experiments: an immediate-recall task. The results of the research suggest that when reconstructing a sentence from memory, speakers first retrieve the words and then apply the syntactic building procedures called on by the lexical items. This study provides support for the assumptions of lemma-driven speech production models, which hypothesize that when constructing an utterance, first words are accessed and words further activate the appropriate syntactic building procedures.

5. Roelofs, A. (1997). The WEAVER model of word-form encoding in speech production. *Cognition, 64,* 249–284. The article contains a detailed discussion of Roelofs WEAVER (Word-form Encoding by Activation and VERification) model. The model assumes that word form retrieval takes place by spreading activation and that phonological representations of words are constructed in a rightward incremental fashion based on the principle of active syllabification. Roelofs compares this latter process to weaving a fabric, hence the name WEAVER model. In this model, it is also hypothesized that syllables are processed anew each time they are called on rather then being stored as preassembled units. Roelofs postulates that the checking of the encoding processes takes place through a verification mechanism called binding by checking. The article discusses how findings of previous studies on phonological encoding can be accommodated by the WEAVER model and how computer simulations are able to predict the basic tenets of the theory.

6. Postma, A. (2000). Detection of errors during speech production: A review of speech monitoring models. *Cognition, 77,* 97–131. Postma's article is a detailed and up-to-date review of theories and empirical research on speech monitoring. In the first sections of the article, a definition of errors, self-corrections, and various types of self-repairs is provided. This is followed by the overview of feedback loops in speech production and the levels of monitoring proposed in the literature. Finally, the major theories of monitoring are described and evaluated on the basis of research findings with emphasis on recent studies on the timing of self-repairs. Postma concludes that with modifications

Levelt's perceptual loop theory is able to account for most of the results of studies on monitoring.

7. van Turennout, M., Hagoort, P., & Brown, C. (1999). The time course of grammatical and phonological processing during speaking: Evidence from event-related brain potentials. *Journal of Psycholinguistic Research, 28*, 649–676. The study described in this article provides new insight into the issue of what the order of lexical and phonological encoding is and whether activation in speech production can cascade from one level of processing to a lower level. The study is also interesting because of its research methodology. In this research, participants' brain activity was recorded while performing two types of decision tasks. The participants were presented pictures and had to decide whether they saw animate or inanimate concepts and whether they started with a particular phoneme. The observations concerning the participants' brain activity showed that semantic information was available earlier than phonological information. The findings of van Turennout, Hagoort, and Brown's research are often taken as counterevidence to the cascaded flow of activation in speech production.

4 Lexical Encoding and the Bilingual Lexicon

This chapter discusses the most important theoretical issues and findings of empirical research about lexical encoding and the organization of the lexicon in a second language. Lexical processes have received distinguished attention in bilingual language production research for several reasons. First of all, it is a widely accepted view among language teachers and researchers of the field that the knowledge of vocabulary is essential for being able to communicate in a second language. One might be able to speak using just a few rules of grammar and might still be understood, but without using appropriate vocabulary, communication can hardly be successful (Widdowson, 1978). Second, one can observe the highest level of interaction between L1 and L2 at the level of vocabulary. A high percentage of intentional code-switching involves just the use of a single lexical item (Poplack, 1979/1980), and meanings and forms of L1 words are also frequently transferred to L2 (N. Ellis, 1997; Jiang, 2004; Odlin, 1989, 2003). Unintentional code-switching resulting from the competition of L1 and L2 lexical items is also more frequent than unintentional switches occurring at any other level of speech encoding (Poulisse, 1999). Finally, in one of the most influential theories of speech production, the modular model proposed by Levelt and his colleagues (Levelt, 1989; Levelt et al., 1999), lexical encoding plays a central role because lexical items govern syntactic processing (see the section titled Levelt's Modular Model of Speech Production in chap. 1). Therefore, if one is able to gain a good understanding of how lexical access takes place, a major mechanism of speech production can be explained. Based on all this, it is no wonder that lexical encoding and the bilingual lexicon are the most widely researched areas of L2 speech production.

In this chapter, I first review lexical encoding in L2 speech. Next, mechanisms of lexical access are discussed, then lexical selection procedures are described. The second part of this chapter is devoted to the organization of the bilingual lexicon. Here I start with the discussion of conceptual representation in bilingual memory, which is followed by the analysis of the work on the organization of the bilingual lexicon. I argue that although we have a fairly good understanding of lexical encoding, which is mainly due to the careful theoretical and empirical work in the field of cognitive and experimental psychology, there is a great terminological and theoretical confusion in the research of the organization of bilingual lexicon. I point out that issues of access and representation are often confounded (see also Grosjean, 1998), and many of the claims made by researchers in the field do not accord with the results in the field of lexical access nor with well-received theories of language production. This chapter also discusses code-switching and transfer at the lexical level, as well as the psycholinguistic mechanisms involved in acquiring vocabulary in L2.

LEXICAL ACTIVATION AND SELECTION IN L2

As we saw in chapter 3, there is general agreement among researchers that the language that one wants to use for communication is selected in the conceptualization phase. In Levelt's (1989, 1999a) model, this is the stage where information concerning the communicative situation is available and where it can be decided which language is appropriate for the given interaction. When discussing lexical selection, we need to understand an important distinction: activation and selection, namely that activation does not necessarily mean selection. From L1 speech production research, we know that when we want to encode a concept such as TABLE, not only the concept of TABLE but related concepts such as CHAIR, DESK, and so on are also activated to some degree. Because our intention is to express the concept of TABLE, this concept will receive the highest level of activation; thus it will be selected. The activation of other related concepts will be lower than that of TABLE. As activation spreads from the conceptual to the lexical level, the lemma for TABLE will again be the most highly activated one. Nonetheless, the concept of TABLE also activates semantically related lemmas such as "desk" and "chair," though to a lower degree than the lemma "table" (for a detailed discussion of this issue, see Bloem, van den Bogaard, & La Heij, 2004). Thus, at both the conceptual and lexical levels, activation and selection need to be distinguished. In sum, we can say that selection always entails activation, but activation does not always lead to selection.

The question that is first asked in L2 lexical encoding research is whether the conceptual system spreads activation only to the lexicon of the intended language or to that of the nonintended language as well. Early studies in this field assumed that the most economical solution to this question would be if activation spread only to the words of the selected language, and the lexical items in the other language were not activated (McNamara, 1967; McNamara & Kushnir, 1972; cf. Costa, 2005). In other words, when having to name a picture showing a chair in English, a Hungarian native speaker would activate only words in English, and the Hungarian words for the target concept, such as "szék" and items related to it, would not receive any activation. Recent research, however, shows that this is not the case.

A number of studies provide evidence for the fact that the conceptual system sends activation to both L1 and L2 lexical items. Among the first ones is Poulisse and Bongaerts' (1994) and Poulisse's (1999) research involving slips of the tongue. In a large corpus of slips of the tongue produced by Dutch speakers of English at various levels of proficiency, Poulisse and Bongaerts (1994) and Poulisse (1999) found that a high number of slips were L1 lexical substitutions (e.g., "she *hheft,* uh she has eh, big ears"; Poulisse, 1999, p. 148). L1 lexical substitutions are hypothesized to occur as a result of the fact that the concept to be encoded erroneously sends activation to both the L1 and L2 lemmas, which then further activate the phonological forms of both L1 and L2 words (lexemes), and because L1 lexemes are more frequently used in general than L2 lexemes, they will be selected for further phonological processing.

Hermans et al. (1998) conducted a series of experiments with upper-intermediate Dutch speakers of English, in which the participants had to name pictures in their L2 and ignore distractor words written in the picture. The distractor words were in either English or Dutch, and they were either semantically or phonologically related to the picture, or they were not related to it at all. From research in L1 production, it is well known that distractor words that are semantically related to the target picture slow down picture naming. This is due to the fact that the presentation of a semantically related word raises the level of activation of the related lexical item, which is high anyway because conceptually related words also receive a certain level of activation from the target picture. In this way the difference between the level of activation of the target word and the distractor word becomes smaller, which slows down production. This effect is called *semantic interference.* Picture interference studies in L1 have also demonstrated that phonologically related distractors facilitate selection because they spread activation to the target concept, thus raising the difference in the level of activation between the target lexical item and the semantically related competitors (see Fig. 4.1). This effect is generally referred to as the *phonological facilitation effect* (for a review of L1 research using the picture-word interference paradigm, see MacLeod, 1991). Because Hermans et al. wanted to test whether Dutch words were also activated when the participants had to name words in English, another picture-word interference situation in their study was when the distractor word presented in Dutch (e.g., dal–[valley]) was semantically related to the Dutch translation equivalent (berg) of the target word (mountain). If both languages are activated, one

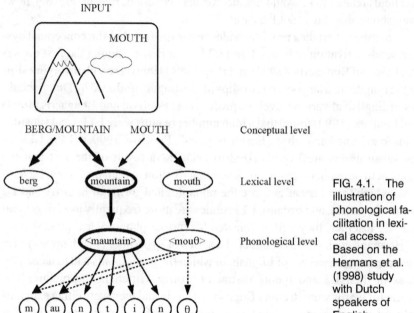

- - - - ▶ indicates possible cascading of activation.

FIG. 4.1. The illustration of phonological facilitation in lexical access. Based on the Hermans et al. (1998) study with Dutch speakers of English.

would observe slower picture naming than in the case of unrelated items because two semantically related words—the Dutch "berg" and the English "mountain"—compete for selection. The study supported this assumption, as significantly longer naming latencies were observed in this condition than in cases when the distractor words were in no way related to the picture name (see Fig. 4.2).

Using different research methods and a different L2 speaker population, Colomé (2001) also came to the conclusion that both languages are active in lexical encoding based on the results of a series of phoneme-monitoring tasks. In her study, highly proficient Catalan-Spanish bilinguals had to decide whether letters corresponding to one of the sounds either in the Catalan word or in the Spanish word or to a sound that is not included in the words in any of the two languages were part of the Catalan name of the presented picture. For example, she found that both languages receive activation because semantic interference arose when a phoneme (e.g., [s]) that was contained in the Spanish translation equivalent (e.g., silla) of the Catalan word (e.g., cadira) was presented along with the drawing. She argued that in this case the phoneme [s] activates the Spanish translation equivalent of the target Catalan word ("silla"), which then competes with the Catalan lexical item ("cadira") for selection. Therefore, the fact that more time is needed to decide whether the presented phoneme is part of the word depicted by the drawing can be taken as support for the coactivation of both languages.

Whereas Hermans et al.'s (1998) and Colomé's (2001) study provided evidence for the coactivation of L1 and L2 lexical items based on semantic interference, Costa et al. (2000) found phonological facilitation across languages. In their research, bilingual speakers of Catalan and Spanish had to name pictures whose names were phonologically similar in the two languages (called *cognates*) and pictures whose names were not related in any way in Catalan and Spanish (see Fig. 4.3). If both languages are activated in lexical access, bilinguals can name cognates faster than noncognates because of the phonological facilitation effect of the translation equivalent, but this difference in naming latencies should not be present in monolingual speakers. The results supported this hypothesis and were also replicated by Kroll et al. (2000). From this review of research, it becomes apparent that studies using different research methodologies and participants speaking different languages with vari-

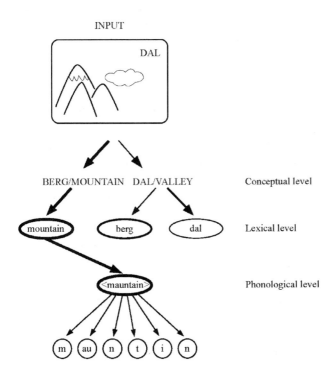

FIG. 4.2. The illustration of semantic interference in L2 lexical access. Based on the Hermans et al. (1998) study with Dutch speakers of English.

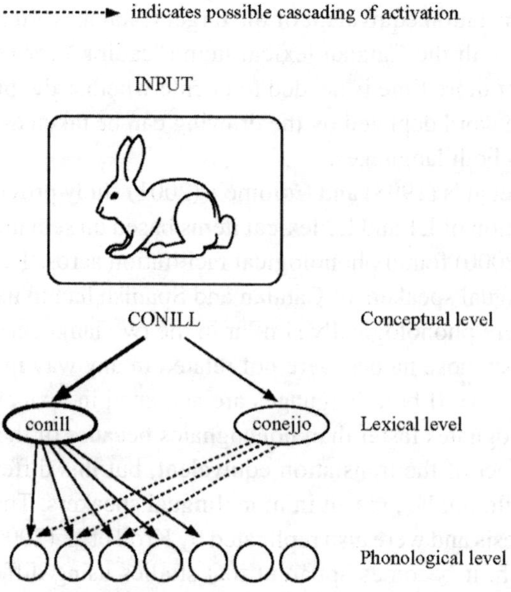

---------------▶ indicates possible cascading of activation

INPUT

CONILL · · · Conceptual level

conill · · conejjo · · Lexical level

○○○○○○ Phonological level

FIG. 4.3. Illustration of the cognate facilitation effect in Catalan-Spanish bilingual speakers. Based on Costa, Caramazza, and Sebastian-Gallés (2000).

ous levels of proficiency all came to the same conclusion as regards lexical access in bilingual language production, namely that the conceptual system sends activation to lexical items in both languages: the selected language and the nonselected one as well.

We have seen that words belonging to both the intended and nonintended language are activated in lexical encoding. One would logically assume that this also means that every activated word is a possible candidate for selection and further phonological processing. This is, however, not the case. There are two views concerning how activated words are selected: one called the *non-language-specific selection* view, which argues that every word no matter what language it belongs to is considered for further processing, and the other that only words in the intended language are possible candidates for selection, which is generally referred to as *language-specific selection*.

Let us first look at experimental evidence for the view of non-language-specific selection. As described earlier, both Hermans et al. (1998) and Colomé (2001) observed semantic interference between L1 and L2 lemmas, which indicated that not only are both L1 and L2 lemmas activated in lexical encoding, but they also compete for selection. Poulisse (1999) also explained the occurrence of blends that involved parts of words from both L1 and L2 (e.g., "springling" from the English "spring" and German "Frühling") with reference to the competition of L1 and L2 lemmas for selection. She claimed that blends are produced as a result of this competition, in the course of which incidentally both lemmas are selected for further phonological processing, and the phonemes of both words are combined into a single new word. Lee and Williams (2001) investigated the relationship of language switching and lexical selection. In their study, participants had to name three words described by three different definitions after each other (e.g., Edam is a kind of Dutch ... [cheese], The Queen lives at Buckingham ... [palace], and An animal that travelers ride in a desert [camel]) and then name two presented pictures (e.g., a house and an apple). In the priming condition, the word described by the middle one of the definitions was semantically related to the target word (e.g., the definition of the word "palace" acted as a prime for the picture of the house). In other conditions, there was no relationship between the pictures and the definitions. The participants were English-French bilinguals, who had to respond in English to the definitions, which were also presented in English, and had to name the pictures either in English or in French, or switch languages between the first and the second picture. We return to Lee and Williams' results when discussing inhibition in lexical selection; what is important for us here is that their study also showed that there is a competition between L1 and L2 lexical items in L2 production, which slows down production in the case of semantically related English and French word pairs (see Fig. 4.4).

◄────► indicates competition between lexical entries.

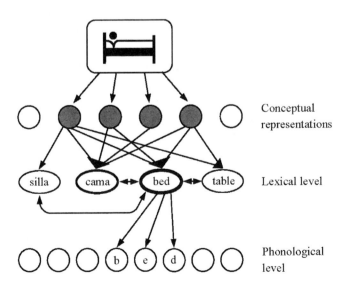

Conceptual representations

Lexical level

Phonological level

FIG. 4.4. Illustration of the non-language-specific selection hypothesis in the case of Spanish-English bilingual speakers. Based on Costa, Miozzo, and Caramazza (1999).

On the other hand, there also seems to be support for the assumption that lemma selection is language-specific. Proponents of the language-specific view cite evidence for their position based on the results of another type of experiment where the distractor words printed in the pictures to be named were the translation equivalents of the target word depicted by the picture (Costa & Caramazza, 1999; Costa et al., 1999; Hermans, 2000). The logic of the semantic priming experiments described previously (e.g., Hermans et al., 1998) would suggest that the translation equivalent in the nonintended language would act as a competitor for the target word to be produced in the selected language. For example, if an English-Spanish bilingual has to name a picture depicting a bed in Spanish ("cama"), and sees the word "bed" written in the picture, one would assume that the lemma "bed" enters into competition with the Spanish lexical item "cama," and this will slow down production. Contrary to these expectations, in all of these experiments, which involved speakers of various languages, the presentation of the translation equivalent facilitated picture naming. This effect is called the *translation facilitation effect*. Costa and Caramazza (1999) and Costa et al. (1999) explained this effect by arguing that lexical selection is non-language-specific, and therefore in Spanish-English bilingual word production, the English word "bed" sends activation to its Spanish equivalent "cama," and because lemmas from the nonintended language do not enter into competition with words in the intended language, it is easier to select an item the activation level of which rests higher (see Fig. 4.5).

Costa, Colomé, et al. (2003) made an attempt to explain the contradictory findings in the field of lexical selection. First of all, they were interested in whether they could replicate the semantic interference effect that Hermans et al. (1998) found with upper-intermediate Dutch speakers of English in the case of highly proficient Catalan-Spanish bilingual speakers. This was important because one possibility might be that depending on proficiency, L2 learners differ as regards their ability to keep the two languages apart in lexical encoding. Costa and his colleagues obtained the same interference effect as Hermans et al., which indicates that at some level of encoding there is a competition between the items of the selected and nonselected languages regardless of the participants' level of proficiency. The question is where this competition occurs. One possibility is that as Hermans et al. (1998) and Lee and Williams (2001) proposed, lexical nodes compete with each other. In Costa, Colomé et al.'s view, another explanation for the interference effect might be that the competition takes place at the phonological level, and in lexical selection the lemmas of the nonintended language are not considered. This is, however, highly unlikely because it is inconceivable how the phonological representa-

◆━━━▶ indicates competition between lexical entries.

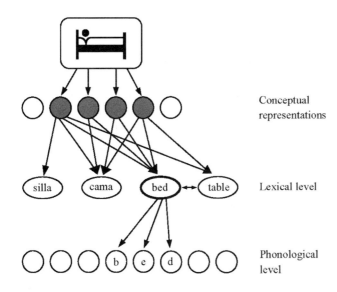

Conceptual
representations

Lexical level

Phonological
level

FIG. 4.5. Illus-
tration of the lan-
guage-specific
selection hypoth-
esis in the case
of Spanish-
English bilingual
speakers. Based
on Costa,
Miozzo, and
Caramazza
(1999).

tions of competitor words would receive activation if the words themselves are not activated. Hermans (2000) seemed to provide a sound explanation for the translation facilitation effect by claiming that when participants see the translation equivalent and the picture at the same time, the concept to be encoded receives activation from two sources, the written word and the drawing. This speeds up concept selection to such an extent that the competition at the lexical level is compensated for; moreover, the speed-up of concept selection is higher than the decrease in speed at the lexical level due to the interference of the nonintended language, and thus we can observe a facilitation effect. La Heij's (2005) view of control in lexical encoding discussed in the section titled Syntactic Processing in chapter 2 also supports this explanation because he argued that tasks send additional activation to concepts; and in this case the same concept is activated from two different tasks (for a detailed discussion of the translation facilitation effect, see Bloem et al., 2004).

From the review of research on language selection, it can be concluded that there is stronger evidence for the non-language-specific selection hypothesis, namely that in lexical encoding both L1 and L2 lemmas enter into competition, than for the language-specific selection hypothesis, which claims that lexical items in the two languages do not compete for selection.

The non-language-specific selection hypothesis seems to be able to account for most research findings with speakers of any level of proficiency.

CONTROL IN LEXICAL ENCODING

Previously we argued that there is now sufficient evidence that lemmas in both L1 and L2 are activated in lexical encoding. How is it possible then that bilinguals retrieve the situationally appropriate lexical item and rarely use words in the nonintended language? How is it that intentional code-switching at the lexical level is executed smoothly most of the time? How is it possible to explain the occurrence of blends at the lexical level? These three related questions need to be answered by any theory that intends to account for control in lexical encoding. The issue of control in bilingual access can be approached from two perspectives: from the angle of language-specific versus non-language-specific selection and from the aspect of the complexity of the access and selection mechanisms (La Heij, 2005).

We saw in the previous section that there are two possible ways one can conceive of competition in lexical encoding. One of them is that even though lemmas in the nonintended language are also activated, they are ignored in selection. In the language-specific selection models, lemmas are assumed to carry a language tag (Costa et al., 1999), and lexical concepts are supposed to be language-specific. Costa (2005) argued that, for example, a Spanish-English bilingual speaker might have a different lexical concept for DOG and for PERRO (dog in Spanish). If this speaker wants to produce words in English, the concept DOG spreads activation to the lemma "dog" that carries the language tag "English," and a checking mechanism establishes whether the selected lemma indeed matches the intended concept. This assumption is an example of the "simple access and complex selection" type of control process because it presumes straightforward correspondence between concepts and lemmas and the existence of a checking mechanism, which determines whether the right lemma has been selected. Roelofs (1998) also proposed a similar lexical control mechanism as outlined by Costa (2005). When discussing lexical access in L1 in the Lexical Encoding section of chapter 2, I have already pointed out that one of the main problems with including checking mechanisms in lexical encoding is that it is not specified where these mechanisms derive the knowledge from to control selection. Moreover, supposing that different conceptual representations exist for all the words in L2 is against the findings in the field of the organization of the mental lexicon (see the next section). We have also seen that the language-specific selection hypothesis cannot account for a number of research findings in the field of lexical encoding (e.g., Hermans et al., 1998).

In the non-language-specific selection models, control can be conceived of in different ways. One possibility is to assume the existence of inhibitory mechanisms, which is also a type of the "simple access and complex selection" hypotheses. The most famous of the inhibitory theories is that of D. W. Green's (1998) inhibitory control (IC) model. In this model, first a conceptual representation of the message to be conveyed is generated. This conceptual plan sends activation to the lexicon and to an attentional system that controls language processing, which is called the supervisory attentional system (SAS). Green assumed that when speaking, one activates different task schemas such as a task schema for picture naming in L1, or translating words from L2 to L1. It is the job of SAS to control the activation of the task schemas. Thus, when one has to name a picture in L2, SAS activates the appropriate task schema, which in turn sends further activation to the lexical level, where lemmas carry language tags. Because both lemmas in the intended and the nonintended language receive activation, the task schema is responsible for raising the activation level of L2 lemmas and inhibiting the selection of L1 lemmas. Because task schemas are supervised by an attentional system, inhibiting words in the language not in use requires conscious effort on the part of the speaker (see Fig. 4.6).

D. W. Green's (1998) model has been tested in experiments where participants were asked to switch languages during task performance, and the time interval needed to select the other language was taken as an indication of

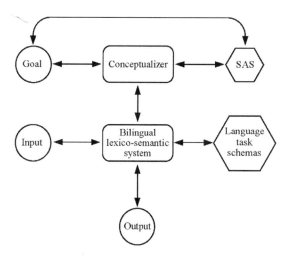

FIG. 4.6. The inhibitory control model. From D. W. Green (1998). Copyright 1998 by Cambridge University Press.

switching costs. Somewhat counterintuitively, the model predicts that proficient bilinguals need more energy to suppress words in L1 when talking in L2, which is explained by Green in the following way. Due the frequent use of L2, L2 words also have a high resting level of activation, and the smaller the difference in activation between L1 and L2 words, the more attention is needed to control selection. Meuter and Allport (1999) examined the switching costs involved in changing from L1 to L2 and from L2 to L1 in a digit-naming task. As predicted by Green's model, it took more time to switch back from L2 to L1 than from L1 to L2. In the experiment that I described in the previous section, Lee and Williams (2001) also found that when speaking in L2, L1 words are strongly inhibited, but in L1 production there is only moderate or no inhibition of L2.

D. W. Green (1998) also claimed that the amount of attention necessary to control lexical selection also depends on the task itself, more precisely on the level of activation of the lemmas in the nonselected language. For example, it is easier to prevent L1 words from being selected in a simple L2 picture-naming task, than in a so-called Stroop task when a distractor word in L1 is also printed in the picture that needs to be named in L2.

Another assumption of D. W. Green's (1998) IC model is that with the development of proficiency the inhibition of the unwanted language gets increasingly difficult. This follows from the fact that the more frequently the L2 is used, the higher the resting level of L2 words' activation becomes, thus the smaller the difference between the resting levels of L1 and L2 words is. Therefore, more-proficient bilinguals are assumed to need more energy to suppress L1 words. This positive relationship between speakers' level of proficiency and the amount of switching cost hypothesized by Green was not confirmed by Meuter and Allport's (1999) study. As one would assume based on general theories of automaticity in L2 production (see chap. 3), and as Meuter and Allport's research also showed, with the increase of L2 competence the attention needed to control performance decreases. This is an important finding that runs counter to Green's IC model. Green's model has also been criticized on other grounds. Both Kroll and Tokowitz (2005) as well as Costa (2005) pointed out that Green did not specify the scope of the inhibitory mechanisms. It is unclear whether in his model words are inhibited at the lemma level or at the phonological level or both. Costa, Colomé, et al. (2003) and Kroll et al. (2000) found that the phonological features of the words in the nonintended language are also activated, which is difficult to explain if we assume that lexical nodes from which activation could spread forward are inhibited. The occurrence of blends cannot be explained in inhibitory models either, because these models do not allow for the parallel selection of L1 and L2 lemmas.

Moreover, inhibition was not observed in research on L1 production, therefore assuming its existence makes theories of L2 encoding unnecessarily complicated (Costa, 2005).

One of the simplest ways to exercise control in lexical encoding is assuming that the preverbal message contains all the necessary information to retrieve the appropriate word (complex access, simple selection). Poulisse and Bongaerts (1994) proposed that the preverbal message contained a language cue in addition to the conceptual specifications. In their view, lemmas also carry language tags, and selection simply involves matching the conceptual specifications and the language cue with the appropriate lemma. If the speaker wants to use L2, the L2 language cue raises the activation level of L2 words, thus L1 words will not be selected. Intentional code-switching can also be explained by assuming that if the speaker wants to insert an L1 word into an L2 utterance, all he or she needs to do is to change the language cue of the concept corresponding to the word. Unintentional use of words from the nonselected language can be due either to the erroneous specification of the language cue or to the incidentally higher level of activation of the lemma in the nonintended language. La Heij (2005) further elaborated Poulisse and Bongaert's theory of control in lexical access. He argued that assuming the existence of a language cue at the conceptual level is sufficient because it ensures that lemmas in the language in use receive higher activation than lemmas in the nonselected language. Words in the selected language also rest at a higher level of baseline activation because repeated use raises their level of activation, making their selection easier (this is called the frequency effect; see Morton, 1969, and for a review, Levelt, 1989). The only minor difference between Poulisse and Bongaert's and La Heij's views is that Poulisse and Bongaerts proposed that lemmas have language tags, whereas La Heij argued that the language cue should be added at the conceptual level because in Levelt et al.'s (1999) recent model of lexical encoding, lemmas do not contain semantic information (see the section 7 below).

We have seen that there exist three possible ways of how one can conceive of control in lexical selection. One of them involves the use of a checking mechanism; the other presumes the existence of inhibitory processes; and the third one postulates that lexical selection is only based on the word's activation level, which is regulated by the language cue and the frequency of use. The first two theories can be criticized on both theoretical and empirical grounds, whereas besides being simple and theoretically sound, the third, activation-based view of control is able to account for most phenomena observed in research on lexical encoding.

CONCEPTUAL AND LEXICAL REPRESENTATION
IN BILINGUAL MEMORY

Although the bilingual lexicon is one of the most widely researched knowledge stores of the L2 speech production system, little is known about its structure and the information it contains. This is partly due to the fact that there is no agreement among researchers concerning what aspects of word knowledge are stored in the lexicon, and what the relationship between concepts and word meanings is.

Pavlenko (1999), who recently called attention to the theoretical and terminological debate in this respect, argued that research on the bilingual memory has been plagued by a number of problems. One of these is that semantic information (word meaning) and conceptual knowledge are neither clearly defined nor appropriately distinguished in the literature. The question is partly a philosophical one, namely, whether concepts can exist independent of word meanings. One standpoint in the psycholinguistic literature is that concepts should be distinguished from word meaning (e.g., Paradis, 2000; Pavlenko, 1999). In this view, it is claimed that concepts are "multisensory units of meaning independent of whether a corresponding word exists" (Paradis, 2000, p. 22) and that "language is only one way to access concepts" (Paradis, 2000, p. 22). On the other hand, several researchers argue that semantic and conceptual representations do not need to be distinguished (de Groot, 2000; Francis, 2005). Their arguments are based on the assumptions of Hintzman's (1986) work, who claimed that abstract knowledge such as that of word meanings is not distinct from the knowledge of concepts because both are built up of memory traces that one's experiences leave in the mind. A concept or the meaning of a word is made up of the complete set of the memory traces related to this exemplar, and when one accesses a specific word such as "sorrow" all the traces that contain relevant information related to this concept are activated. This view also implies that in different contexts and in different languages various features or traces of concepts are in the foreground.

The fact that researchers disagree on whether word meaning and concepts can and should be differentiated, also results in two theoretically different approaches to how concepts and word meanings are represented in the language-processing system. In one view it is proposed that semantic and conceptual representations are stored at distinct levels, whereas in the other it is supposed that these two types of knowledge are interdependent and represented at the same level. Roelofs' (1992) and Levelt et al.'s (1999) model of lexical access is an example of an integrated conceptual and semantic level, in which concepts are represented by nodes that are connected with each other (for a discussion of this specific issue, see Roelofs, 2000). In this view, concepts are undivided wholes that are activated in their entirety. Concepts can be both lexical, that is, expressed by a single word, and nonlexical, which means that they can be encoded only by multiple words, phrases, or sentences. Concepts can be culture or language specific; thus, it is possible for a speaker to have a different conceptual representation for the English word "winter" and the Hungarian "tél," the latter involving associations to snow and cold, and the former to rain, fog, and mild weather. Moreover, lexical concepts can also be connected to imagery and background knowledge. Lexical access involves the activation of concepts, which then further spread activation to lemmas, which contain syntactic information about the lexical entry but no information on meaning. Lemmas are also stored in an interconnected network, where related items can spread activation to each other. Roelofs (2000) explained certain aphasics' failure to access lexical representations who are nevertheless able to retrieve the conceptual features of a word with reference to the damage in the connections between the conceptual and lemma level.

In the other view, which was first advocated by Paradis (1997, 2000) and is also held by Pavlenko (1999), a distinction is made between the semantic and conceptual level of representation. Paradis (2000) claimed that a "concept includes all the knowledge that an individual has about a thing or event" (p. 22). Thus Paradis, just like de Groot (2000), also saw concepts as interconnected networks of features, which might be activated to a different degree depending on the communicative situation. However, Paradis (2000) argued that "the lexical and semantic components of a lexicalized concept are not part of the concept but of the language system" and that conceptual and lexical properties "map onto each other, but are distinct entities" (p. 24). He interpreted the observations of aphasic research, which describes that certain patients might not be able to access lexical representations (e.g., word forms), but the conceptual representations for the lexical entries are available for them (i.e., they can characterize the object they cannot name), as support for the distinction of semantic and conceptual levels. Pavlenko (1999) also argued for the necessity of differentiating the semantic component and conceptual component of lexical concepts from the perspective of cultural relativity. In an earlier study, Pavlenko (1997) investigated how different types of Russian-English bilingual speakers, namely those who learned English in a decontextualized classroom setting in Russia and those who acquired English in the United States describe a scene illustrating an event of the invasion of privacy. The results showed that students who learned the language in a foreign language environment were able to define the term "privacy" but had no episodic knowledge related to this word. This was caused by the fact that in a number of languages such as Russian and Hungarian there is no word for privacy, which also entails that there is no lexical concept for it either. Based on this finding, Pavlenko (1999) argued that lexicalized concepts have a distinct semantic and conceptual component. By semantic component, she meant "explicitly available information, which relates the word to other words, idioms and conventionalized expressions in that language" (p. 211.), whereas the conceptual component is characterized by "multimodal-information, which includes imagery, schemas, motor programs, auditory, tactile and somatosensory representations, based on experiential world knowledge" (p. 212). Jarvis (2000) criticized Pavlenko's definitions of semantic and conceptual knowledge by arguing that they are not derived from a model of bilingual memory, fail to consider implicit knowledge of semantics and concepts, and exclude the denotations and connotations of words from semantics. He also pointed out that the most convincing support for the necessity to differentiate between the semantic and conceptual level of representation would be if evidence was found that an aphasic patient is able to retrieve semantic information related to a word but can access neither its form nor its conceptual features (for an overview of theories of semantic and conceptual representation, see Table 4.1).

TABLE 4.1
Overview of Theories of Semantic and Conceptual Representation

	Separate Conceptual and Lexical Level	Nature of Concepts	Relationship of L1 and L2 Concepts	Empirical Evidence
Roelofs (1992, 2000)	No	Undivided units	Concepts can be language specific	Computational test of the WEAVER model
de Groot (1992, 2000)	No	Network of features	Conceptual features/memory traces of L1 and L2 concepts overlap	Word association research
Paradis (1997, 2000)	Yes	Network of features	Conceptual features/memory traces of L1 and L2 concepts overlap	Aphasic research
Pavlenko (2000)	Yes	Network of features	Conceptual features/memory traces of L1 and L2 concepts overlap	Intercultural comparison of bilingual speakers

From the preceding review, it becomes apparent that the question of how semantic and conceptual knowledge is represented in the bilingual memory is a controversial issue. Pavlenko (1999) explained that this was due not only to the lack of agreement among researchers concerning the differentiation of semantic and conceptual levels of representation but to the fact that most of the research in this respect involved decontextualized experimental tasks in laboratory settings. She called attention to the need to consider cultural and contextual factors in the study of bilingual memory representation. Nevertheless, research evidence from studies on brain damage and on the organization of memory in experimental psychology seems to be in favor of the combined storage of semantic and conceptual information.

MODELS OF THE ORGANIZATION
OF THE BILINGUAL LEXICON

As shown in the previous section , the bilingual lexicon can be seen in different ways: It might be the store of conceptual and semantic information, the depository of words forms only, or a memory store for both word forms and semantic information. One of the basic problems in this field is that most of the researchers do not make clear what exactly they mean by the bilingual lexicon; therefore, it is often difficult to decide whether they refer to the semantic/conceptual and/or to the linguistic structure of the lexicon when discussing the organization of bilingual lexical memory. Bilingual lexical representation research would greatly benefit from defining these key concepts.

In this section, I first present the hierarchical models of the bilingual lexicon, and then evaluate them critically and provide alternative explanations for the empirical research findings in the field. Following this, I describe studies that examine the structure of the mental lexicon.

In the early work on bilingual lexical representation, three important distinctions were made concerning the organization of the lexicon. Weinreich (1953) argued that speakers of a second language might represent words in a *compound, coordinate,* or *subordinate* manner. This means that in compound storage, the conceptual representations of a given word are shared, and the speaker has two words for the same concept in the languages spoken. For a German speaker of English, this would mean that he or she has the same concept for the word "fall," and the English and German words are connected to this shared concept (see Fig. 4.7). In the coordinate mode of representation, speakers have separate concepts in their two languages, and these concepts are lexicalized by the respective words in the two languages. For example, in the case of another German-English bilingual, slightly different concepts might

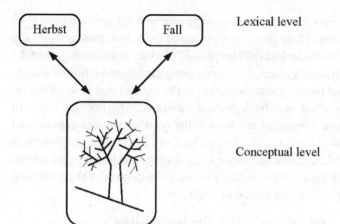

FIG. 4.7. Compound model of representation.

exist for the German word "Herbst" and for the English "fall" (see Fig. 4.8). In the subordinate manner of representation, the concept for a given lexical item is directly linked to the L1 word, which is connected to the L2 word; thus, a different German native speaker of English retrieves the word "fall" via the L1 lexical item "Herbst" (see Fig. 4.9).

Whereas Weinreich (1953) used the previously described categorizations for lexical storage only, Ervin and Osgood (1954) extended them to learners who acquired their two languages in different situations. One is likely to develop a coordinate system of representation if he or she learns the two languages in two different cultural contexts, or if he or she learns one language in a particular setting, for example, at home, and the other in other circumstances, for example, at school. In these situations, there is great likelihood that many words will be linked to slightly different conceptual representations. Bilinguals who learn their two languages simultaneously might have a compound mode of representation. These learners generally use the two languages interchangeably in the same situation with the same people, for example, in a bilingual family. Students who typically learn the second language in a foreign language environment and in a classroom situation might store many of the words in a subordinate manner, through associating L2 words with their L1 equivalents. Although Ervin and Osgood's recognition of the fact that the context in which words are learned might influence how they are stored is important, this static view about the type of bilingual speakers is not tenable anymore. First of all, the characteristics of the words, such as their similarity in the two languages, the word class they belong to, and abstract versus concrete status (for a recent review, see Kroll & Tokowitz, 2005), are assumed to influence the manner they are encoded in the lexicon. Second, it has been proposed that lexical representation changes with the development of language proficiency; for example, with more experience in L2, a word initially stored in a subordinate manner might become represented in a compound manner (for a review, see Kroll & de Groot, 1997; Kroll & Tokowitz, 2005).

The reformulation of the classic compound versus subordinate distinction can be found in Potter, So, von Eckardt, and Feldman's (1984) so-called hierarchical model. The model is called hierarchical because it assumes separate levels for concepts and word forms. Potter et al. argued that there are two dif-

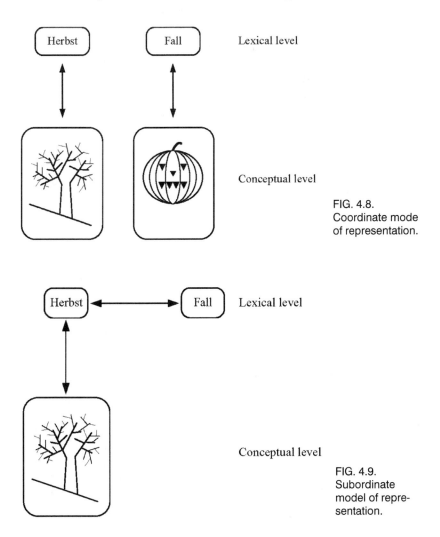

Herbst Fall Lexical level

Conceptual level

FIG. 4.8.
Coordinate mode
of representation.

Herbst Fall Lexical level

Conceptual level

FIG. 4.9.
Subordinate
model of repre-
sentation.

ferent ways in which concepts can be related to words in L2. In the *concept mediation* alternative, both the L1 and L2 words are associated with the same concept, and similarly to the L1 word, L2 lexical entries are also accessed through this shared concept. This is the same as compound lexical representation (Weinreich, 1953), which in the case of a Spanish-English bilingual means that he has a shared concept for a given word (e.g., CHAIR/SILLA), for which two independent lexical representations exist in L1 ("chair") and L2 ("silla"). In the *word association* alternative, L2 words have no links to the concepts; they are associated with their L1 translation equivalents. In other words, there is a direct link between the translation equivalents, and when translating an L1 word to L2 there is no need to retrieve the concept (see Figs. 4.10 and 4.11). For example, when a Spanish learner wants to say "chair" in English, he or she accesses this word by first retrieving the Spanish word "silla," and through it the L2 word "chair."

Potter et al. (1984) tested these models by examining the time course of picture naming and word translation in the case of proficient and less proficient

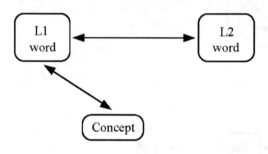

FIG. 4.10. Word association model. Adapted from *Journal of Verbal Learning and Verbal Behaviour, 23,* M. C. Potter et al., Lexical and conceptual representation in beginning and more proficient bilinguals, pp. 23–38. Copyright © (1984), with permission of Elsevier.

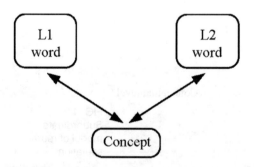

FIG. 4.11. Concept mediation model. Adapted from *Journal of Verbal Learning and Verbal Behaviour, 23,* M. C. Potter et al., Lexical and conceptual representation in beginning and more proficient bilinguals, pp. 23–38. Copyright © (1984), with permission of Elsevier.

L2 speakers. They found that picture naming took approximately the same time as translation in the case of both competent and less competent learners, which they took as a support for the concept mediation alternative. Subsequent studies (H.-C. Chen & Lueng, 1989; Kroll & Curley, 1988), however, found that speakers who were less proficient than the lower proficiency group in Potter et al.'s study were faster at translation than picture naming. Other evidence for the fact that beginning L2 students use the word association strategy when retrieving words in L2 comes from studies examining the difference in the speed of translating cognates and noncognates (Dufour, Kroll, & Scholl, 1996; cf. Kroll & de Groot, 1997). The results of this study indicated that regardless of language proficiency, L2 speakers translated words that were cognates faster than noncognate words, and that less proficient speakers benefited more from the cognate facilitation effect than their more proficient counterparts. Talamas, Kroll, and Dufour's (1995; cf. Kroll & de Groot, 1997) research, in which speakers at two different levels of proficiency were asked to judge whether words are translation equivalents, found that advanced speakers were slower to reject word pairs as equivalents in which the meaning of the words was related, whereas less competent speakers found it more difficult to decide on word pairs the form of which was similar.

Kroll and Stewart (1990, 1994) drew up a new model of lexical and conceptual representation called the revised hierarchical model (RHM), which incorporated both the earlier concept mediation and word association model and assumed different strengths of links between concepts and words at various stages of language development. In this model, conceptual representations for words were assumed to be shared. The model presumed that at the beginning of L2 acquisition links between L1 words and concepts as well as between L2 words and L1 translation equivalents are stronger than links between L2 words and the corresponding concept, and that with the development of proficiency the weak conceptual links between L2 words and concepts become stronger (see Fig. 4.12). To illustrate this for a Spanish learner of English, this means that links between Spanish words and concepts such as "silla" and CHAIR are stronger than links between English words and concepts (i.e., chair and the concept of CHAIR). This theory therefore does not claim that there are no conceptual links between L2 words and concepts in the case of beginning learners, but that these links are not strong enough to allow direct access from L2 words to concepts. The model also proposes that there are asymmetrical links between L2 and L1 words, namely that L2 words are more strongly related to their L1 translation equivalents than vice versa, which results in L2 to L1 translation being faster than L1 to L2 translation. The model has been tested by a number of studies, and

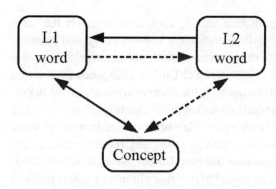

FIG. 4.12. The revised hierarchical model. Based on Kroll and Stewart (1994). Adapted from *Journal of Memory & Language, 33*, J. F. Kroll & E. Stewart, Category inference in translation and picture naming: Evidence for asymmetric connections between bilingual memory representations, pp. 149–174. Copyright © (1994), with permission from Elsevier.

its predictions concerning the differences in the speed of translation from L1 to L2 and from L2 to L1 have largely been borne out (e.g., Keatley, Spinks & de Gelder, 1992; Kroll & Stewart, 1994; Sholl, Sankaranarayan, & Kroll, 1995; but see, de Groot & Poot, 1997; La Heij, Kerling, & van der Velden, 1996).

The hierarchical models outlined previously raise a number of questions that have received little attention in the literature. First of all, it is often claimed that these models are models of lexical and conceptual representation (Kroll & de Groot, 1997; Kroll & Stewart, 1990, 1994; Kroll & Tokowitz, 2005), but in fact they attempt to explain lexical access. The hierarchical models are not concerned with how concepts are represented (e.g., what the relationship of L1 and L2 concepts is), they merely state that concepts are stored at a different level of production than words. Neither do they specify what is meant by lexical representation. Questions such as whether the lexical level contains information about word meanings, and if not what the relationship is between word meanings (semantics) and concepts (see the previous section), are not addressed. Therefore, these models do not account for how words are represented in the bilingual lexicon but aim to explicate word retrieval in different tasks. A further problem is that these models do not distinguish between automatic access from concepts to words and conscious, effortful processing, and problem solving. Kroll and de Groot often used the term "translation strategy," which indicates that they regarded word association as a conscious problem-solving mechanism and not as an instance of automatic retrieval process, but they did not make this distinction clear in their model.

Another problem with the hierarchical models is that they compare word translation and picture naming based on the argument that word translation involves lexical processing, whereas picture naming entails accessing conceptual representations as well. If we analyze the psycholinguistic processes involved in word translation, we see that translation comprises a number of substeps. If one is asked to translate a visually presented word from L1 to L2, first he or she has to recognize the word (lemma). This L1 lemma will spread activation to the concept linked to it via a concept node and to other L1 and L2 lemmas that are associated with it (e.g., semantically related lexical items) (see Dijsktra, Van Heuven, & Grainger, 1998). For the sake of simplicity, now let us assume that concepts are shared in L1 and L2. Based on the task instructions, a language cue is added to the conceptual representation, and the concept will activate the L2 lemma (La Heij, 2005). The important argument here is that translation cannot simply involve accessing the equivalent L2 word through the L1 lemma. There is no theory of lexical access in which one lexical item can retrieve another one; lemmas are always accessed through conceptual representations (see La Heij, Hooglander, Kerling, & van der Velden, 1996, for a similar line of argumentation). It is possible, though, that because L2 words are learned through associating them with their L1 equivalents, very strong associative links are formed between them. Thus perceiving the word in one of the languages will raise the activation level of its translation equivalent to such an extent that its selection through the conceptual representation can become very fast. This is probably what happens in the case of learners who acquire words by linking them to their L1 counterparts, and because this is typical at the early stage of acquisition, beginning learners are fast at translating words. In picture naming, the picture activates the concept associated with the picture, and the concept spreads activation to the L1 and L2 words related to it. Because the task instructions specify that the word has to be named in L2, the lemma corresponding to the concept and the language cue will receive the highest level of activation. Due to the fact that the L1 word was not presented earlier, there is nothing that would boost the initial level of activation of the L2 lemma; thus, selection will be slower for less advanced speakers. The reason for the finding that more proficient learners perform translation and picture naming during a similar amount of time (Potter et al., 1984) is that above a certain level of proficiency learners acquire words associating them with their conceptual representations and not with their L1 counterparts; thus, the strong associative links between L1 and L2 words become weaker and do not facilitate translation any more.

We also have to note that it would deserve more careful consideration under what circumstances strong associative relationships between L1 and L2 lexical items are established. It might be supposed that this is not just the function of proficiency, but might depend on the context of acquisition, the methods of teaching, and individual learning strategies. In naturalistic learning environ-ments (L2 context), word-association might be less frequent than in a foreign language classroom situation. If teachers consistently present new vocabulary by relying on the L1 and if the learner prefers learning words by associating them with their L1 equivalents, it is more likely that strong connections be-tween L1 and L2 words develop, and perhaps these connections remain active even at a higher stage of proficiency.

The argument just outlined, that translation is always conceptually medi-ated, can explain why less competent speakers are faster at word translation than at picture naming, but there are other studies that have been taken as sup-port for the word association model. One of them is Dufour et al.'s (1996) re-search that compares the time needed to translate cognates and noncognates. When discussing research on lexical access, we have seen that the fact that names of pictures that are cognates in the two languages are retrieved faster is due to the facilitation effect arising at the phonological level (Costa et al., 2000). Therefore, it can be assumed that when an L1 word the phonological form of which is similar to the L2 translation equivalent has to be translated, the L1 lemma passes on activation to its phonological form, which facilitates the phonological encoding of the L2 word. This might be the reason why cog-nates are translated faster than noncognates. What is more difficult to explain, however, is why the facilitation effect is higher for less competent speakers than for advanced speakers as found by Dufour et al. One possible solution to this problem might lie in the differing levels of automaticity with which word form encoding is performed at different levels of L2 competence. Advanced learners might access the phonological form of words in an automatic fashion, which means that this process is generally fast, and the phonological facilita-tion effect has a less noticeable effect. However, phonological facilitation might be more apparent in the case of beginning learners, for whom phonolog-ical processing is effortful and slow. Talamas et al. (1995; cf. Kroll & de Groot, 1997) study, which found that less competent L2 learners took longer to decide whether orthographically similar L1 and L2 words are translation equivalents also has a similar explanation. For learners at the beginning stage of L2 acqui-sition, the lemma to word form mappings are not yet strongly encoded; there-fore, they pay attention to these aspects of words first. For more proficient learners, accessing the phonological form of the lemma is automatic; there-fore, their attention is freed for considering different shades of meaning. In sum, the three studies that have so far been regarded as support for the existence of the word association alternative can be explained without recourse to this model as well.

The RHM can be criticized on other grounds as well. As I have argued previously, theories of lexical access do not allow the retrieval of lexical entries without activating their conceptual representations; therefore, I do not find that the claim included in the RHM, that is, that at an early stage of acquisition lexical links between L1 and L2 words are stronger than conceptual links between the concept and the L2 word, is justified. Conceptual links in this model are the concept nodes through which activation spreads from concepts to words, whereas lexical links are associative links established in the network of L1 and L2 words stored together in the speaker's lexicon. Access from concepts to L2 lemmas either is automatic, and in that case only the extent of competition between the lexical entries in the lexicon determines the speed of retrieval, or is effortful and involves a search mechanism or the use of lexical communication strategy, which slows down lexical encoding to a considerable extent and might even render it unsuccessful. The RHM, however, is not concerned with this latter alternative.

The model of bilingual lexical memory that is indeed concerned with lexical and conceptual representation is de Groot's (1992) conceptual feature model. In this theory, it is presumed that words are linked to concepts, which are made up of a set of interconnected features. The theoretical assumptions underlying this model are based on theories of memory representation (Hintzman, 1986; see earlier discussion), namely that both concepts and word meanings are represented as a network of interconnected features or memory traces, a certain group of which is activated together to form a unit (concept or lexical meaning). The most important claim of the distributed feature model is that conceptual representations in the two languages of a bilingual speaker are not necessarily shared; they might only overlap. Van Hell and de Groot (1998) argued that cognates, concrete words, and nouns generally share more conceptual features than noncognates, abstract words and verbs, which they supported with the results of a series of word association tasks. A series of translation experiments involving cognate and non-cognate as well as concrete and abstract word pairs also showed that words that share more conceptual features are translated faster than those where the concepts in the two languages differ to a great extent (e.g., Kroll & Stewart, 1994; Schwanenflugel, Harnishfeger, & Stowe, 1988). Figure 4.13 illustrates the distributed feature model by depicting the conceptual feature overlap between the cognate word pairs of the English word "lamp" and its German counterpart "Lampe" and the abstract words "love" and "Liebe."

Having presented the most important models of bilingual lexical representation, now I discuss what it means to know a word and how the different types

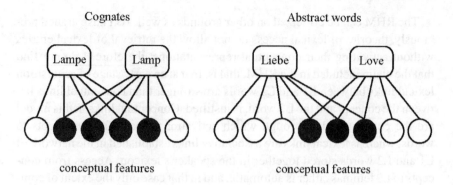

FIG. 4.13.   Illustration of the conceptual feature model.

of knowledge might be represented in the bilingual mind. It is an accepted view in general L2 vocabulary research that when learning a new word, the following types of information need to be acquired: (a) phonological, (b) orthographical, (c) syntactic, (d) morphological, (e) semantic, (f) pragmatic/sociolinguistic, and (g) idiomatic (Nation, 1990). There seems to be an agreement among researchers concerning the first four types of knowledge: The phonological characteristics of a word are stored in the mental lexicon at the level called the lexeme and the syntactic and morphological information is represented at the lemma level (see the section Levelt's Modular Model of Speech Production in chap. 1). In L1 production, idioms are also assumed to be stored as one lemma in the mental lexicon (Levelt, 1989), and once acquired, L2 idioms are also represented as one unit.

We have seen that there is considerable disagreement among researchers as regards where information regarding semantic features is encoded. Levelt et al. (1999) and Roelofs (1999) assumed that there is a separate conceptual level where word meanings are stored. De Groot (1992) in her distributed feature model also postulated that conceptual and semantic information are stored together in lexical memory, whereas Paradis (1997, 2000) and Pavlenko (1999) argued that concepts are located outside the lexicon, which, however, contains semantic as well as syntactic information. As regards L2 representation, de Groot (1992, 2000), Paradis, and Pavlenko all agree that L1 and L2 concepts are not separate entities but share a certain number of features or memory traces. In both theories of semantic and conceptual representation, it is also assumed that the meanings of translation equivalents overlap but are not completely identical. The storage of pragmatic and sociolinguistic information associated with a particular word has received little attention. Although Paradis', de Groot's, and Pavlenko's views differ on levels of representation, they all imply that the pragmatic and sociolinguistic information is stored at the conceptual level. L2 pragmatic research suggests that especially in decontextualized classroom settings pragmatic and sociolinguistic information is difficult to acquire; thus, even advanced L2 speakers frequently rely on the pragmatic and sociolinguistic knowledge associated with the L1 word (Kasper, 1992).

As regards the organization of the bilingual lexicon, the final issue addressed in this section concerns the relationship between the items stored in it. The lexicon is frequently characterized by the network metaphor and is often conceived of as a "gigantic multidimensional cobweb" (Aitchison, 1987, p.72, quoted by Wilks & Meara, 2002). Wilks and Meara called attention to the need to refine this view of the mental lexicon. On the basis of computer simulations and word association data collected from native and nonnative speakers of French, they pointed out that in the core lexicon of both native and nonnative speakers one can find a high number of connections between lexical items, and that there are more connections between L1 items than L2 ones. Their results suggest that in reality there are fewer connections between items than it would be possible in the model, which is against the view that the mental lexicon has very high network density. Wilks and Meara also speculated that the network structure of L1 and L2 lexicon might be different, and that certain lexical items might play a central role in the network (i.e., they might have connections to a high number of other items), whereas others might be found at the periphery of the network.

Wolter (2001) examined the structure of the mental lexicon based on the associations that exist between lexical items.[1] Despite the fact that he started out from the assumption that the L1 and L2 mental lexicons are separate, which is hotly debated by most researchers in the field of psycholinguistics, his findings are important concerning the relationship of lexical entries and can be easily adapted to models that assume one single store of vocabulary in L1 and L2. He argued that L2 words are organized in a network in which depth of world knowledge determines whether the items occupy a central or a peripheral position. Well-known words are located at the core of the lexicon, and the less words are known, the further away they can be found from the center of the network (see Fig. 4.14). Wolter found that words that are well known by speak-

---

[1]It is unclear in both Wilks and Meara's (2002) and Wolter's (2001) studies what information the bilingual lexicon contains: semantic, syntactic, or both. This is especially problematic in Wolter's research, who discussed semantic and phonological relations between items, and it is not explicit whether semantical information and phonological information about words is represented at the same or different levels of the lexicon.

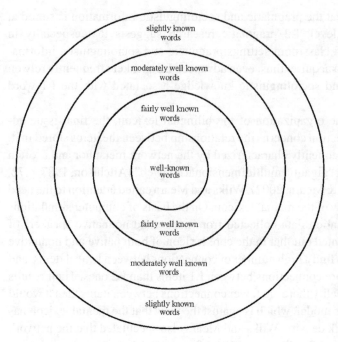

FIG. 4.14.
Depth of word
knowledge model
of the mental lexi-
con. From Wolter
(2001). Copyright
2001 by Cam-
bridge University
Press.

ers tend to have semantic connections with other items in the lexicon, whereas words on the periphery seem to have phonological or nonsemantic connections with other words. Wolter also noted that connections between L2 items in the lexicon are not stable. In the course of learning, they might be strengthened and the nature of the connection might change; moreover, connections between words might also be lost (see also Meara, 1984, 2004). Although Wolter examined word knowledge primarily from the perspective of knowing the meaning of the word, his research is important because it charts the way for further studies that are needed to have a better understanding of what kind of associative links exist between words in the mental lexicon and how these links change with the development of proficiency.

CODE-SWITCHING AND LEXICAL PROCESSING

In discussing lexical selection and control, we have already mentioned the issue of code-switching, but here we elaborate on code-switching and lexical encoding in more detail from the point of view of theories of speech production. Code-switching involves the use of two or more languages in the same discourse (Myers-Scotton & Jake, 1995), and is obviously constrained by a number of pragmatic and sociolinguistic phenomena such as the relationship of the speakers, the status of languages involved, and so on, which we do not discuss in this book. Here we differentiate between intentional and unintentional code-switching, the former being conscious whereas the latter results from accidental slip of the tongue. Unintentional code-switching might take place in situations where the two speakers only share the language used in communication, whereas intentional code-switching is applied in the bilingual mode of communication (Grosjean, 1998).

When discussing code-switching the first important question that needs to be addressed is how the languages for communication are chosen. In the case of unintentional code-switching, the language choice is outside the speaker's control, therefore here this question is not relevant. As regards intentional code-switching, it needs to be decided which language should serve as the dominant mode of communication, which, as mentioned earlier, is primarily determined by sociolinguistic factors. There is considerable agreement among researchers that the decision about which language to speak is made in the conceptualizer, as this is the module, which, on the basis of the speaker's knowledge of the situation, can choose the situationally appropriate language (de Bot, 1992, 2002; de Bot & Schreuder, 1993; Myers-Scotton & Jake, 1995; Poulisse, 1999; Poulisse & Bongaerts, 1994). Therefore, most researchers assume that the preverbal message—in addition to conceptual information—also contains a language-specifying feature or language cue.

De Bot (1992) assumed that code-switching can be explained by proposing that L2 speakers formulate two parallel speech plans, one for the selected language (e.g., L2) and one for the active language, which is not used at the moment of speaking (e.g., L1). If problems occur in encoding the speech plan for the selected language, speakers can stop and resort to the available L1 speech plan. This solution was criticized for being highly uneconomical (Poulisse, 1997b), and de Bot and Schreuder (1993) soon worked out another hypothesis, namely, that code-switching comes about when speakers ignore the language cue that is added to the preverbal plan. This is again problematic because if it is possible to ignore the language cue (either consciously or unconsciously), the semantic specifications in the preverbal plan could also be disregarded; thus, it would be impossible to account for how the appropriate lexical entries are selected in error-free production (Poulisse, 1997b).

Recent theories of code-switching (de Bot, 2002; Myers-Scotton & Jake, 1995; Poulisse, 1999; Poulisse & Bongaerts, 1994) all assume that the information on which language to use needs to be included in the preverbal plan in the form of a language cue. Myers-Scotton (1993) also added that one language is always the more dominant mode of communication, which she called Matrix Language. It is on the basis of this language that the basic grammatical frame for the specific unit of discourse is established, and elements into this frame might be inserted from the so-called Embedded Language, which is the less dominant mode of communication.

The most comprehensive account of how intentional and unintentional code-switching takes place in lexical encoding was provided by Poulisse and Bongaerts (1994) and Poulisse (1999) and was also adopted by La Heij (2005). Poulisse and Bongaerts (1994) and Poulisse (1999) proposed that besides having semantic and syntactic tags, lemmas are also labeled with a language tag, and lemma activation will take place only if all the features of the preverbal message, including the language specification, match those of the lemma. As mentioned in the section Control in Lexical Encoding, the only difference between La Heij's views and Poulisse and Bongaerts (1994) and Poulisse's (1999) proposal is that La Heij argued that the lemmas do not need to contain a language tag. Rather, a language cue at the conceptual level is sufficient because in Levelt et al.'s (1999) more recent model of lexical encoding, lemmas do not contain semantic information; only syntactic information is stored at this level. Poulisse and Bongaerts (1994) and Poulisse (1999) as well as La Heij agreed that unintentional code-switching can occur due to the fact that the concept to be encoded erroneously sends activation to both the L1 and L2 lemma. These lemmas then further activate the L1 and L2 lexemes, and because L1 lexemes are more frequently used in general than L2 lexemes and rest at a higher level of activation, they will be selected for further phonological processing. In this theory, it is also assumed that intentional switches are produced when speakers intentionally replace the L2 specification in the preverbal plan with an L1 specification. This can have several reasons: the lack of knowledge of the appropriate L2 lexical item (see chap. 7) or because the L1 lexical item meets the conceptual (semantic and/or lexical) specifications better than the L2 word (see Myers-Scotton & Jake, 1995).

THE INFLUENCE OF L1 ON LEXICAL ENCODING

Various definitions of transfer exist (for a review, see Odlin, 2003), but for the sake of simplicity, we take transfer to be the influence of L1 on acquisition, language use, and comprehension. In terms of lexical processing, transfer can arise at several levels. If we follow the steps in the process of lexical encoding, the first level is conceptual transfer. Research on the conceptual system of bilingual speakers shows that "L2 acquisition largely involves learning a new system of linguistic forms to be mapped onto an already existing system of mental concepts that has been constructed and organized according to a person's total experience with language and concepts" (Jarvis, 1998, p. 25). This means that the L1 conceptual system is an important source of influence in L2 vocabulary use and acquisition. Swan (1997) distinguished various sources of conceptual and semantic transfer. It is possible that both L1 and L2 have the same concept for an entity or action, but the two languages "stick the linguistic labels on in different places" (p. 157). He cited Clark (1993), who gave the example of talking about dressing in English and Japanese. Although both English and Japanese speakers conceptualize putting on a garment in a similar way, in English the verb "put on" is used for every kind of garment, whereas in Japanese different verbs are used for different body parts. Another source of conceptual transfer can be the case when entities or actions are categorized differently in terms of both concepts and lexis in the two languages. Swan illustrated this with the example of the color spectrum, because it is well known that different languages divide the color spectrum in different ways. Finally, another source of transfer can be when languages conceptualize things (especially abstract concepts) so differently that it is hardly possible to match the L2 concept with an L1 equivalent. Pavlenko's (1999) example of the problem Russian speakers of English have conceptualizing the English word "privacy" can serve as an illustration for this.

In psycholinguistic models of speech production, pragmatic, stylistic, and frequency information concerning a particular word is also located in the conceptualizer, and until learners acquire these aspects of lexical knowledge, they might transfer this information from L1 as well. If we accept the mainstream position in lexical processing research, namely that word meanings are also stored at the conceptual level (see the section Models of the Organization of the Bilingual Lexicon), transfer of word meanings also occurs in the conceptualizing phase. In terms of de Groot's (1992) distributed feature model, transfer of semantic and conceptual information (including pragmatic, stylistic, and frequency information) can be conceived of in a fairly straightforward way. There is consensus in L2 vocabulary research that when learners first store an L2 word in their mental lexicon, they tend to associate it with almost identical conceptual features as its L1 translation equivalent (see, e.g., N. Ellis, 1997; Jiang, 2004). As a result of more encounters with the word, they will slowly establish new L2 specific conceptual features and memory traces encoding these features, but as word association studies show (see, e.g., Jiang, 2004; N. Schmitt, 1998; N. Schmitt & Meara, 1997), L2 learners hardly ever succeed in building up as rich a conceptual structure for an L2 word as a native speaker.

Transfer can also occur at the lemma and lexeme level. Studies of vocabulary acquisition show that it is not only word meanings that are frequently transferred from L1 but also the syntactic information concerning L2 words (for a review, see Swan, 1997). It is possible that in the L2 learners' mental lexicon L2 lemmas point to the diacritic parameters of the corresponding L1 lemma. In this way, features such as gender and countability for nouns, transitivity for verbs, as well as information about optional and obligatory complements might be transferred from L1. For example, a French learner of Italian might transfer the French gender values for a particular word in Italian. The transfer process might be intentional and conscious, in which case the learner applies a communication strategy, or might be unintentional, when the L2 speaker does not even realize the gap in his or her knowledge. Transfer might result in both a correct and incorrect L2 structure. Transfer at the lexeme level is less frequent, and mostly occurs in the case of cognates. Though phonemes are often transferred from L1 to L2 (see the section titled The Role of L1 in Phonological and Phonetic Encoding and the Acquisition of L2 Phonology in chapter 5), it is rare for learners to pronounce an L2 word as if it was an L1 word (Poulisse, 1999). This process can be conceived of as the recall of the phonological structure of the L1 lemma as one unit, and probably occurs when the L2 speaker believes that because the L2 word is a cognate it is also pronounced in a similar way as its L1 translation equivalent. An example for this is the case of beginning Hungarian learners of English who frequently pronounce the English word "museum" in the same way as its Hungarian cognate "múzeum." If this happens consciously due to the lack of knowledge of the phonological form of the L2 word, it can be considered a communication strategy (see the section titled Communication Strategies and Language Learning in chapter 7).

THE ACQUISITION OF L2 LEXICAL KNOWLEDGE

Although it is a well-received view in SLA research and language pedagogy that learning vocabulary is essential for being able to communicate in L2, we know surprisingly little about the mental processes involved in vocabulary acquisition. As Meara (1997) pointed out, there is an abundance of studies concerning what techniques are helpful in vocabulary learning (for a recent review of this line of research, see de Groot & van Hell, 2005), but hardly any attempts have been made to construct a model of vocabulary acquisition, not to mention the scarcity of studies on the process of word learning. Based on the available literature and our knowledge of lexical encoding and the bilingual lexicon, the following issues can be identified in vocabulary acquisition research. One line

LEXICAL ENCODING AND THE BILINGUAL LEXICON

of studies in this field has been concerned with how memory traces for newly acquired lexical items develop and how different aspects of word knowledge are encoded (Meara, 1997; N. Schmitt, 1998; N. Schmitt & Meara, 1998; Truscott & Sharwood-Smith, 2004). Another group of researchers have addressed how the organization of the mental lexicon changes as a result of the development of L2 proficiency. This includes the hierarchical and revised hierarchical models described earlier in the section titled Models of the Organization of the Bilingual Lexicon (for a review, see Kroll & de Groot, 1997; Kroll & Tokowitz, 2005) and connectionist models of the lexicon (Meara, 1997). Studies have also investigated what factors influence the retention of lexical knowledge (Hulstijn & Laufer, 2001; Laufer & Hulstijn, 2001).

Interestingly, one of the most detailed accounts of how memory traces of lexical entries are established comes from a model that is primarily concerned with the acquisition of syntactic knowledge, namely Truscott's and Sharwood-Smith's (2004) acquisition by processing theory (APT). We do not discuss the model in detail here (for a description, see the section Transfer and the Acquisition of Syntactic Knowledge in chap. 5), but concentrate only on vocabulary acquisition. Truscott and Sharwood-Smith claimed that once a speaker meets an unknown lexical item such as "horse," it first creates an empty syntactic structure that corresponds to the phonological form of the given word. Next, the syntactic processor establishes the grammatical category for the syntactic structure of the word based on the word's syntactic environment (and the constraints of Universal Grammar). The following step is assigning meaning to the word, which is often based on contextual clues. Syntactic information concerning a word such as the complements of verbs are assumed to be encoded by raising the activation level of the various syntactic features associated with the verb such as [transitive] for the verb "hit." Truscott and Sharwood-Smith adopted the connectionist position that learning takes place through the increase of the activation level of items and through the strengthening of connections between layers. In our example, if an L2 learner repeatedly hears the sound string [ho:s] and infers from the context that it refers to a four-legged animal that one can ride, the link between the conceptual representation of HORSE and the phonological form of the word will be strengthened, which will aid the understanding and production of this word upon future use.

Meara (1997) considered the acquisition of a vocabulary from a slightly different perspective and argued that "an acquisition event consists of the building of a connection between a newly encountered word, and a word that already exists in the learner's lexicon" (p. 118). Meara claimed that the word with which associative links are established can be either the L1 translation equivalent or an L2 word (e.g., a synonym or antonym). He did not make a distinction between the conceptual and lemma level in his definition of acquisition, nor did he discuss the creation of memory traces, which makes this model simplistic, as he himself admitted. Nevertheless, the model is very useful in explaining changes that take place in the lexicon with the development of language proficiency.

The two theories of vocabulary acquisition that we have discussed so far have been concerned with rather limited aspects of vocabulary knowledge—word meaning and syntax—and have ignored other information that is necessary in order to know a word: orthography, phonology, style, frequency, and collocation. Unfortunately, none of the existing models covers these aspects of word knowledge. N. Schmitt (1998), however, made an attempt to explore how different aspects of lexical knowledge are acquired in a small-scale study, which investigated four advanced learners' acquisition of the spelling, grammatical information, meaning, and associations of 11 words. He found that the knowledge of word meaning "moved from receptive to productive and from unknown to receptive" (p. 301). Related to this, most students' associations became more nativelike. Schmitt's results also indicated that his participants had appropriate knowledge of the grammatical information concerning the investigated words even if they knew the meaning(s) of words only partially, and they made very few spelling errors. Schmitt also attempted to set up a developmental hierarchy for word knowledge types assuming that if such hierarchy exists in the case of syntax, it is logical that different kinds of lexical knowledge would be learned in a specific sequence. He did not succeed in establishing a development order for word knowledge types, which, however, might not mean that such an order does not exist. It is more likely that this is due to the fact that few participants took part in his study, and he used only a small number of words.

After discussing the first step in vocabulary learning, which is the establishment of memory traces and the encoding of various types of information related to word knowledge, the next issue that we explore is how relationships between lexical items change as a result of the development of language proficiency. In the section Models of the Organization of the Bilingual Lexicon, we have seen that the mainstream position in the cognitive view of vocabulary learning is represented by the RHM (Kroll & Stewart, 1994), which claims that at the beginning of the acquisition process L2 words are generally associated with their L1 translation equivalents and through them with the corresponding concepts, and that direct links to concepts develop only at later stages of learning. Criticism of this view was also discussed in that section. Meara's (1997) theory of vocabulary learning seems to be more detailed and with fewer problems than the RHM. As mentioned earlier, Meara claimed that vocabulary learning consists of the establishment of associative links, which might not mean connections only to L1 items but also to other L2 words. He also argued that links might be unidirectional (e.g., only from word A to word B and not vice versa) and bidirectional allowing for the flow of activation in both directions. The existence of these two types of links can explain why certain words can be characterized as active/productive (bidirectional links) and others as passive/receptive (unidirectional links). Meara postulated that words that are well known by the speaker have a high number of links to other words in the lexicon, whereas poorly known lexical items have few links to other items. In other words, Meara saw acquisition as a link-building mechanism, in the course of which new links can be established and unidirectional links can become bidirectional (for a similar view, see also Wilks & Meara, 2002, and Wolter, 2001).

In the case of the acquisition of vocabulary, memory plays an important role because the words one learns need to be stored in long-term memory. Early studies of encoding processes in long-term memory claimed that for some piece of new information to be stored in long-term memory, in-depth processing is necessary (Craik & Lockhart, 1972). Though it is intuitively correct that the intensity of processing affects the success of memorization, it is unclear what Craik and Lockhart meant by depth of processing (Baddeley, 1978). Nevertheless, there seems to be an agreement among researchers that new information is retained better if learners pay sufficient attention to it, and if they form a high number of and rich associations between old and new knowledge. Laufer and Hulstijn (2001) drew up a model of L2 vocabulary memorization, called the involvement load hypothesis, which aimed to apply findings of cognitive psychology concerning the depth of processing and elaboration to the task of L2 vocabulary learning. In their theory, involvement in processing is assumed to consist of three components: *need* (to learn the given word), *search*, which refers to how the meaning of the word is found out, and *evaluation*, which "entails the comparison of the word's meaning with other words, a specific meaning of a word with its other meanings, or comparing the word with other words in order to assess whether a word does or does not fit its context" (p. 544). These three factors can be either present or absent in vocabulary-learning instructional tasks and natural situations and can have different degrees. The components of involvement can be described by what Laufer and Hulstijn called the *involvement index*. Laufer and Hulstijn hypothesized that the higher the involvement index is, the better words will be retained in long-term memory. The assumptions of their model were largely borne out by the experiments Hulstijn and Laufer (2001) conducted in Israel and the Netherlands, which investigated how tasks with different involvement load affect the success of vocabulary learning.

SUMMARY

This chapter explored what processes are involved in lexical encoding, what the structure of the bilingual lexicon is like, as well as how code-switching and transfer take place at the level of words and how lexical items are acquired. Investigations in the field of cognitive psychology seem to suggest that in lexical encoding both L1 and L2 lemmas are activated; moreover, there is converging evidence that these lemmas are not only active but also compete for selection. Researchers disagree, however, on the issue of how lexical selection is controlled. The most convincing view seems to be that of "complex access and simple selection" (La Heij, 2005; Poulisse, 1999; Poulisse & Bongaerts, 1994), in which it is hypothesized that the preverbal plan contains all the necessary specifications to recall the appropriate word in the intended language. Concerning the organization and structure of the bilingual lexicon, one of the basic questions that has been addressed is whether conceptual and semantic information are represented at a single shared level or at separate levels. The mainstream position in this respect suggests that there is no need to presume that semantic information is distinct from conceptual information. In the section Models of the Organization of the Bilingual Lexicon, I reviewed the hierarchical models of the lexicon and pointed out a number of problematic aspects of these models. I also argued that the network model seems to be a more viable theory of how words are organized in the mental lexicon. Psychological mechanisms involved in code-switching and transfer have also been discussed in this chapter. It was shown that not only is La Heij's (2005), Poulisse and Bongaerts' (1994), and Poulisse's (1999) theory of complex access and simple selection the most viable model of control in lexical access, but it is also able to provide adequate explanation of intentional and unintentional code-switching. In discussing lexical transfer, an attempt was made to account for how L1 influences the use of lexical items at every level of vocabulary knowledge, namely semantics, syntax, morphology, phonology, style, and pragmatics. As regards the acquisition of vocabulary, views on how memory traces for newly learned words are established and retained as well as on how the associations between words develop as a result of learning have also been described.

5   Syntactic and Phonological Encoding

A GENERAL OVERVIEW OF SYNTACTIC ENCODING PROCESSES

As we saw in chapter 2, syntactic encoding comprises a number of subprocesses such as the activation of the syntactic information stored at the lemma level and of grammatical morphemes, the selection of syntactic rules that build phrases and clauses, and the application of word order rules that determine the sequence of the sentence constituents. Some of the processes involve the use of declarative knowledge, whereas some others entail the automatic application of rules, which is also referred to as procedural knowledge (see chap. 3). The syntactic information encoded at the lemma level can be considered declarative knowledge, whereas phrase and clause building as well as word order rules are part of an L1 speaker's procedural knowledge. Ullman (2001) and Paradis (1994) cited empirical evidence from aphasic and modern brain-imaging research, which supports the procedural versus declarative distinction by showing that these two types of knowledge are stored in different parts of the brain

Before discussing syntactic processing in L2 in detail, it is important to review the basic characteristics of the processes. This description is based on Levelt's (1989) and Kempen and Hoenkamp's (1987) model of grammatical encoding, because as argued in chapter 2, this model is the most detailed one and has also been supported by a number of empirical studies. The model has undergone several modifications, but the new theory called the unification space model has been elaborated only for sentence comprehension (for the most recent version of the model, see Vosse & Kempen, 2000). The basic processing principles underlying Incremental Procedural Grammar (IPG) developed by Kempen and Hoenkamp's have, however, remained mostly unchanged. We also have to note that a number of other grammatical theories exist to date (e.g., Chomsky's Minimalist Program [Chomsky, 1995]; optimality theory [Prince & Smolensky, 1993]), but they are concerned with the general principles and properties that govern language and not with how language is processed in psychological terms.

Four basic assumptions underlie IPG, the first of which is that "processing components are autonomous specialists, which operate largely automatically" (Pienemann, 1998, p. 2) at least in L1 production. In other words, in syntactic encoding subprocesses work autonomously without conscious supervision, which ensures that processing can proceed parallel and automatically. The processing components work with their characteristic input; for example, noun phrase (NP)-building procedures are triggered by the activation of a lemma that belongs to the lexical category of nouns. The next principle of IPG is *incrementality,* which means that a processing component can already start working with a fragment of its characteristic input; that is, it does not have to wait until the previous component delivers a "finished product." In order for this to work, it has to be assumed that certain bits of the already processed message sometimes need to be "put aside" for a while, that is, stored somewhere, because the order of conceptual information does not always translate directly into the order of the sentence constituents. Therefore, the third principle of IPG states that "the output of the processor is linear, while it may not be mapped unto the underlying meaning in a linear way" (Pienemann, 1998, p. 2). This *linearization problem* (Levelt, 1989) might refer to conceptual components, such as in the sentence "Before going to university, he served two years in the army"; the proposition "he served two years in the army" might be conceptualized earlier than the one "before going to university." In this case once the first proposition is encoded, it has to be deposited in a memory store until the second proposition is processed. Grammatical information might also need to be stored temporarily, for example, in the case of subject–verb agreement, where information about the person and number of the subject needs to be deposited so that it becomes available when the verb phrase is encoded. The fourth principle of IPG is concerned with the storage of this information and states that there exists a special grammatical memory store, where the output of intermediary processes can be held temporarily.

In chapter 2, we saw how grammatical encoding is envisaged to take place in IPG, but I describe it here once more in detail. The first step in the process is the activation of the lemma, which entails access to the syntactic properties encoded at this level. The syntactic information of a lemma includes its syntactic category (e.g., noun, verb, adjective, pronoun), diacritic parameters such as gender, singularity, transitivity, and so on, and specifications concerning obligatory and possible complements. The next step is the so-called category procedure, which "inspects the conceptual material of the current iteration (the material currently being processed) for possible complements and specifiers and provides values for the diacritic features" (Pienemann, 1998, p. 4). Following this, the phrasal procedure assigns a grammatical function to the phrase, for example, whether an NP is the subject or object of a sentence. Finally, the so-called S-procedure builds the syntactic structure of the sentence and calls on the word order rules to arrange the processed constituents in appropriate order. If the sentence contains a subordinate clause, an additional subordinate clause procedure encodes it. In the following, we look at each phase of grammatical encoding and discuss the relevant research findings and theories.

DIACRITIC FEATURES: THE ENCODING OF GRAMMATICAL GENDER

One of the few areas of second language syntactic processing that has been studied by means of experimental techniques is the encoding of grammatical gender in a few Indo-European gender-marking languages. I describe gender encoding in L2 in this section in detail, not only because this is the only diacritic feature that has been investigated in the L2 field, but because whatever we can conclude from studies on gender might refer to the encoding of other types of grammatical information stored together with a lexical item such as countability status and plural markers of nouns, transitivity of verbs, and so forth.

In L1 production, it is assumed that grammatical gender is the lexico-syntactic property of nouns, which is looked up when the noun is produced (e.g., Roelofs et al., 1998; B. M. Schmitt et al., 1999; Schriefers & Jescheniak, 1999). In monolingual models, all nouns of a given gender are connected to gender nodes that specify gender; in other words, there is one abstract gender node for each gender. In L2 research, the question is whether the L1 and L2 gender systems can be shared across languages if both languages have similar gender structure. Logically two possible answers exist to this question. One possibility is that the gender system of the two languages is shared and L1 and L2 words that have the same gender in the two languages are connected to the same gender node (see Fig. 5.1). Costa, Kovacic, et al. (2003) called this the *gender-integrated view,* for whose plausibility they referred to the correlation of grammatical and semantic gender as well as the relationship between phonological features and gender found in many languages. In gender-marking languages, it is common that words referring to concepts that have male or female gender also have corresponding grammatical gender values (e.g., man, woman, actor, actress). Moreover, in some languages certain phonological features such as the last phoneme of the word often mark a particular gender

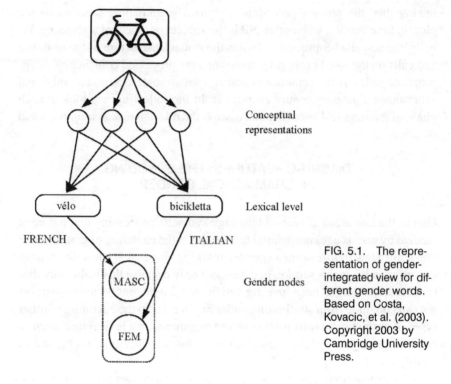

FIG. 5.1. The representation of gender-integrated view for different gender words. Based on Costa, Kovacic, et al. (2003). Copyright 2003 by Cambridge University Press.

(e.g., in Italian the majority of nouns ending with -o are masculine). If similar correlations exist in gender marking in L1 and L2, L2 speakers might be led to assume that a particular gender value in L2 is the same grammatical property as in L1; thus, they might connect the acquired L2 words to the existing L1 gender nodes. The other possibility is that the gender systems of the two languages are separate, and therefore separate gender nodes exist for L2 words (see Fig. 5.2), which Costa, Kovacic, et al. term the *language autonomy view*. They did not list any supporting evidence for this view, but it is possible that languages that have different gender systems (e.g., have three different gender values: masculine, feminine, neuter in one of the languages, and only two values: masculine and feminine in the other language) or in which the gender value has different consequences for NP encoding might not share the same gender system. It might also be the case that L2 learners start out with a separate gender system at the beginning stage, which becomes integrated with the development of language proficiency or vice versa. As pointed out previously, the two possible views as regards the relationship of gender information of L1 and L2 words might also be extended to other diacritic features, and one might ask the question of whether information on the countability status of nouns or the transitivity of verbs is stored together or separately in the mental lexicon of an L2 speaker.

The other theoretically relevant question in gender encoding is whether the selection of the gender feature is an activation-based mechanism or an automatic process. In L1 processing, a number of researchers (e.g., Schriefers, 1993; Vigliocco et al., 2002) argue that the speed with which the gender value of a noun is encoded is dependent on the level of the activation of the given gender node. In other words, if a feminine noun needs to be encoded and previously also a feminine noun was accessed, the selection of the feminine gender value will be faster than in the case if the previous noun was of masculine gender. In some other studies, it is proposed that the gender value of a noun is always accessed when the noun itself is activated; therefore, this process is automatic and does not depend on activation levels (Caramazza, Miozzo, Costa, Schiller, & Alario, 2001; cf. Costa, Kovacic, et al., 2003; Schiller & Caramazza, 2003). Costa, Kovacic, et al. concluded that following from the fact that there are two options as regards the relationship of L1 and L2 gender systems and another two concerning the selection of the gender value, four possibilities exist. Both in the gender-integrated view and in the language autonomy view, gender features might be accessed either automatically or with the help of an activation spreading mechanism. If the two gender systems are

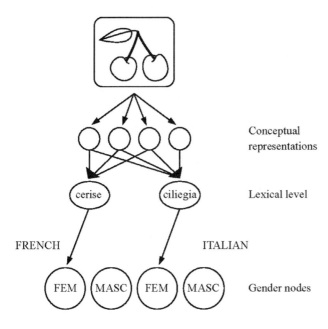

FIG. 5.2. The representation of gender in the language autonomy view for same-gender words. Based on Costa, Kovacic, et al. (2003). Copyright 2003 by Cambridge University Press.

separate, the fact that L1 and L2 values are the same does not facilitate gender encoding. Therefore, in the language autonomy view neither the automatic access account nor the spreading activation account would predict any difference in the speed of the encoding of nouns whose gender is the same in L1 and L2. Moreover, in the automatic access view no difference is assumed to exist in the retrieval speed of same gender words even if the gender systems of the two languages are shared. The only situation when facilitation can be observed is if the gender system is integrated and access is based on spreading activation, as in this case naming latencies had been affected by the gender of the L1 translation equivalents. In the review of lexical encoding in L2 in chapter 4, we have seen that in L2 lexical access L1 words also become activated to some extent. Thus, if the activated L1 word has the same gender value, it also spreads additional activation the relevant gender node, which results in quicker selection (for a review of the four options, see Table 5.1).

Costa, Kovacic, et al. (2003) carried out a series of experiments with participants speaking languages whose gender system is structurally similar (French-Italian, Catalan-Spanish) and also with languages where the gender systems differ in their structure (Croatian-Italian). With minor variations, the basic experimental procedure involved naming pictures in L2 whose gender values were either shared or different in the two languages. The results in all of the experiments with the three language pairs showed no difference in the time needed to name the pictures, from which one conclusion can be drawn, namely that if the gender system of the L1 and L2 is integrated, access of the gender feature is not based on spreading activation. Therefore, further research is needed to test whether L2 speakers rely on a single gender system for the two languages, and if not, whether gender values are accessed automatically or based on spreading activation. On the basis of more conclusive future studies, inferences could be made concerning how other types of syntactic information related to a given word are stored and accessed in L2 production.

TABLE 5.1

Description of the Predictions for the Naming Performance of L2 Speakers for Words That Share the Gender Value in the Two Languages.

	Selection Based on Activation Spreading	Automatic Selection
Gender-integrated view	Facilitation	No effect
Language autonomy view	No effect	No effect

Note. Table Based on Data From Costa, Kovacic, et al. (2003)

ACCESSING GRAMMATICAL MORPHEMES

Words are generally classified as content versus function words, or as open- versus closed-class words in descriptive grammar; in psycholinguistic terms, however, morphemes, that is, the smallest units of language that carry meaning, are characterized from the perspective of how they are stored and accessed. Myers-Scotton and Jake (2000) developed the 4-M model, which delineates four different types of morphemes, based on code-switching and L2 developmental data as well as research on aphasic language production. In this model, two basic types of morphemes are differentiated: *content morphemes,* which are words that assign and receive thematic roles (e.g., agent, patient) and head their maximal projections (e.g., nouns head NPs), and *system morphemes,* which do not assign or receive thematic roles. Typical content morphemes are nouns and verbs, whereas system morphemes include among others determiners, inflections, and some prepositions. System morphemes are further subdivided into three groups. The so-called *early system morphemes* are conceptually activated and are dependent "on their content morpheme heads in their immediate maximal projections for their form" (Myers-Scotton, 2005, p. 338). For example, early system morphemes include determiners that are activated based on the feature [+ accessible] (e.g., "the" in English) or [– accessible] (e.g., "a" in English) specified by the preverbal plan, the plural marking of nouns, and derivational affixes. *Late system morphemes* can be of two types: *bridge late system morphemes* and *outsider late system morphemes.* Bridge late system morphemes are used to connect elements and ensure that the constituents are well formed. An English example for this type of morpheme is "of" in the phrase "the book of the prophets." "Outsider late system morphemes are called outsiders because they depend for their form on information from outside their immediate maximal projection" (Myers-Scotton, 2005, p. 338). An example for outsider late system morpheme is subject–verb agreement, in the course of which the inflection of the verb is dependent on information from the subject of the clause. Table 5.2 contains a summary of the characteristics of the four different types of morphemes.

Primarily based on code-switching data, which is discussed in more detail in the section Code-Switching and Syntactic Encoding, Myers-Scotton (2005) assumed that the four different types of morphemes are accessed differently in both L1 and L2, as well as in situations of the simultaneous use of the languages. She argued that content morphemes and early system morphemes are activated in the mental lexicon based on the conceptual specifications of the preverbal message. Once content morphemes and early system morphemes are selected, they further activate the syntactic building procedures that call

TABLE 5.2

Description of the Four Different Types of Morphemes in Myers-Scotton
and Jake's (2000) 4-M Model

Morphemes	Conceptually Activated	Thematic Role Assignment	Require Operations Outside the Maximal Projection
Content	+	+	–
Early system	+	–	–
Bridge late system	–	–	–
Outsider late system	–	–	+

the late system morphemes. On the basis of the assumptions of IPG, Pienemann (1998) also classified morphemes in a similar way. He distinguished lexical, phrasal, and interphrasal morphemes. Lexical morphemes are similar to Myers-Scotton and Jake's (2000) early system morphemes, because they are specified by the diacritic features of lemmas; that is, they are conceptually activated at the lemma level. Pienemann cited the example of the English determiners because their selection is based on whether the head of the phrase (i.e., the noun) is singular or plural; thus the information concerning this diacritic feature of the head has to be deposited in the NP-building procedure and called on when the determiner is activated (e.g., "a" or "an" as in "a book" or a zero determiner as in "books"). Outsider late system morphemes (Myers-Scotton & Jake, 2000) correspond to Pienemann's interphrasal morphemes, the selection of which is governed by agreement between phrases of a sentence (e.g., person marking of verbs). IPG assumes that first lexical morphemes are activated, and this is followed by the selection of phrasal and finally by interphrasal morphemes.[1] A basic tenet of processability theory (PT) formulated by Pienemann is that highly proficient L2 speakers also encode the three different types of morphemes in this order; but if learners have not acquired the procedures necessary for activating the morphemes at a given level, they will not be able to process their intended message grammatically at a further level, and they will simply map the conceptual structures on the surface form. A more detailed discussion of PT can be found in the section Transfer and the Acquisition of L2 Syntactic Knowledge.

---

[1]For Pienemann (1998), some of Myers-Scotton and Jake's (2000) early system morphemes are phrasal morphemes because they are dependent on the agreement between the head of the phrase and another phrasal constituent. Pienemann did not discuss morphemes that would correspond to Myers-cotton and Jake's content morphemes. It is also difficult to establish direct correspondence between bridge late system morphemes in Myers-Scotton and Jake's taxonomy and Pienemann's categorization of morphemes.

THE ACTIVATION OF SYNTACTIC BUILDING PROCEDURES

Very few experimental studies have been conducted on the activation of syntactic building procedures, which is partly due to the fact that even in L1 production this is a less frequently researched topic. In chapter 2, we have seen that syntactic processing at the level of phrases and clauses is primarily investigated with the help of the method called syntactic priming. The major finding of syntactic priming experiments was that the use of one syntactic structure in a sentence (called the prime) increases the likelihood of the use of the same structure in another sentence, which is called priming effect (Bock, 1986). The experiments also showed that it is only the similarity of syntactic structure that produces the priming effect, and that lexical, thematic, metrical, or phonological similarities between the prime and target do not result in priming (for a review, see Bock & Levelt, 1994; Levelt, 1989). This indicates that one syntactic structure can activate another similar structure, and therefore the mechanisms of spreading activation are also at work in syntactic encoding. In extensions of the classical syntactic priming experiments (Potter & Lombardi, 1990; Tree & Mejer, 1999) it was also found that L1 speakers use recently activated words to reconstruct the sentence they have to recall, which supports the assumption that syntactic encoding is lexically driven. The question that is asked in L2 production as regards the activation of syntactic building procedures is whether L2 lemmas activate specifically L2 syntactic building procedures or can they point to processes in L1. De Bot (1992) and Pienemann (1998) assumed that phrasal- and clausal-structure-building processes are language specific; that is, L2 lemmas do not trigger L1 grammatical encoding processes. Pienemann et al. (2005) added that transfer of L1 syntactic procedures is possible only if L2 learners have already acquired earlier processes in the processing hierarchy (for more detail see the next section). In their APT, Truscott and Sharwood-Smith (2004) stated exactly the opposite and proposed that if L1 syntactic procedures are more highly activated than L2 processes, they are selected instead of the target language process. As is shown in the next section, although there is ample evidence for the viability of Pienemann et al.'s argument, the APT model has not been empirically tested yet.

Meijer and Fox Tree (2003) asked the question what happens if L1 and L2 syntactic procedures for specific structures are the same in both languages and investigated this issue by means of syntactic priming. The participants of their study were highly proficient Spanish-English bilinguals, whose first task was to recall sentences containing dative verbs in English that can take either an NP-NP structure as a complement (e.g., The mother gave the child the ice cream.) or an NP-PP structure (e.g., The mother gave the ice cream to the child). The target sentence presented in English was followed by a Spanish prime sentence containing either the same or a different complement structure than the one in the English sentence. Following this a distractor word was presented, for which participants had to decide whether it was included in the sentence or not. Finally, participants had to recall the originally presented English sentence. In another experiment, the order of the direct-object pronoun was manipulated in Spanish target sentences, and English prime sentences were used. In addition, they also investigated the use of the double negative as opposed to single negation, which are both permissible in Spanish. The main question of the study was whether seeing a different structure in the Spanish or English prime sentence induces participants to use this structure in the sentence to be recalled in the other language. In other words, they wanted to test whether the activation of one particular phrase-building procedure in one language affects selection of procedures in the other. Meijer and Fox Tree found that speakers in both L1 and L2 switched from one structure to the other possible syntactic structure if they saw it in the prime sentence, with the exception of double negative, which turned out to be a semantically marked structure in Spanish. On the basis of this result, they argued that "syntactic rules necessary for both languages are centrally stored" and that they "are not labeled with respect to language" (p. 193). We have to note that they are probably right assuming that syntactic rules for L1 and L2 are stored at the same place once the L2 rules become fully proceduralized, that is, when L2 speakers are able to apply them automatically. At lower proficiency levels, however, rules are often used consciously and are stored in declarative memory, which has been found to be located in a different part of the brain than procedural knowledge (Paradis, 1994; Ullman, 2001). Pienemann et al. (2005) also argued that even if L1 and L2 rules are the same, L2 learners have to acquire lower order syntactic procedures first to be able to transfer this knowledge from their L1. In sum, it is unlikely that unbalanced bilingual speakers store L1 and L2 syntactic procedures in the same place.

TRANSFER AND THE ACQUISITION OF L2 SYNTACTIC KNOWLEDGE

Transfer and the acquisition of L2 syntactic knowledge have often been regarded as two interrelated processes in L2 acquisition, because it was frequently assumed that learners start out by applying L1 rules to construct L2 utterances, and the developmental path they take slowly reaches a state where L2 rules are correctly used (see, e.g., Selinker's, 1972, interlanguage hypothesis). Somewhat later it was acknowledged that the acquisition of syntax does not simply involve the transformation of the L1 grammatical system into the L2 system, but also the application of creative construction processes (Dulay & Burt, 1974), which are independent of both L1 and L2. In this section, I give a brief overview of how major theories of language learning view the acquisition of L2 syntactic encoding processes and also discuss PT (Pienemann, 1998), which is concerned with the psycholinguistic constraints of syntax learning and not with the actual process of how acquisition takes place. An important question in the acquisition of L2 grammatical encoding processes is how L2 rules learners know consciously become automatic, in other words, how declarative knowledge gets transformed into procedural knowledge, is not elaborated here; I postpone the discussion of this process to chapter 8, where it will be discussed together with other issues of the automaticity of speech production processes.

The issue of the transfer of L1 knowledge and the use of cognitive construction processes in the learning of L2 syntax was first addressed from the perspective of Chomsky's (1965) Universal Grammar, which assumes that humans are equipped with a specific *language acquisition device* (LAD) that helps them acquire their first language from the impoverished input they receive as young children. The LAD contains principles that are universal for all languages and parameters that need to be set for the particular language to be learned, which together are referred to as Universal Grammar (UG). For a long time, in L2 research the question was whether L2 learners have access to UG, and if so, whether they can access it fully or only partially (the study of transfer and the role of UG is a wide area of SLA research, which we do not explore in great detail here; for the most recent review, see White, 2003). A number of studies in the nativist paradigm have proposed that L2 learners have full access to UG, and that learning L2 syntax involves resetting the parameters established for L1 in order to conform to the rules of L2. Among these researchers the positions differ as regards the constraints on L1 transfer. In the most extreme view, held by Schwartz and Sprouse (1996), it is argued that every aspect of L1 syntax might be transferred, and the fact that L2 syntax is often not acquired fully is explained with reference to fossilization, which takes place if input necessary for restructuring L1 knowledge is not available or salient. Other studies pose several restrictions on L1 transfer. For example, Vainikka and Young-Scholten (1994) argued that transfer is limited to lexical categories and word order rules, whereas Eubank (1993) allowed for the transfer of lexical and functional categories. A number of other researchers, such as Felix (1985) and Clahsen and Muysken (1989), however, assume that L2 learners have limited or indirect access to UG, which explains why perfect acquisition of L2 above a certain age is hardly possible. Finally, there are views that claim that L2 learners no longer have access to UG, and they apply general problem-solving strategies to reconstruct the L2 grammar from the available input (Meisel, 1991). White (1996) pointed out that the theory of UG has been mistakenly applied to explain the acquisition of grammar because it is a theory of representation and not of development. Therefore, the question of whether L2 learners have access to UG has recently been reformulated as whether the grammatical system of learners' interlanguage follows the same principles as natural languages or it is impaired in certain respects (see, e.g., Hawkins & Chan, 1997). This question, however, is outside the scope of this book.

Connectionist approaches to language learning deny the existence of an inborn language acquisition device and claim that language learning is not different from any other kind of learning (for a review, see N. Ellis, 2003). The most well-known model of language acquisition in the connectionist paradigm is the competition model originally developed by MacWhinney and Bates (for a recent review of the model, see MacWhinney, 2001). In this model, learning is influenced by the frequency and complexity of the relationship of grammatical forms and communicative functions, and the existence of UG is denied. It is assumed that learning L2 means acquiring how particular surface forms express communicative intentions, which is called form-function mapping, and that learners do not need to have an innate language capacity; they simply rely on available input. The aspects of input learners need to process and acquire are called "cues." The strength or salience of cues is determined by the frequency and availability of the particular form-function mapping in the input. Cues can also compete with each other, and certain cues might override others. MacWhinney (1997) cited the example of Dutch word order and case marking. In Dutch the noun phrase before the modal verb is usually the subject of the sentence, which can be regarded as a word order cue. However, when the noun phrase before the modal verb is marked accusative, it is the object of the sentence; thus here the case-marking cue is stronger than the word order cue. The competition model predicts that in both L1 and L2 acquisition cue strength influences the order in which the various cues are learned.

As regards the acquisition of L2 syntax and transfer, the competition model assumes that learners start out by attempting to transfer the form-function mappings of the L1 to L2. MacWhinney (1997) argued that "because connectionist models place such a strong emphasis on analogy and other types of pattern generalization, they predict that all aspects of the first language that can possibly transfer to L2 will transfer" (p. 119). If transfer does not produce the correct output, the learners will further attend to cues in the input and assemble the structure step-by-step. The model also predicts that if a particular structure has the same function in both languages, acquisition of the structure will be facilitated, whereas syntactic structures that are formally similar in the two languages but have different communicative values will be difficult to learn. The competition model has mainly been applied to examine bilingual and monolingual sentence comprehension; very few studies have been conducted in the framework of this theory on acquisition of L2 grammatical knowledge in speech production. One of them is Döpke's (2001) investigation of bilingual children's production of L2 syntactic structure over the period of 1–3 years. Döpke argued that her data support that in bilingual-child first and second language acquisition, syntactic knowledge is built up by learners through attending to the surface structure of the utterances and by slowly establishing the correct form and function mappings in both L1 and L2.

A new development in the field of connectionism concerning the acquisition of syntax is that successful computer simulations were carried out that were able to show that if a connectionist architecture is exposed to vast amount of input, it is able to generalize from the exemplars in the input and build morphological, phonological, and syntactic structures (for a review, see N. Ellis, 1998; Murre, 2005). Though most of this type of work has been performed using L1 input, some studies in the L2 field have also been conducted. N. Ellis and Schmidt (1998) recorded how a group of learners acquire morphology in an artificial grammar and then modeled the learning process with a connectionist computer network. The system showed a similar developmental pattern as that of the language learners and was able to reproduce rulelike behavior without actually being equipped with prior knowledge of the rules; in other words, it was able to infer rules from the input alone. Kempe and MacWhinney (1998) also successfully modeled the acquisition of German and Russian case marking in a connectionist network.

APT, developed by Truscott and Sharwood-Smith (2004), views acquisition and transfer from a different perspective than the previously described models and theories, although it draws heavily on the work of connectionism just like the competition model. The theory is based on Chomsky's (1995) Minimalist Program and Jackendoff's (2002) view of modularity, in which it is claimed that the message is constructed by three independent processors: the conceptual processor, which is outside the language module, and the syntactic and phonological modules, which together make up the language module. The syntactic module is invariable across languages and has full access to UG. The source of interlanguage variation is located in the lexicon. In simple terms, Truscott and Sharwood-Smith proposed that learning by processing involves adding additional activation to items, whether words, functional categories, inflections, and so on, which results in these items being more readily available for processing in the future. In the case of syntactic representations that can have different features in L1 and L2 (e.g., strong vs. weak feature), the activation level of the L2 target feature is increased as a result of learning so that it finally exceeds that of the L1 feature. As a consequence, Truscott and Sharwood-Smith assumed that transfer, as seen in previous research, does not exist. For them transfer means that in certain cases, especially at the beginning of the acquisition process, the activation of L1 syntactic features is at higher resting level, and therefore they will be selected instead of the L2 feature. Although the activation-based explanation for learning and transfer has great potential for SLA research, in its current state APT is not yet fully developed and lacks empirical support. Table 5.3 contains a summary of how different theories view the role of UG and transfer in the acquisition of L2 syntax.

PT, developed by Pienemann (1998), is primarily concerned with the constraints of acquisition and not with the representation of grammatical knowledge. In this theory it is hypothesized that "L2 learners can produce only those linguistic forms for which they have acquired the necessary prerequisites" (Pienemann et al., 2005). PT is based on IPG (Kempen & Hoenkamp, 1987) and assumes that processing components are autonomous specialists, which work incrementally, and that the intermediary products of processing are stored in grammatical memory (see the section Diacritic Features). In accordance with Kempen and Hoenkamp, Pienemann postulated the following sequence in which syntactic encoding takes place: (a) lemma access, (b) category procedure

TABLE 5.3
Overview of Theories of the Acquisition of Syntax by L2 Learners

Theory	The Role of Universal Grammar	Transfer
Nativists	Views range from limited to full access to UG.	Views range from no constraint on transfer to the existence of various constraints (developmental, universal, etc.).
Competition model	No UG	Transfer is not constrained.
Acquisition by processing theory	There is full access to UG.	Transfer does not exist.
Processability theory	It does not consider the question of UG.	Transfer is developmentally constrained.

(builds the phrasal category), (c) phrasal procedure (encodes the phrase), (d) the S-procedure (establishes the place of the phrase within the sentence), and (e) subordinate clause procedure (for examples, see the detailed description of Kempen and Hoenkamp's, 1987, model in chap. 2). He also assumed that lemmas are separate for L1 and L2 words and contain language-specific diacritic features as well as information on complements and specifiers, and that all the syntactic procedures are language specific. The most important hypothesis of PT is that because the syntactic encoding processes form a hierarchy, in which each subordinate phase needs to be at least partially completed before the next phase can start working, learners also need to acquire lower order grammatical encoding procedures before they can process the following stage. In other words, the acquisition of syntactic knowledge follows the order of the procedures of syntactic encoding. Pienemann argued that if the learner has not acquired procedures at a specific stage and above, he or she will have to resort to mapping concepts to surface form from that level on. As de Bot (1998) rightly pointed out, the question of what happens if processing is cut off at a particular stage due to lack of knowledge is not explained in great detail by Pienemann. De Bot suggested that one possible solution L2 learners can apply in this case is resorting to communication strategies to compensate for their lack of knowledge (see chap. 7 for more detail).

Pienemann also described his hierarchy in terms of the processing of different morphemes. He proposed that lexical morphemes such as the marking of past tense on English verbs can be produced without having recourse to phrase-building procedures; therefore, they are the first types of morphemes in the acquisition hierarchy. At the next stage of learning, phrasal morphemes, the production of which is dependent on the agreement of the phrase, and another phrasal element can be found (e.g., determiners in English that contain information on the singularity of the head noun). Finally, interphrasal morphemes (e.g., verbal inflections expressing agreement with the subject of the sentence) are acquired (see Table 5.4). Empirical support for the PT has been primarily provided by studies investigating the order of acquisition of specific syntactic structures, in which it was found that syntactic structures indeed emerged in L2 learners' speech as predicted by the theory. Pienemann (in press) reanalyzed Johnston's (1985) and Pienemann and Mackey's (1993) studies investigating learners of English from various L1 backgrounds and the work on learners of the ZISA (Zweitspracherwerb Italienischer und Spanisher Arbeiter [Second Language Acquisition of Spanish and Italian Workers] research group on learners of German (e.g., Clahsen, 1980; Clahsen, Meisel, & Pienemann, 1983; Meisel, Clahsen, & Pienemann, 1981; Pienemann, 1980),

TABLE 5.4
Hierarchy of Processing Procedures

Stage	Processing Procedure	L2 Process	Morphology	Syntax
5	Subordinate clause procedure	Main and subclause		Cancel inversion (e.g. I wonder what he means)
4	S-procedure	Interphrasal information exchange	S–V agreement (e.g., Anna loves swimming)	Do2nd (e.g. Do you like swimming?)
3	Phrasal procedure	Phrasal information exchange	Possessive pronoun (e.g., This is my room)	Do-fronting (e.g., I do not like this)
2	Category procedure	Lexical morphemes	Plural (e.g., two cats)	Canonical word order (e.g., Me no live here)
1	Word/lemma	Words	Invariant forms Single constituents	

Note. Table based on data from Pienemann et al. (2005).

and found that these learners followed the acquisition order described by his theory. Moreover, recent studies with learners of Japanese and Italian (Di Biase & Kawaguchi, 2002), as well as Chinese (Zhang, in press), Swedish (Pienemann & Håkansson, 1999), and Arabic (Mansouri, 2000) as L2 also lend support to PT. Research conducted in the framework of Myers-Scotton and Jake's (2000) 4-M model also came to similar conclusions as Pienemann (1998) as regards the acquisition hierarchy of grammatical morphemes. Wei (2000) claimed that content morphemes (i.e., lemmas that assign thematic roles) are activated first in the processing hierarchy and are therefore the first to be acquired. Next come early system morphemes, which are also conceptually activated and have an important role in conveying one's message. Late system morphemes are the last in the hierarchy because they are structurally assigned, which makes their acquisition difficult. The accuracy order of grammatical morphemes in the speech of Chinese and Japanese learners of English examined in Wei's study reflects a similar sequence as Pienemann's (1998) processing hierarchy.

It is a logical consequence of the processing hierarchy that it is impossible that at the beginning of the L2 learning process students transfer all their knowledge of the L1 syntactic system to L2. Pienemann et al. (2005) argued that instead L2 learners reconstruct the L2 grammatical system from scratch starting from the bottom of the processing hierarchy. They pointed out that "L1 transfer is developmentally moderated and will occur only when the structure to be transferred is processable within the developing L2 system." To illustrate Pienemann et al.'s view, this means that at Stage 1, L2 learners might transfer diacritic features, as well as possible and obligatory complements and specifiers of L1 lemmas to L2; at Stage 2, where syntactic information about lemmas is already acquired, categorial procedures based on L1 knowledge might be applied, and so on. Håkansson, Pienemann, and Sayehli (2002) provided empirical evidence for this view by showing that Swedish learners of German do not transfer rules from their L1 that are also to be found in L2 until they reach the stage where they can process that particular rule. A number of studies with learners from different language backgrounds and acquiring different L2s also support this view (e.g., Haberzettl, 2000; Johnston, 1997; cf. Pienemann et al., 2005).

In this section we have seen that four major theories exist as regards the learning of L2 grammar and the role of transfer: the nativist paradigm, connectionist theory (the most developed representative of which in the field of syntax is the competition model), the acquisition by processing theory, and the processability theory. From the previous discussion, it is also apparent that these four theories approach the question of the acquisition of syntax from different perspectives. Nativists assume the existence of an inborn language acquisition device that is also partly or fully available in L2 learning. The PT focuses on the sequence in which various L2 syntactic encoding processes can be acquired based on the constraints of the syntactic system, whereas the competition model and APT are concerned with how syntax is learned from the available input. The competition model claims that the acquisition of syntactic rules is possible through the analysis of input, whereas in the APT and nativist theories it is argued that even though learning is primarily an activation-based mechanism, there exists a separate innate language module.

CODE-SWITCHING AND SYNTACTIC ENCODING

In one of the first studies on bilingual code-switching behavior it was observed that code-switched utterances of proficient bilinguals are rule governed (Poplack, 1981), and since then the syntax of code-switching has received distinguished attention. Several constraints on code-switching and rules concerning the structure of code-switched sentences have been proposed, mostly in the framework of various grammatical theories. Due to the complex nature of the theories underlying these studies and to the fact that most of the research in this vein does not consider the cognitive aspects of speech production, only one study, Myers-Scotton's (1993) Matrix Language Frame, which has cognitive psychological background, is discussed here (for linguistic theories on the grammatical structure of code-switched utterances, see Belazi, Rubin, & Toribio, 1994; MacSwan, 2000; Poplack, 1981; Woolford, 1983).

Myers-Scotton (1993) drew up her model based on psycholinguistic theories of speech production (primarily on Levelt's, 1989, model), in which she claimed that one language is always the more dominant mode of communication (Matrix Language), and that the basic grammatical frame for a specific unit of discourse is established on the basis of this language. Elements might be inserted into this frame, called Matrix Frame, from the so-called Embedded Language, which is the less dominant mode of communication. Myers-Scotton established two constraints on code-switching: the morpheme order principle, which claims that the Matrix Language determined the order of morphemes within a bilingual constituent, and the system morpheme principle, which states that system morphemes that indicate grammatical relations between phrasal constituents (called late system morphemes in the 4-M model; Myers-Scotton & Jake, 2000—see the Accessing Grammatical Morphemes section) also need to come from the Matrix Language. This model is motivated by the assumption that certain grammatical morphemes might be conceptually specified in the preverbal plan (early system morphemes), whereas others are called on by syntactic building procedures, and therefore they behave differently in code-switching. MacSwan (2000, 2003) cited several counterexamples to the rules proposed in the Matrix Language Frame model and pointed out an important problematic aspect of the model. He argued that Myers-Scotton's assumptions concerning the existence of language frames in syntactic processing were not supported by grammatical theory. Moreover, the idea of syntactic frames is against the view that syntactic encoding is lexically driven, which is also a basic assumption of Myers-Scotton's model. This results in a contradiction within the model, which, however, is the only available psycholinguistic theory of syntactic processes operating in code-switching to date.

SUMMARY OF GRAMMATICAL ENCODING PROCESSES

As the previous sections show, we are left with more questions than answers in the field of syntactic encoding, and many of the issues in the field have not yet been given sufficient attention. As regards the diacritic features of lemmas, it is only gender that was investigated in a recent study by Costa, Kovacic, et al. (2003). All they were able to conclude is that for advanced L2 speakers the encoding of gender might be either activation based or automatic, and either gender features might be stored separately or L1 and L2 words might share the same gender node, but out of the four combinations that arise only one can be ruled out: If L1 and L2 gender systems are integrated, gender values are not accessed based on activation levels. The access of other diacritic features of nouns and verbs has not been studied yet. We seem to have more insight into the issue of activation of grammatical morphemes than the access of diacritic features, and there also appears to be a consensus in this respect. Researchers tend to agree that grammatical morphemes can be activated in two different ways—by the specifications of the preverbal plan and by syntactic encoding procedures—and that the way these morphemes behave in L2 processing, acquisition, transfer, and code-switching is largely dependent on the mode by which they are accessed. There is more disagreement concerning the question as to whether L2 lemmas can activate L1 syntactic building procedures or only L2 ones. The investigation carried out by Meijer and Fox Tree (2003) shows that if certain grammatical processes are identical in L1 and L2, they can be merged and might not have a specification for language in the case of advanced L2 speakers. The PT (Pienemann, 1998; Pienemann et al., 2005), however, claims that there is a processability hierarchy of syntactic structures, and L2 learners cannot process a structure if they have not yet acquired the procedures to be found at earlier stages of the hierarchy. This also means that they cannot transfer or apply an L1 process instead of the L2 one if they are not yet at the stage where the L1 process is located in the hierarchy.

In the field of transfer and the acquisition of syntactic encoding processes, we have reviewed three theories: the PT, the competition model, and the APT. The main concern of PT is the sequence in which various L2 syntactic encoding processes can be acquired based on the constraints of the syntactic system, whereas the other two models concentrate on how syntax is learned from the available input. PT has been extensively tested with learners acquiring different languages and having various L1 backgrounds, and its assumptions have largely been borne out. The competition model has been mainly applied to studies of comprehension, and studies on its implications for bilingual syntax acquisition are scarce. APT is a new theory that needs to be submitted to empirical testing. Further psycholinguistic investigation of the syntactic processes involved in code-switching is also imminent.

GENERAL OVERVIEW OF PHONOLOGICAL ENCODING PROCESSES

In chapter 2, we reviewed Roelofs' (1997b) WEAVER model of phonological encoding, which presents one of the most detailed accounts of how phonological processing might work in monolinguals. Let us recapitulate the basic steps in this model here once more. The first step in the phonological encoding process is accessing the mental representation of the phonological word, which contains information on the metrical structure of the word and the phonological segments that constitute it. The syllabification process, which is the next step, assigns the segments their position within the syllables based on the syllabification rules of the given language. When producing words that consist of several morphemes and connected speech, this process also takes neighboring morphemes and words into consideration. Syllabification proceeds from the first segment to second, from second to third, and so on, which Roelofs compared to weaving a fabric (hence the name WEAVER model). In phonetic encoding, metrical representations are used to set parameters for loudness, pitch, and duration, and the program is made available for the control of the articulatory movements. The model assumes incremental production, which means that a fragment of the input is enough to trigger production. Therefore, syllabification can start on the initial segment of a word if the metrical structure is available, and the interim results of the syllabification process can be stored in a buffer until further segments are ready. In the articulation phase, motor programs are retrieved from a store of learned programs, which is called the syllabary. Syllables are produced as packages of scores for the articulatory movements to be made. Scores also specify the gestures and their temporal relationships. Assimilation of sounds is assumed to be the result of the overlap of gestural scores. In the model, only forward spreading of activation is allowed.

Phonological encoding in L2 has received little attention by researchers working in the field of psycholinguistics. In line with L1 research, one of the issues that has been addressed is whether the phonological form of nonselected but activated words can be activated, that is, whether activation cascades from the lemma to the lexeme level (Colomé, 2001; Costa et al., 2000; Hermans, 2000; Hermans et al., 1998; Kroll et al., 2000). The other question that has been recently tested by means of experimental techniques is whether representations of phonemes are shared or separate in L1 and L2 (Roelofs, 2003b). Poulisse (1999) investigated phonological slips of the tongue and drew conclusions concerning L2 phonological encoding processes from the types and distributions of the slips in her corpus. An attempt was also made by Laeufer (1997) to set up a typology of bilingual phonological and phonetic representation. As regards the role of L1 in phonological encoding and the acquisition of L2 phonology, most studies apply a linguistic theory to address these issues. Research that is concerned with the psycholinguistic processes of learning L2 phonological encoding mechanisms is scarce (but see Flege, Frieda, Walley, & Randazza, 1998; Hancin-Bhatt & Bhatt, 1992).

THE ACTIVATION OF THE PHONOLOGICAL FORM
OF LEXICAL ITEMS

In chapter 2 we saw that one of the central questions in psycholinguistic research on word form encoding is whether activation can cascade from the lemma to the lexeme level, in other words, whether the phonological form of a given lexical item can receive activation from a nonselected, but nonetheless, activated lemma. In L1 production research, support for the cascading of activation was found by, among others, Jescheniak and Schriefers (1997) and Peterson and Savoy (1998), but counterevidence also exists (see, e.g., Jescheniak et al., 2003; van Turennout et al., 1997). Interestingly, in L2 production most studies have found that the phonological form of words in the nonselected language also becomes activated.

The first piece of evidence for the assumption that activation spreads to the phonological form of both L1 and L2 words comes from studies investigating naming latencies of cognate words. A number of researchers (e.g., Costa et al., 2000, for Spanish-Catalan bilinguals; Kroll et al., 2000, for Dutch-English bilinguals) have observed that participants were faster naming pictures that can be described by similar-sounding words in the two languages than pictures where no phonological relationship exists between the words. The explanation for this finding probably lies in the fact that in the case of cognates the phonological form of the lemma in the nonselected language also becomes activated and sends additional activation to the phonological features of the lemma in the selected language (see chap. 4, Fig 4.3, for an illustration), and this speeds up picture naming (see also Gollan & Silverberg, 2001).

Colomé (2001, Spanish-Catalan bilinguals) and Hermans (2000, Dutch-English bilinguals) used a so-called phoneme-monitoring task to investigate whether activation cascades to the phonological level. The task of the participants was to decide whether a given phoneme can be found in the word describing an object. There were two different conditions in the experiment: The phoneme was either present or not in the word to be named in the selected language, and the phoneme was either present or not in the translation of the given word in the other language, which yielded four different types of trials. Colomé and Hermans both observed that decisions concerning the presence of the given phoneme were slower if the phoneme was present in the translation equivalent of the target word but not in the target word itself, which they explained with reference to the fact that the phonological form of the word in the language not in use is also activated and interferes with the selection of the phonological form of the word in the selected language.

SHARED VERSUS SEPARATE PHONOLOGICAL
AND PHONETIC SYSTEMS

As at every phase of speech production, one of the central questions for researchers in the field of bilingualism is to what extent encoding processes and representations are shared. In a recent study, Roelofs (2003b) investigated to what extent memory representations of phonological segments that are common in L1 and L2 are shared, and whether phonological encoding in advanced bilinguals proceeds in the same rightward incremental fashion as described by the WEAVER model (Roelofs, 1997b) for monolingual speakers. Roelofs was also interested in whether phonological segments common to both languages are stored and accessed as one unit or as a combination of phonological features. In the experiments that aimed to give insight into these questions, he used the form preparation paradigm (also called implicit priming), which we described in chapter 2. In the first experiment, Roelofs replicated Meyer's (1990, 1991) experiments in English with Dutch participants who were advanced speakers of English. In the first phase of the research, the students had to learn pairs of words. When the first word of a pair was presented visually, participants had to produce the second word. Three different sets of words were involved in the experiments: two homogenous sets, when response words shared either their first or their last syllable, and a heterogeneous set, when there were no similarities between the forms of words. The focus of interest in this experiment was to what extent similarities speed up the production of the response. Roelofs (2003b) found that producing the first syllable of the word in a previous response helped participants to encode the target word faster in L2, but no such effect was detected when the previous response and the target word shared their last syllables, which results are in line with Meyer's study (1990, 1991) with L1 speakers. From this Roelofs concluded that the predictions of the WEAVER model for L2 phonological encoding are right as far as rightward incrementality is concerned; in other words, L2 speakers also encode words phonologically starting from the first segment on the left and move segment by segment to the right.

In the second experiment, the same design was used as in the first one, but here word pairs came from mixed languages. For example, a Dutch-English homogeneous set involved the following word pairs: punt-stip, vapor-steam, ijzer-staal. Just as in the monolingual task, Roelofs (2003b) found a facilitation effect when the response words shared their first segment, which he explained by arguing that mental representations of phonological segments that are common in both languages are shared. In the final experiment, Roelofs' (1999) study, which was described in chapter 2, was replicated for L2 production. Here the research question was whether the facilitation effect arises as a result of segmental or feature overlap. In other words, this experiment aimed to find an answer to the question of whether L2 phonemes are stored as one unit (e.g., [b]) or L2 phonemes are represented as a list of features (e.g., [+ voiced] [+ labial] [− nasal] in the case of the phoneme [b]). Therefore two different types of homogenous word pair sets were used: those containing words that share their initial consonant (e.g., river-boat, girl-boy) and those sharing the first segment except for one phonological feature (e.g., cat-dog, sugar-tea). The results of the experiment indicate that only complete segmental overlap speeds up production of the following word (i.e., if words start with the same sound), and that partial overlap (e.g., if a word starting in [d] is followed by another one whose first sound is [t]) does not produce any effect on phonological encoding, which suggests that L2 phonological segments are also stored as one unit and not as a set of features. This is in complete accord with Roelofs' (1999) results in L1 speech production.

Poulisse (1999) investigated the phonological slips of the tongue in the speech of Dutch learners of English at different levels of proficiency. She found that sometimes it occurs that instead of the L2 phoneme, L1 phonemes are accidentally activated and used in syllables that are otherwise constituted of L2 sounds. Based on the existence of these types of slips of the tongue, she claimed that L1 and L2 phonemes are probably stored in one single network and are labeled for language. She noted that these lapses of performance are rather rare, and that L2 words are usually encoded with L2 phonemes, and L1 words even when used in code-switching, that is, in an L2 utterance, also activate L1 phonemes.

As Roelofs' (2003b) experiments show, it is possible that advanced L2 speakers have shared memory representations of phonological segments that are common to L1 and L2; the picture, however, is more complicated in the case of phonological segments that are different in the two languages and the ones whose phonetic realizations are different in L1 and L2. Based on Weinreich's (1953) typology of bilingual representation, Laeufer (1997) argued that phonological systems might also be of three types: coexistent, merged, and supersubordinate. She illustrated these three different systems with stop consonants ([b], [d], [g], [p], [t], [k]), which are present in many languages of the world and which can be realized phonetically in three basic and universal ways along the continuum of voice onset time (VOT) (time between the release of a stop and the onset of voicing for the following vowel) (Keating, 1984). Stops can be produced with a so-called lead; these are the voiced stops such as English [b]. Stops can have short-lag VOTs, which results in voiceless unaspirated consonants such as French [p], and long VOTs in the case of voiceless aspirated consonants such as English [pʰ]. A French speaker of English might have coexistent representations of the phoneme [p], which means that two different phonological representations exist for this sound, which are also realized phonetically in separate ways (see Fig. 5.3a). In the merged system, speakers have a common representation of the phoneme for L1 and L2, which is phonetically encoded separately for L1 and L2 (see Fig. 5.3b). In the supersubordinate system, no separate memory representation exists for the L2 phoneme; and the L2 phoneme is realized phonetically similarly to the phoneme from L1 (see Fig. 5.3c). Lauefer argues that nativelike realization of L2 sounds is possible only in the coexistent system, and in the merged and supersubordinate system we can see various degrees of interaction between L1 and L2 at the phonetic level. Lauefer reviewed research on the pronunciation of stop consonants, and concluded that there is experimental evidence for the existence of each of the different representation systems. With a few exceptions, studies cited by Lauefer also suggest that coexistent systems mostly emerge in the case of L2 speakers who acquired their L1 and L2 simultaneously or started learning the L2 before the age of 7. Lauefer proposed that the merged system is characterized by nonnative realizations of both the L1 and L2 phonemes, which usually happens in situations where L2 is the dominant mode of communication and the L1 attrition has already begun. Supersubordinate systems are typical in the speech of beginning to advanced speakers who acquire the L2 after the age of 7, and for whom mainly L1 is used for everyday communication.

If one considers Roelofs' (2003b) research and psycholinguistic theories of speech production, Lauefer's (1997) typology seems problematic for several reasons. First of all, we have to note that the typology proposed by Lauefer might not characterize every sound of the L2 because as Roelofs' study suggests, sounds that are phonologically and phonetically identical in the two languages might share phonological representations and gestural scores used to produce these sounds. Moreover, it is also possible, especially at the beginning phase of the L2 learning process, that L2 speakers simply equate the L2 phoneme with the L1 phoneme at the phonological level and also produce it identically as the L1 sound (see e.g., Flege, 1987). In terms of mental representation and phonetic realization, there does not seem to be a difference in these two cases: There is a shared representation that triggers a non-language-specific phonetic encoding process. The other problem in Lauefer's model is whether it is possible that one shared phonological representation can activate two different phonetic encoding mechanisms; in other words, how would the processor know which gestural score to access: the one for L1 or that of the L2? Because

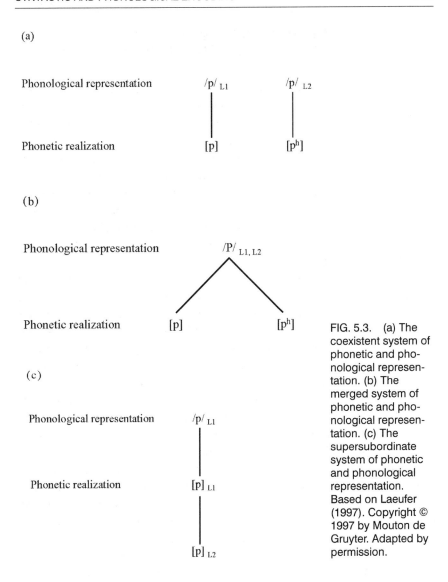

(a)

Phonological representation   /p/ L1   /p/ L2

Phonetic realization   [p]   [pʰ]

(b)

Phonological representation   /P/ L1, L2

Phonetic realization   [p]   [pʰ]

(c)

Phonological representation   /p/ L1

Phonetic realization   [p] L1

[p] L2

FIG. 5.3. (a) The coexistent system of phonetic and phonological representation. (b) The merged system of phonetic and phonological representation. (c) The supersubordinate system of phonetic and phonological representation. Based on Laeufer (1997). Copyright © 1997 by Mouton de Gruyter. Adapted by permission.

there is a shared representation, we cannot assume that a language tag would guide the encoding process; the only possible way of controlling language selection would be inhibition, which we saw in chapter 4 gives rise to several unresolved issues. In psycholinguistic terms, it seems more likely that in certain cases representations might be shared, otherwise L2 phonemes are represented separately from L1 sounds.

THE ROLE OF L1 IN PHONOLOGICAL AND PHONETIC EN-
CODING AND THE ACQUISITION OF L2 PHONOLOGY

Just as in the case of syntactic encoding, transfer and acquisition of L2 phonology are strongly related processes. Research evidence suggests that L2 learners start out using L1 phonemes for similar but nonidentical L2 ones, often
apply L1 rules of encoding to L2 phonology, and find it very difficult to modify
gestural scores automatized for L1 production (for a review of these issues, see
Leather, 1999). Similarly to the acquisition of syntactic encoding processes
and in line with major theories of language learning, we can delineate three
different types of theories used in explaining how L2 phonology is learned.
The earliest models of the acquisition of phonological processing are based on
the assumption that the major influence in the course of learning this component of speech production comes from the learners' L1 (e.g., Broselow, 1984).
These theories were soon refined by models that argued that in addition to
transfer, universal linguistic principles also play an important role in language
learning including the acquisition of phonology. One of the important models
in this vein is Eckman's markedness differential hypothesis (1977), which de-
fines markedness as the frequency of a particular linguistic structure in the
world's languages: If a specific linguistic feature frequently occurs in languages, it is considered as unmarked, and if it occurs rarely, it is marked
(Eckman, 1977). The main assumption of the markedness differential hypothesis is that those L2 structures that are more marked than the corresponding L1
structure are more difficult to acquire. Since the publication of Eckman's paper, several studies in the field of phonology have provided counterevidence
against this hypothesis and have criticized it on theoretical grounds (for a review, see Major & Kim, 1999). A relatively recent development in the theories
of linguistic universals is *optimality theory* (Prince & Smolensky, 1993),
which instead of universal principles and parameters found in UG, assumes
that there exists a set of universal constraints that speakers of all languages
share. The novelty of the theory is that certain constraints might be violable
and might have different degrees of importance in constructing grammatically
acceptable utterances. Speakers of a language aim to produce optimal output
(hence the name optimality theory) that violates only those constraints that are
violable and that are shaped by constraints that they regard important.
Optimality theory has been used in explaining the acquisition of syllable structure of English by speakers of Spanish and Japanese (Hancin-Bhatt & Bhatt,
1997) as well as of Mandarin (Broselow, S.-I. Chen, & Wang, 1998). The third
important theory in the universalist tradition is Major's (1987) *ontogeny*

model, which argues that universal developmental processes and transfer play different roles at various stages of L2 phonological development. At the beginning of the acquisition process, transfer exerts the greatest influence on L2 phonological encoding, but its role decreases with the development of L2 phonological competence. Parallel to the diminishing influence of transfer, universal developmental processes begin to affect acquisition. Connectionist theories, which do not presume the existence of linguistic universals, have become influential in explaining how L2 phonological processing is learned only recently; Hancin-Bhatt and Bhatt (1992), Hancin-Bhatt and Govindjee (1999), and Keidel, Zevin, Kluender, and Seidenberg (2003) used models of phonological feature acquisition that are based on connectionist architectures that extract regularities from the input. In what follows next, I concentrate on the acquisition of phonological encoding processes in speech production and not on the entire process of learning L2 phonology. We look at four levels of phonology—segments, syllables, stress, and intonation—and discuss how L1 comes to play role at these levels and how these aspects of L2 phonology are acquired.

As regards acquisition and transfer at the level of single phonemes, four important theories are reviewed: feature geometry, the feature competition model, lexical phonology, and the speech learning model. We also discuss the study conducted by Flege et al. (1998), who investigated the factors affecting the production of phonemes and whether it is sound-size phonemes that are the targets of learning or L2 learners or sound patterns of entire words. The theory of feature geometry is based on the assumption that phonological features are organized in a hierarchical way; that is, certain features often occur together, whereas certain others are dependent on each other (Rice & Avery, 1995). It is also proposed that the structure of a phonological segment is determined by contrastive features that make the segment different from other segments in the phonological inventory of the given language. Rice (1995; cf. Archibald, 1998a) illustrated this with the example of liquids in English and Japanese: The English featural inventory contains the features [approximant] and [lateral], whereas the Japanese inventory includes only [approximant]. As a result, the phonemes [l] and [r] are not contrastive in Japanese and occur in free variation, which means that they have one single phonological mental representation. Brown (1998) investigated Japanese and Chinese speakers' production and perception of the English phonemes [l] and [r] and came to the conclusion that if a particular feature is missing in the L1 feature geometry, L2 speakers are unable to create the appropriate mental representation for the L2 phoneme. Representations for new segments in L2 can, however, be created by the combination of existing features in L1. We have to note that this possibly does not apply to L2 learners starting to acquire the language in their childhood.

Hancin-Bhatt's (1994) feature competition model draws on the competition model of MacWhinney and Bates (for a review, see MacWhinney, 1997) and claims that the acquisition of L2 phonemes is influenced by the prominence of phonetic features available in the L2 input. L2 phonological features compete to be noticed in the input, and those features that are more salient are perceived and learned more easily. Though Hancin-Bhatt's proposal is appealing because it considers the important role input plays in the acquisition of segments, it poses several problems, the most important of which is how to establish the prominence of phonological features. Hancin-Bhatt simply equated the frequency of the particular feature in the L2 sound inventory with perceptual salience instead of establishing prominence based on empirical research (Archibald, 1998a). Moreover, the results of her own study do not fully support the model.

The third important theory concerning phonological segments is based on lexical phonology (Mohanan, 1986), which assumes the existence of two types of phonological rules: lexical and postlexical. Lexical rules operate at the word level and produce phonemes that are contrastive in the given language, whereas postlexical rules can be applied across word boundaries and can result in allophones, that is, sounds that are not contrastive in the language.[2] Research evidence suggests that postlexical rules are frequently transferred from L1 to L2, whereas lexical rules are less susceptible to transfer (Broselow, 1987; Rubach, 1984; Young-Scholten, 1997). Eckman and Iverson (1995; cf. Archibald, 1998a) argued that when L2 learners want to acquire an L2 sound that is an allophone in L1, they have to suppress the application of L1 postlexical rules in L2 phonological processing. Unfortunately, no studies have been published yet on how the transfer of phonological rules takes place in psycholinguistic terms.

Flege (1995) in his speech learning model proposes that when beginning L2 learners encounter an L2 sound that is not part of the L1 phonological inventory, they first substitute the nearest L1 sound for the target phoneme. With more exposure to L2, learners gradually establish a new phonological category, that is, underlying mental representation for the L2 sound as well as gestural scores and motor programs to produce the sound. As regards the factors

---

[2]In this context, contrastive means that the given language uses this sound to differentiate the meaning of words from each other. For example, the English phonemes [d] and [t] are contrastive because their exchange alters the meaning of words, for example, bed and bet.

that influence this learning process, Flege synthesized many of the previously described findings of L2 segmental phonology when he claimed that the acquisition of L2 phonemes is constrained by the phonetic difference between the target L2 sound and the corresponding most similar L1 sound and the feature inventory of the L1. In addition, he proposed that the age when L2 speakers started learning the language and the frequency of L2 use also affect the success of the acquisition process. Flege's model was recently tested by Keidel et al. (2003) with the help of a connectionist learning network, which was able to reproduce how English speakers assimilate Zulu sounds to English phonemes in real-life circumstances. In another study, Flege et al. (1998) were primarily interested in whether the assumption of the speech learning model and other theories of phonological learning are right in assuming that sounds are the basic units of acquisition and not combinations of sounds as found in entire words or morphemes. The other important question that they addressed in this investigation was whether the cognate status of words in L1 and L2 influences pronunciation. If evidence was found that sounds are produced differently in cognate words from sounds in noncognates, it would support the assumption that in phonological encoding L2 cognates are accessed indirectly through the phonological form of the L1 translation equivalent. Flege et al. asked 20 native speakers of English and 40 Spanish-English bilinguals to produce 60 words beginning in /t/ and analyzed the VOT of this sound. Some of the words in the list were Spanish-English cognates. In addition to calculating word frequency from existing corpora, they also investigated how well the participants knew the words, how familiar they were with them, when they learned them, and how concrete they judged them to be. Regression analysis was applied to establish the importance of various factors. The major finding of the research was that regardless of their level of L2 competence the participants were not influenced by lexical factors in producing the sound under investigation. Although Flege et al. warned against drawing far-reaching conclusions from their study, they claimed that their results indicate that assumptions concerning sounds being the basic unit of phonological acquisition might be right. Furthermore, it seems that their participants did not access the phonological form of L2 cognate words through their L1 counterpart.

Syllables have also been the subject of extensive research in L2 phonology. Because the production of syllables is governed by the application of phonological rules, most studies in this field have been interested in the workings of these rules from the perspective of theoretical linguistics. With the exception of connectionist theories, we can find investigations carried out in the framework of the different models of phonological acquisition outlined earlier. The conclusions that can be drawn from these studies is that syllable production is affected by the transfer of L1 syllable structure to L2 as well as by universal markedness and universal constraints (for recent reviews, see Cutillas Espinosa, 2002; Hansen, 2004). It has also been shown that the acquisition of syllabification rules in L2 often takes place simultaneously with learning new L2 phonological feature distinctions (Archibald, 1998b). Furthermore, re- search evidence also suggests that L2 learners' acquisition of syllable structure can be characterized more accurately as U-shaped rather than as being linear. Studies reviewed by Abrahamsson (2003) indicate that beginning speakers' production of L2 syllable structure is fairly accurate, but with general profi- ciency development taking place, learners' attention is diverted to other aspects of speech production and thus a high number of syllable errors are made. At further stages of development, the accuracy of L2 learners' syllable structure increases again.

The way stress is assigned in L1 at both the word and sentence level seems to influence L2 speech to a great extent (Archibald, 1997, 1998a; Trammell, 1993). Archibald (1997, 1998a) investigated the production and perception of English stress by native speakers of accentual languages (i.e., languages that use pitch to signal stress) and of nonaccentual languages such as Chinese and Japanese, in which pitch and/or tone is stored as part of the lexical entry. His results suggest that participants whose L1 was an accentual language (Polish and Hungarian) transferred the principles and parameters of L1 metrical struc- ture to L2, but because Chinese and Japanese participants could not make use of transfer, they stored L2 stress specifications for each lexical item in L2 rather than computed it on the basis of stress assignment rules. In an opposite situation, when native speakers of accentual languages learned a tonal lan- guage, L2 learners were found to transfer their knowledge of how tone is used in intonation in their L1, which can be regarded as transfer across structural levels (Leather, 1997). Intonational patterns also tend to be transferred from L1 to L2 (Archibald, 1998a); moreover, speakers' attitude as expressed by intonation might also be interpreted based on L1 values (Holden & Hogan, 1993).

SUMMARY OF PHONOLOGICAL ENCODING PROCESSES

It is apparent from the preceding review of studies on phonological encoding that this topic is a neglected area of psycholinguistic research. Whereas in the case of syntactic encoding I have concluded that we are left with more ques- tions than answers, in the psycholinguistic field of L2 phonology we do not even find a sufficient number of questions that have been raised. The classic issue of shared versus separate representations that has been addressed at every stage of bilingual speech production also appears in the case of L2 phonemes but is neglected in the case of syllables and the application of phonological rules. Moreover, we also have very little insight into the cognitive processes involved in learning L2 phonology. At the moment, the following assumptions concerning L2 phonological encoding mechanisms have gained support. First of all, there seems to be ample evidence that the phonological form of translation equivalents in the nonselected language also becomes activated when accessing the phonological form of the word in the target language; in other words, activation can cascade from the lemma in the language not in use to its phonological form. As regards phonemes that are identical in two languages, Roelofs' (2003b) research suggests that in the case of advanced speakers they have shared memory representations; whereas concerning nonidentical L1 and L2 phonemes, Poulisse (1999) argued that they are retrieved from a common store of L1 and L2 phonemes. Flege et al.'s (1998) study indicates that L2 phonemes are acquired on an individual basis, and that combinations of sounds constituting words or morphemes are not learned as one unit. Studies in phonological acquisition all attribute a central role to L1 influence, but there is considerable disagreement with respect to factors constraining transfer. At the moment, no unitary theory of how L2 phonological encoding takes place and is acquired exists, and until more psycholinguistic research is done in this field it is hardly possible to devise such a model.

6   Monitoring

In chapter 2, we saw that three basic psycholinguistic models of monitoring exist in L1 speech production research: the editor theories (Baars et al., 1975; Laver, 1980; Motley et al., 1982), the activation spreading theory (Berg, 1986; Dell, 1986; Dell & O'Seaghda, 1991; MacKay, 1987, 1992; Stemberger, 1985), and the PLT (Levelt, 1983, 1989, 1993; Levelt et al., 1999). Editor theories of monitoring assume that the editor can veto and replace the incorrect output of the speech production processes. In this model, the editor has its own system of rules against which the output is checked (Baars et al, 1975; Motley et al., 1982). In order to account for the occurrence of errors, these theories presume that either the system of rules the editor uses is incomplete (e.g., Garnsey & Dell, 1984) or the rules used at a given moment vary (e.g., Motley et al., 1982). The major shortcoming of these types of models is that the editor can only check the final outcome of the processes and is unable to intercept erroneous output at intermediary levels. Several researchers working in the paradigm of editor theories of monitoring (e.g., Laver, 1980; Nooteboom, 1980) proposed that there should be a specialized monitor at each stage of the processing system, which checks the correctness of the outcome of each process. Such a model is called the *distributed editor theory* because the monitor has access to the different stages of production. In Stemberger's (1985) and Dell's (1986) model of interactive activation spreading, speech perception is assumed to proceed through the bottom-up flow of activation, and this mechanism is in operation when speakers monitor their own speech. Therefore, in this theory, monitoring is "an automatic by-product of bottom-up activation spreading" (Berg, 1986, p. 139). In chapter 2, two basic problems were pointed out concerning this theory of monitoring: It does not account for the fact that many errors remain unnoticed by speakers (Levelt, 1983) and nor that monitoring also involves perceiving the pragmatic inappropriacy of the message and the inadequacy of the information conveyed (Levelt, 1992). In chapters 1 and 2, I also argued that Levelt's (1983, 1989, 1993; Levelt et al., 1999) PLT seems to provide the most detailed and reliable account of how monitoring takes place in L1 production. In this theory, it was proposed that the speech comprehension system is used for attending to one's own speech as well as that of others and that there are three loops for inspecting the outcome of processes. In the first loop, the preverbal plan is compared to the original intentions of the speaker; in the second loop, the message is monitored before articulation (called *covert* or *prearticulatory monitoring;* see also Postma & Kolk, 1992, 1993), and finally, the generated utterance is also checked after articulation, which constitutes the final, external loop of monitoring.

Models of monitoring have been put to the test not only in L1 production, but also in L2 research (Kormos, 1999, 2000b; van Hest, 1996). In L2 production, the investigation of monitoring involves the analysis of various types of self-repairs found in the speech of learners, their syntactic structure, and the timing of corrections. The study of monitoring also yields insight into how L2 learners allocate their attention to various aspects of speech processing. The issue of how monitoring behavior changes with the development of proficiency has also been addressed by a number of researchers. Monitoring is also considered to be an important process of L2 production because it is believed to contribute to language learning by making learners notice deficiencies in their knowledge of the target language (Izumi, 2003; Kormos, 1999).

MONITORING PROCESSES IN L2

In both L1 and L2 research, monitoring is most frequently investigated by means of analyzing the self-repair behavior of speakers based on the assumption that self-corrections are overt manifestations of the monitoring processes. A self-initiated self-completed correction comes about when the speaker detects that the output has been erroneous or inappropriate, halts the speech flow, and finally executes a correction. In many cases, however, the speaker notices the error prior to articulation and either repairs it before the utterance is articulated (this is called a covert repair) or decides not to correct the mistake in the utterance. Before I go on to discuss monitoring research, it is important to note that these two phenomena cause serious methodological problems for studying monitoring via the investigation of self-repairs. Covert repairs can be explored reliably only under laboratory conditions or with the help of verbal reports, whereas the decisions of the speaker not to correct an error can be analyzed only with the help of retrospection or by investigating the recognition of errors rather than their production. Unfortunately, research on L2 self-repairs has made limited use of these research methods (but see Kormos, 2000a, 2000b, 2003). In this section, I discuss the psycholinguistic processes underlying various types of self-corrections, as well as what the structure and timing of self-repairs reveal about the cognitive mechanisms involved in producing self-repairs. In the light of the findings of self-repair research in these areas, I argue that with minor modifications PLT is the model of monitoring that can best account for L2 behavior among the various theories of monitoring.

Inferences concerning basic psycholinguistic processes involved in monitoring are most frequently made by analyzing the types of repair that occur in speech samples elicited from participants in various ways. The description of monitoring processes presented here is based on Levelt's (1989) and Levelt et. al.'s (1999) speech production model. The first type of monitoring mechanism discussed involves the realization that the content of the preverbal plan needs to be changed. In the case of an error in the conceptualizing phase of the speech production process, speakers might decide to encode new and different information from the one they are currently formulating, or they might modify the informational content of their current message. The former type of repair is called *different information (D-) repair,* whereas the latter is often referred to as *appropriacy (A-) repair* (Levelt, 1983). Levelt (1983) identified two reasons why one might want to choose to convey different information: first, one can realize that parts of the intended message need to be ordered differently, as in Example 1, and second the information content of the message can prove to be inappropriate or incorrect, as in Example 2. Examples with retrospective comments are taken from the speech samples elicited in a research project on L2 monitoring behavior (for reports on the project, see Kormos, 2000a, 2000b):

1. Uhm well there's a big dining table for forty person. And then <u>we've also got er well it's well the dining table</u> occupies half of the room. Retrospection: I thought, I did not tell you first how big the room was, so I said that the dining table occupies half of the room, and then I said what I originally wanted to say.
2. <u>you have to we have</u> to make a contract Retrospection: I realized that it is stupid to say that you have to make a contract, it's the restaurant that has to write it.

The analysis of L2 self-correction behavior has revealed that there might be a third reason why L2 speakers might decide to encode new or different information in the preverbal plan. It is especially characteristic of L2 learners that in certain cases they might abandon their originally intended message all together and replace it with a completely new one (Kormos, 2000a). This usually happens due to limited L2 competence, as in Example 3.

3. <u>we have some er er v ... maybe you have vegetarians</u> in your group Retrospection: Here the idea of vegetarians suddenly popped up, and I abandoned what I was going to say because I would not have been able to list any more types of food anyway.

It has to be noted, however, that in some cases this type of repair is very similar to the problem-solving strategy of message replacement, as the speaker does not feel capable of executing the original preverbal plan, and, therefore interrupts the encoding of the original message and substitutes it with a different one. In the case of the communication strategy of message replacement, however, very often the original message is not articulated and the replacement process takes place even before the preverbal plan is sent to the formulator.

Appropriacy repairs also involve the modification of the preverbal plan, but they are different from different-information repairs in that they are employed when the speaker decides to encode the originally intended information but in a modified way (Levelt, 1983). Speakers resort to appropriacy repairs when they have encoded (a) inaccurate (Example 4) or (b) ambiguous information (Example 5) that needs to be further specified, or if they have used (c) incoherent terminology (Example 6) or (d) pragmatically inappropriate language (Example 7). The first three classes of self-corrections were identified by Levelt (1983), and the fourth one by Brédart (1991). He called this latter type *repair for good language,* which included both pragmatic and good-language repairs. Kormos (1999), however, proposed that these two groups of self-repairs be more clearly separated, as their sources are different. Pragmatic self-corrections concern meaning in context, whereas repairs of good language are carried out to ensure a more sophisticated manner of expression (see Example 8). Here are Examples 4 through 8:

4. There are very wide choice of er main courses er er <u>steak er er several kinds of steak</u>.
   Retrospection: I wanted to say it more precisely that we do not only have one kind of steak but several kinds of steak.
5. In this um in this part of the town er there are many vegetarians. Er this is because the university is here and vegetarians <u>like it er like this restaurant</u>.
   Retrospection: I noticed that "it" could also mean the university, so I wanted to make it clear that it is the restaurant that the vegetarians like and not the university.
6. Participant: In this case er if it is so urgent and important for you, we would like er you to to write us <u>an order</u> er in er 24 hours that you make sure that you will er come and book this er room.
   Researcher: I see, all right and then I can only pay the deposit next week when I er find out how many people come and when I have talked to all of the people.

Participant: Er but <u>this letter is er the order</u> is er anyway needed and we ...
Retrospection: I remembered that I had used the word "order" earlier, and
I wanted to stick to the same terms, so I replaced "letter" with "order."
7. It doesn't it's not a problem.
Retrospection: First I wanted to say "it does not matter" but I realized
that in a business deal you cannot say "it does not matter."
8. Thirty-five <u>per ... people</u>.
Retrospection: First I wanted to say "persons" but I had used "persons" several times before, so I said "people."

The second psycholinguistically different monitoring mechanism is the
correction of linguistic errors which results in *error (E) repairs*. In the case of
these errors the preverbal plan is appropriate, but in the course of the message
formulation either an erroneously activated word, or an inappropriate syntactic structure, or a wrong phoneme is selected. Levelt (1983) labeled these
lexical (Example 9), syntactic (Example 10), and phonetic repair (Example
11), respectively corresponding to the three main levels of processing in his
model:

9. Will er have to pay er <u>five</u> er sorry er <u>twenty-five</u> percent.
Retrospection: Here I said "five" instead of "twenty-five" accidentally.
10. I think <u>it</u> a very nice <u>it's</u> a very nice
Retrospection: I left out "is," and I corrected it.
11. We could arrange er more smaller <u>[teibiə] [teibəl]</u> if you would like
that better.

Kormos (1999) identified a third type of repair mechanism, called rephrasing repair. As opposed to error repairs, when the same preverbal plan is issued,
this type of repair involves the modification of the preverbal plan but leaves the
content of the message unaltered. Rephrasing repairs are employed when L2
speakers are uncertain about the correctness of their utterance, which makes
this type of repair similar to communication strategies (Example 12). Rephrasing repairs indicate underlying competence problems, whereas error repairs
signal lapses of performance:

12. Uhm our fish fish meals er foods are very good too.
Retrospection: I corrected "fish meals" for "fish food" because I was
not sure you can say "fish meals" and "fish foods" sounded a bit better.

Having reviewed the basic psycholinguistic processes involved in self-correction behavior, let us examine what the timing of self-corrections reveals
about monitoring mechanisms. As we saw in chapter 2, a number of studies
have investigated the exact timing of different types of self-repairs and the relevance of timing data for different theories of monitoring (e.g., Blackmer &
Mitton, 1991; Hartsuiker & Kolk, 2001; Levelt, 1989; Oomen & Postma,
2001; van Hest, 1996). Research on speech comprehension has shown that
word recognition takes place about 200 ms after word onset (Marslen-Wilson
& Tyler, 1980). On the basis of this, Levelt (1989) assumed that, in the case of
overt repairs, the shortest time between the detection of the error and the cutoff
point is also 200 ms. He estimated that the recognition of one's internal speech
lasts for approximately 150 ms, and the time between the delivery of the phonetic plan and the articulation is between 200 and 250 ms. Thus, speakers have
a maximum of 100 ms for prearticulatory monitoring, which may not be
enough to prevent the articulation of the erroneous utterance. In this case, the
erroneous word is interrupted shortly after its articulation begins; that is, the
time between the onset of the error and the point of interruption will be less
than 200 ms. As Levelt's (1989, 1993) model allows for parallel processing, it
is possible that there is already some processed material ready for articulation
in the articulatory buffer; consequently, speakers can intercept erroneous
output before it is articulated (covert repair).

In order to verify Levelt's (1989) estimations, Blackmer and Mitton (1991)
carried out an empirical study in which they found a high number of repairs
with short error-to-cutoff and cutoff-to-repair intervals (less than 150 ms).
They argued that, with respect to corrections with cutoff-to-repair intervals
shorter than 150 ms, it is unlikely that the replanning of the utterance could
take place within this period of time. Therefore, they assumed that speakers often start processing the repair before the flow of speech is interrupted. This hypothesis was confirmed by significant negative correlations between the
error-to-cutoff and the cutoff-to-repair intervals in the case of fast repairs in
their database. On the basis of these results, Blackmer and Mitton did not accept the cutoff point as a reliable measure of the point of the recognition of the
error, and they also argued that the cutoff-to-repair intervals do not equal the
total period of time spent replanning the utterance. Hartsuiker and Kolk (2001)
ran computer simulations using timing data collected by Oomen and Postma
(2001) to test the assumption that interruption and repair are "simultaneously
starting parallel processes, beginning immediately upon error detection" (p.
148), which is similar to Blackmer and Mitton's conclusion outlined previously. Hartsuiker and Kolk's research showed that the computer model could

successfully reproduce the timing patterns if parallel interruption and planning were supposed. From the timing research on L1 monitoring, it becomes apparent not only that interruption and the planning of repair can proceed parallel, but also that the very short cutoff times found in these studies do not lend proof to the existence of distributed editors (Laver, 1980; Nooteboom, 1980), because in the distributed editor models, detection is assumed to take at least 200 ms, and parallel processing is not allowed.

In the field of L2 monitoring, only two studies have been conducted on the timing of self-corrections. Van Hest's (1996) research was based on a corpus of self-repairs produced by Dutch speakers both in their mother tongue and in English in three different types of tasks (picture description, storytelling, and personal interview). The results of her project suggest that phonological errors are detected and interrupted faster than lexical errors, whereas inappropriate words seem to be recognized with the slowest speed. Van Hest explained these findings by arguing that, in Levelt's (1989, 1993) model, the correction route of phonological errors is the shortest, as all the other types of errors or inappropriacies need to be checked in the conceptualizer against the original communicative intention. This study also revealed that the cutoff-to-repair intervals of L2 speakers were longer than those in L1 speech, which van Hest assumed was due to a lower degree of automatization of the L2 production processes.

Kormos' (2000b) research involved the analysis of the timing of self-repairs in the speech of 30 Hungarian learners of English at three different levels of proficiency. One of the most important findings of the project was that, on the basis of the difference in the detection times of error, appropriacy, and different-information repairs, the assumption of both the activation spreading theory and the PLT—that monitoring involves the same mechanisms as speech comprehension—gained support. The study also revealed that the speed of detecting pragmatically inappropriate words and lexical errors was very similar, which might mean that during monitoring the pragmatic features of the lexical entry are checked simultaneously with its phonological and semantic form, as well as its argument structure. This finding therefore provides indirect evidence for the assumption that lexical entries do not contain only semantic specifications, but also information concerning their pragmatic value (Dörnyei & Kormos, 1998; La Heij, 2005; for more detail, see chap. 4, the Control in Lexical Encoding section). The analysis of detection times supported the need for the distinction of error and rephrasing repairs, because it revealed that the uncertainty of speakers about the correctness of the utterance in the case of rephrasing repairs slows down the detection process to a considerable extent. The results concerning the cutoff-to-repair intervals indicated that slight modifications in the linguistic form (e.g., error and rephrasing repairs) and in the informational content of the utterance (e.g., appropriate-level-of-information repairs) take less time to implement—that is, they require less processing effort—than large-scale changes in the informational content of the message (e.g., message abandonment repairs). The similarity of the time periods necessary for replanning the utterance, in the case of error repairs and rephrasing repairs, suggested that L2 speakers used the psycholinguistically simplest strategies in the case of uncertainty about the correctness of the output.

Whereas the analysis of different types of self-repairs yields insight into the various types of monitoring processes, the timing data are useful in making inferences about how these processes work. The study of the structure of self-corrections can further refine our understanding of the mechanisms of monitoring. Several studies have investigated whether the syntactic structure of self-repairs shows any signs of systematicity (e.g., De Smedt & Kempen, 1987; Levelt, 1983) and found that the majority of self-corrections follow a specific rule, which was named the well-formedness rule by Levelt (1983). According to the rule, "an original utterance <O> plus repair <OR> is well-formed if and only if there is a string of zero or more words <C> to complete the utterance so that the string <OC or R> is well-formed, where C is a completion of the constituent directly dominating the last element of O" (p. 78). In other words, this rule says that the utterance and the repair have to follow to the rule of syntactic coordination. Example 13 illustrates a well-formed repair, and Example 14 an ill-formed one:

13. all chairs have handles. And er sorry arms
14. you can this er reserve this er er room

Two studies have investigated the well-formedness of L2 self-repairs (Kormos, 2002; van Hest, 1996), which found little difference between L1 and L2 self-repairs in this respect. Following Levelt's (1983) rule of classification, 80% of the L2 self-repairs were well-formed in Van Hest's corpus whereas in Kormos' database 87.3% of the repairs followed the well-formedness rule. On the basis of van Hest's and Kormos' results, it seems that the self-repair behavior of L2 learners also follows the well-formedness rule. These results seem to be explicable only in terms of the modular models of speech production (Levelt, 1989, 1993; Levelt et al., 1999) as they indicate that L2 learners, just like L1 speakers reprocess the relevant parts of the speech plan when making a correction and do not restart the utterance from an intermediary level of production as assumed by the activation spreading theories of monitoring.

THE ROLE OF ATTENTION IN MONITORING L2 SPEECH

The role of attention in L2 acquisition has recently become an important issue in SLA research (for a current review, see Robinson, 2003). In a series of studies Schmidt (1990, 1993, 1994; Schmidt & Frota, 1986) claimed that conscious attention to input (noticing, in his terminology) is necessary for learning to take place. Robinson (1995) refined the conditions that are essential for acquisition by asserting that input will become intake if the detection of input is followed by rehearsal in working memory. VanPatten (1990, 1994, 1996; VanPatten & Cadiorno, 1993) conducted a number of experiments in which he examined how attention is divided between form and content in input processing. It is well known from earlier studies on attention that due to working memory constraints, attentional resources are limited (Broadbent, 1958; Gathercole & Baddeley, 1994). These limitations play an essential role in L2 speech processing, as its mechanisms are only partially automatic and require conscious control, that is, attention (de Bot, 1992). How L2 speakers manage their attentional resources influences their performance; consequently the investigation of this phenomenon is of crucial importance not only in SLA but also in L2 production research. Therefore, an increasing number of studies have been conducted on the allocation of attention under various constraints and conditions in L2 production (e.g., Bygate, 1996, 1999; Foster & Skehan, 1996; Skehan & Foster, 1997, 2001; Tarone, 1983, 1985; Tarone & Parrish, 1988).

The role of attention in speech monitoring, however, has been a slightly neglected area of investigation despite the fact that the issue of the frequency of certain types of self-corrections has been one of the most widely explored aspects of the self-repair behavior of L2 speakers. Most studies in this field were only concerned with establishing the distribution of various types of self-repairs, and did not attribute high importance to the discussion of the allocation of attention. These studies mostly used raw percentages of occurrence rather than standardized frequency data (e.g., Fathman, 1980; Lennon, 1984; van Hest, 1996) to investigate what type of errors L2 speakers' monitor is sensitive to. Thus, the results obtained by calculating only the proportion of various self-repairs might provide a different view about the allocation of attention than results that also take the actual frequency of self-corrections into consideration. Another shortcoming of the research in this field has been that with the exception of Poulisse's (1999) and P. S. Green and Hecht's (1993) research, conclusions concerning the monitoring skills of L2 learners were drawn without the examination of the frequency and the correction rate of errors and their relationship to the frequency of self-repairs. Despite these problematic issues of research methodology, researchers of L2 production assumed that L2 learners pay considerably more attention to lexical appropriacy than to grammatical accuracy (e.g., Fathman, 1980; Lennon, 1984; Poulisse, 1993; Poulisse & Bongaerts, 1994; van Hest, 1996). Investigations concerning L2 self-repairs also revealed that the frequency of repairs concerning the information content of the message varies across different types of tasks (Poulisse, 1993; van Hest, 1996).

Kormos' (2002) study, which investigated the distribution and frequency of self-repairs and the correction rate of errors in the speech of 30 Hungarian learners at three levels of proficiency (preintermediate, upper-intermediate, advanced) and of 10 native speakers of Hungarian, was specifically devoted to the examination of the role of attention in monitoring L2 speech. The global distribution of self-repairs in the research showed that in an information exchange task, Hungarian L2 learners paid approximately equal attention to the appropriacy and adequacy of the informational content of their utterance as to linguistic accuracy. The analysis of the correction rate of lexical and grammatical errors seemed to indicate a similar tendency. Kormos, however, argued that the similarity of the proportion of corrected lexical and grammatical inaccuracies does not necessarily mean that L2 speakers' attention is equally divided between monitoring for the lexical appropriacy and the grammatical accuracy of their message. The lack of observable differences between the correction rate of grammatical and lexical errors might have been caused by the fact that in the study covert repairs were not investigated. The retrospective comments suggested that speakers made conscious decisions concerning the implementation of the repair in L2. Kormos pointed out that this decision can be influenced by several factors such as the accuracy demand of the situation, the learners' perception of how seriously the error impedes successful communication, and to what extent the correction decreases the fluency of the utterance. Therefore, the similar correction rate of grammatical and lexical errors might indicate that upon deciding whether to repair a mistake, the participants in her project did not attribute different importance to grammatical inaccuracies and incorrect lexical choice. These results show that the general claim made by researchers in the field that upon monitoring in L2, attention is focused more on information content than on linguistic form (e.g., Fathman, 1980; Lennon, 1984; Poulisse, 1993, Poulisse & Bongaerts, 1994; van Hest, 1996) does not hold for all types of L2 learners. Formally instructed foreign language speakers in countries where explicit grammar teaching plays a significant role in the curriculum, everyday teaching practice, and state-level language testing, can allocate their attentional resources and make decisions concerning error corrections in a different way from learners in a second language environment or from students instructed with communicative methods.

MONITORING AND SLA

Several studies have been carried out to compare the number and nature of self-repairs with the development of competence and metalinguistic awareness in L1 (e.g., Evans, 1985; Rogers, 1978) and L2 (Kormos, 2002; O'Connor, 1988; van Hest, 1996; Verhoeven, 1989). Overall, the results of these studies indicate that due to limited metalinguistic awareness at the beginning of the acquisition process, learners make more errors and correct a smaller proportion of these mistakes than more-advanced speakers. On the other hand, with the general development of language skills, metalinguistic awareness also increases and speakers make fewer mistakes, and are assumed to have a higher correction rate of their erroneous output. Owing to a higher degree of automatization, learners' attention also seems to shift from lower level lexical, grammatical, and phonological mistakes to problems arising at the discourse level.

In a longitudinal study, Verhoeven (1989) investigated the relationship of L2 self-repairs and the language-learning process of 55 Turkish children living in the Netherlands, who were observed for a period of 2 years. The findings of Verhoeven's study indicated that the number of phonological corrections and restarts sharply decreased between the ages of 6 and 7, but later the number remained constant. He also found a significant positive correlation between restarts and semantic corrections with L2 proficiency at any age, whereas the number of syntactic corrections only increased between the ages of 6 and 8. The results of Verhoeven's study seem to confirm Evans' (1985) findings for L1 self-repairs, namely, that the number and type of self-corrections is related to the children's metalinguistic awareness and oral-language proficiency.

Several studies applied a cross-sectional design to compare the self-repair behavior of L2 learners at different levels of proficiency. O'Connor (1988) analyzed the speech of three beginning and three advanced American speakers of French studying in France. She hypothesized that less-proficient speakers would use more corrective repairs, whereas the self-corrections of advanced learners would tend to be anticipatory in nature; that is, they would be used to avoid possible breakdowns or communication difficulties, and they would involve discourse-level corrections. Her hypotheses were borne out by the analysis of the data. O'Connor also found that it was indeed the nature of the repair that differed in the case of the two groups of learners and not the number of repairs themselves. She interpreted these results by arguing that the lack of automaticity in the speech of beginners reduces their ability and possibility to employ planning techniques to avoid problems. In the case of advanced learners, however, the increase of automaticity frees the attention for the employment of this strategy. A study by Lennon (1990) yielded somewhat different results. He found that after 6 months' residence in England, the speech rate of the participants in his research project went up, and the number of pauses in their speech decreased, but they produced more self-corrections at the end of their stay than at the beginning. Similarly to Evans (1985) and O'Connor, Lennon explained his findings by assuming that with the increase of language competence, more attention becomes available for monitoring and self-repairing. Van Hest (1996) found that beginning and intermediate learners produced about the same number of self-repairs, whereas advanced learners corrected themselves significantly less frequently. She explained this finding by claiming that both the beginning and intermediate group were still in the trial-and-error stage, as opposed to advanced speakers, whose production had become more error-free. Kormos' (2002) investigation of the allocation of attention upon monitoring involved the analysis of the correction rate of lexical and grammatical errors. She found that the amount of attention paid to the linguistic accuracy of the message remained constant at various stages of SLA. Her results also showed that owing to the high level of automaticity of the speech-encoding mechanisms of advanced learners, these speakers had additional attention available for monitoring, which they use for checking the discourse level aspects of their message. The results of the four studies just described show that with increasing L2 proficiency there is a shift from simple error repairs to more complex discourse-level repairs, but the global frequency of self-corrections does not seem to be affected by the level of L2 competence.

The findings of the studies investigating the effect of proficiency on self-repair behavior have special relevance for theories of automatization in SLA. On the one hand, owing to the fact that advanced speakers have more declarative knowledge of the L2—that is, know more lexical entries, rules of grammar, and so on—they make fewer errors due to lack of competence than beginning learners, and as a result, a smaller number of low-level linguistic error repairs can be found in their speech. On the other hand, not only do advanced learners know more about the L2, but they can apply this knowledge in a more efficient way. With the development of language skills, conscious controlled knowledge, which is prone to errors when put to use, is gradually replaced by automatic unconscious rule- or memory-based procedures, which, if stored correctly, is error-free (DeKeyser, 1997; Robinson, 1997; Robinson & Ha,

1993). Moreover, with practice, the strength of connections between stimulus and response becomes stronger (MacKay, 1982), which is especially relevant in lexical retrieval and the access of prefabricated chunks. The increased strengthening of links between the conceptual and lemma level can contribute to the fact that lexical slips of the tongue due to erroneous activation of lemmas are less frequent in the speech of proficient learners than in the output of beginners (Poulisse, 1999). As a result of the various mechanisms of the development of automaticity, advanced learners make fewer errors than less-proficient speakers do, which explains the decreased frequency of low-level linguistic error repairs in their speech. This line of reasoning suggests that error repairs signal not yet fully automatized processes; thus, they can serve as good indicators of automaticity in L2 speech production.

The development of automaticity in L2 acquisition not only accounts for the fact that L2 learners make a decreasing number of linguistic error repairs due to the declining frequency of errors. As mentioned previously, automatic processes do not require attention, so attentional resources are freed for other phases of speech processing. Therefore, advanced learners can have more attention available for monitoring at the level of discourse and content than their less-proficient peers, which is reflected in the finding of a number of studies that advanced learners produce a high number of appropriacy repairs (Kormos, 2002; O'Connor, 1988; van Hest, 1996).

The role of monitoring in SLA has also been studied from the perspective of Swain's (1985, 1995) *output hypothesis,* which claims that output in general as well as pushed output, that is, output that is slightly above the learner's level of competence, promotes second language acquisition. A number of researchers have argued that because monitoring involves both attention and conscious processing as well as producing output, it can enhance the efficiency of acquisition in several ways outlined as follows (de Bot, 1996; Izumi, 2003; Kormos, 1999):

1. Because L2 monitoring involves the checking of both internal and external speech against learner's existing linguistic system, and in PLT (Levelt, 1989, 1993; Levelt et al., 1999) it is assumed to be similar to the processes of comprehension, L2 learners can resort to "receptive knowledge, which is assumed to be more stable and reliable than productive knowledge" (de Bot, 1996, p. 551).The receptive knowledge called for upon monitoring, however, may not always be stable in L2 use; for example, the given linguistic rule or item of vocabulary may not be fully acquired yet, or it may not be sufficiently automatized. In these cases, the L2 speaker sometimes cannot decide with certainty

whether the output is error free (see rephrasing repairs in Example 12 earlier). This can contribute to noticing the gap in one's knowledge, and it can trigger further acquisition processes (Robinson, 1995; Schmidt, 1990, 1993, 1994; Schmidt & Frota, 1986; Swain, 1995; Swain & Lapkin, 1995).

2. Not only perceiving a gap in one's knowledge but also simply noticing an error can promote L2 learning. Robinson (1995) argued that noticing involves "detection plus rehearsal in short-term memory prior to encoding in long-term memory" (p. 296). In the case of monitoring, this means that the erroneous item is detected and the error-free solution is rehearsed before it becomes stored in long-term memory. The memory trace left in this way can contribute to proceduralization of declarative knowledge (see Anderson's, 1995, ACT–R theory), to creating memorized solutions (e.g., Logan's, 1988, instance theory) or to the strengthening of links between various levels of processing (e.g., MacKay, 1982, strength theory), and in turn can facilitate L2 acquisition.

3. Making a self-initiated and self-completed repair in L2 is basically executed in a similar way as the process of making repairs upon the confirmation or clarification requests of the interlocutor. The only difference between the two processes is that in the former case it is the speaker who perceives the error, whereas in the latter case, it is the conversational partner. Instances when corrections or rephrasings of are elicited by the L2 learner's interlocutor have been termed pushed output, and they are believed to contribute to successful L2 acquisition (Swain, 1985, 1995). Thus, just like pushed output, self-initiated self-repairs also serve to test hypotheses about the L2, trigger creative solutions to problems, and expand the learners' existing resources (Swain, 1995; Swain & Lapkin, 1995).

SUMMARY

In this chapter, we have seen that research on L2 self-repairs suggests that mechanisms of L1 and L2 monitoring and self-repair behavior share a number of similarities, in that the distribution and detection of self-repairs display an analogous pattern in the processes of L1 and L2 acquisition and production. However, due to lack of automaticity in L2, monitoring in L1 differs from monitoring in L2 as regards the amount of attention available for error detection. Moreover, due to the fact that the L2 speakers' system of knowledge is typically incomplete and their production mechanisms are not fully automatic, certain repair mechanisms (e.g., message replacement repair and rephrasing repair; Kormos, 1999) occur in L2 speech that are not—or only very rarely—observable in L1 production. Studies on the timing of self-repairs have revealed that the sequence of the detection of different types of errors and inappropriacies is similar to the order in which the interlocutor's speech is processed. Therefore, recent modular and activation spreading models of speech processing (Dell & O'Seaghda, 1991; Levelt, 1989, 1993, 1995; Levelt et al., 1999) rightly assume that monitoring involves the same mechanisms as speech comprehension. From research on the timing of self-repairs, there is also evidence that parallel processing can take place even in L2 speech production. Thus, theories that postulate the existence of distributed editors at different stages of processing (e.g., Baars et al., 1975; Laver, 1980; Motley et al., 1982) cannot be considered viable. The investigations of the syntactic structure of self-repairs also show that speech production does not start from the intermediary level where the error occurred, but from the level of conceptualizing, which provides a strong support for modular models of speech production (e.g., Levelt, 1989, 1993, 1995; Levelt et al., 1999). Thus it can be concluded that both theoretical considerations and the empirical results on monitoring suggest the superiority of Levelt's PLT over the spreading activation and distributed editor models in both L1 and L2 speech processing.

As regards the role of attention in monitoring, we have seen that a large number of studies that have investigated the distribution of different types of self-corrections suggest that L2 speakers tend to pay more attention to the informational content than to the accuracy of their message. On the other hand, Kormos' (2002) research, which also considered the proportion of errors corrected, showed that this may not hold for all formally instructed learners. Students in whose instruction grammar teaching plays an important role might devote more attentional resources to accuracy than to lexical appropriacy than learners taught with communicative methods. In addition, research in this field indicates that with the development of language proficiency, L2 speakers' attention in monitoring shifts from lower level linguistic errors to problems arising at the discourse level. There is now also evidence that monitoring plays an important role in the process of L2 learning. It helps learners notice gaps in their knowledge, proceduralize linguistic rules, and memorize chunks of language, as well as pushes learners to stretch the limits of their language competence.

7　Problem-Solving Mechanisms in L2 Speech

In the introduction of a recent paper on managing problems in speaking, Clark (1994) wrote that "when the participants of a conversation have problems, they manage most of them quickly, skillfully, and without apparent effort" (p. 244). Although this statement is true when the conversation is conducted in the participants' L1, even a brief analysis of any spontaneous piece of L2 oral discourse will reveal that L2 speakers tend to spend a great deal of time and effort negotiating meaning and struggling to cope with the various problems they encounter during the course of communication (cf. Gass & Varonis, 1991). Understanding L2 problem management, therefore, is a principal issue in L2 research, with important potential implications for L2 theory. The language devices applied to overcome communication problems have been the target of extensive research in various subfields of applied linguistics, but very few attempts have been made to provide a comprehensive treatment of the mechanisms L2 speakers employ when encountering communication difficulties. Indeed, Yule and Tarone (1991) pointed out in their discussion of the relationship between the two central domains of problem-management, *meaning negotiation* (for reviews, see Gass & Selinker, 1994; Pica, 1994) and *communication strategies* (for reviews, see Bialystok, 1990; Dörnyei & Scott, 1997; Poulisse, 1994) that the research literatures of the two areas have been almost entirely independent.

The goal of this chapter is to provide a comprehensive overview of problem management in L2 speech production. Following Dörnyei and Scott (1997), three main problem sources in L2 speech are distinguished: (a) resource deficits, (b) processing time pressure, and (c) perceived deficiencies in one's own language output, the last of which was discussed in chapter 6. The fourth type of problem source identified by Dörnyei and Scott—perceived deficiencies in the interlocutor's performance—is not elaborated here because it is not related to speech production (for a discussion of this issue, see Dörnyei & Kormos, 1998). The chapter is structured as follows: First, I review definitions and characteristics of problem-solving mechanisms. Next, I analyze how L2 speakers manage problems in their speech by discussing problem-solving mechanisms related to resource deficits: First lexical communication strategies on the (slightly extended) basis of Poulisse's (1993) framework of strategic language processing are elaborated, then grammatical and phonological problem-solving mechanisms. I also examine problem-solving devices associated with processing time pressure stemming from serial rather than parallel processing in L2. Finally, the role of communication strategies in second language learning is discussed.

REVIEW OF DEFINITIONS AND CHARACTERISTICS
OF COMMUNICATION STRATEGIES

The most extensively researched area of L2 problem-solving behavior has been the study of *communication strategies* (CSs), a term first used by Selinker (1972). Four main views concerning the nature of CSs can be identified in the literature. In what Dörnyei and Scott (1997) called the "traditional view," CSs are seen as "potentially conscious plans for solving what to an individual presents itself as a problem in reaching a particular communicative goal" (Færch & Kasper, 1983, p. 23). In other words, Færch and Kasper consider CSs problem-solving devices that are used to overcome problems of language production arising at the planning stage. In the so-called interactional view, CSs are defined as "a mutual attempt of interlocutors to agree on a meaning in situations where requisite meaning structures do not seem to be shared" (Tarone, 1980, p. 420). In this perspective, CSs are related not only to the speaker's performance problems but also to a range of comprehension problems that occur in communication. In Dörnyei and Scott's extended view, "every potentially intentional attempt to cope with any language related problems of which the speaker is aware during the course of communication" (p. 179) is considered a communication strategy. Dörnyei and Scott conceptualized CSs in the broadest sense, as their definition includes problem-solving devices related to lack of appropriate knowledge, the speaker's own performance, meaning negotiation mechanisms, as well as strategies used to gain time in conversation. Because in this book we are concerned with the psycholinguistic aspects of speech production, I adopt Poulisse's (1997a) definition, which sees CS as "the expression of an alternative speech plan when the original plan proved to be unencodable" (p. 5), and which belongs to the group of studies that take a psycholinguistic perspective in CS research.

In their review of the CS literature, Dörnyei and Scott (1997) established two defining criteria of CS—problem-orientedness and consciousness—and point out that the diversity of definitions and taxonomies in CS research is mainly caused by the fact that these criteria have been inappropriately defined.

One of the major sources of disagreement among researchers comes from the difference in how the problems that arise in the course of communication are defined. Dörnyei and Scott identified four major types of communication problems: (a) resource deficits, which are "gaps in speakers' knowledge preventing them from verbalizing their messages" (p. 183), (b) own-performance problems, which include self-repair mechanisms, and (c) other-performance problems, in other words, meaning negotiation strategies and processing time pressure, which are "associated with strategies such as the use of fillers, hesitation devices and self-repetitions" (p. 183). Table 7.1 contains an overview of how the four main views of CS treat these problems. The second criterion that has resulted in the diversity of approaches to CS is consciousness. We have to note that there is a great controversy both in psychology as well as in SLA research concerning what is meant by consciousness, which we do not discuss here (for a recent review, see Robinson, 2003). Dörnyei and Scott claimed that three aspects of consciousness are relevant concerning CS: (a) consciousness as awareness of the problem, (b) consciousness as intentionality, and (c) consciousness as awareness of strategic language use. They pointed out that in order to distinguish CS from errors and mistakes, it needs to be presumed that when using a CS, speakers are aware that they are having a problem in encoding their message. Consciousness as intentionality is also a necessary criterion because it distinguishes time-gaining strategies from unconsciously applied pauses and hesitations. Dörnyei and Scott also argued that speakers need to be aware of the fact that they are using a strategy, in other words, a less than perfect solution, in order to distinguish situations of CS use and those in which the speakers think they have managed to come up with an acceptable structure or expression in L2.

By incorporating the special features of L2 speech production into Levelt's (1989) model, a comprehensive framework of problem-solving mechanisms

TABLE 7.1
Overview of the Main Views of CS

	Resource Deficit	Own-Performance Problem	Other-Performance Problem	Lack of Processing Time
Traditional view	Included	Not included	Not included	Not included
Interactional view	Included	Included	Included	Not included
Extended view	Included	Included	Included	Included
Psycholinguistic view	Included	Not included	Not included	Not included

in L2 use can be outlined, and it can be discussed how the management of the primary problem areas in the focus of this chapter (resource deficits and processing time pressure) are related to the various phases of speech processing. The first problem area, *resource deficit* (which is a product of L2 speakers' deficient L2 competence), is associated with three problem-solving processes in the planning and encoding of the preverbal message: (a) *Lexical problem-solving mechanisms* handle the frequent inability to retrieve the appropriate L2 lemma that corresponds to the concepts specified in the preverbal plan; (b) *grammatical problem-solving mechanisms* deal with the insufficient knowledge of the grammatical form and the argument structure of the lemma, as well as the phrase and clause structure rules of the L2 (Kempen & Hoenkamp, 1987; Levelt, 1989); and (c) *phonological/articulatory problem-solving mechanisms* help overcome difficulties in the phonological encoding and articulatory phases caused by the lack of knowledge of the phonological form of a word as well as lexical and postlexical phonological rules.

The second main problem area, processing time pressure, is related to the fact that L2 speech processing is (at least partially) serial and, therefore, requires more attentional resources and processing time than speech production in L1 (for a review, see chap. 8). In order to gain time and devote additional attention to processing, L2 speakers can employ various *stalling mechanisms* both when planning the message and when encoding the preverbal plan.

LEXICAL PROBLEM-SOLVING MECHANISMS

Communication strategies have been analyzed most thoroughly with respect to lexical referential communication, where the main obstacle to the encoding process is insufficient L2 lexical knowledge (e.g., Kellerman, 1991; Poulisse, 1993; Yule, 1997). According to Levelt (1989), speech formulation processes are lexically driven; that is, "grammatical and phonological encoding are mediated by lexical entries" (p. 181). This would imply that a great proportion of the problems speakers encounter during speech production are lexis related, which has indeed been found to be the case in past research on communication strategies (see Kellerman, 1991).

Poulisse (1993) assumed that lexical communication strategies were carried out within Levelt's (1989) framework as follows: Having planned the message in the conceptualizer, the speaker issues the preverbal plan. The formulator, however, is unable to retrieve the lemma corresponding to the specific chunk of the preverbal plan, thus the speech production process comes to a halt and an alarm signal is sent to the monitor, which in turn feeds this information back to the conceptualizer. After some modifications are made in the speech plan, the conceptualizer issues a new preverbal plan, which the formulator either manages to process or, upon experiencing another problem, sets the aforementioned mechanism in motion again.

Poulisse (1993) argued that the speaker could resort to one of two main options in case of difficulties in lexical retrieval: They can (a) can abandon or change the original speech plan, or (b) keep the macroplan unchanged and modify the preverbal message only. These two options are analogous to the dichotomy of *reduction* and *achievement behaviors* postulated by Færch and Kasper (1983), and both processes can be further broken down to different types of solutions (for a list of the various mechanisms with definitions, examples, and/or retrospective comments, see Table 7.2).

The first main option the speaker has (i.e., when the intended message or macroplan is reformulated) can be executed in three different ways: (a) The intended message can be given up as a whole, resulting in the avoidance strategy called *message abandonment;* (b) parts of the intended communicative content can be deleted (*message reduction*); or (c) parts of the intended communication content can be replaced with other components (*message replacement*) (cf. also Færch & Kasper, 1983; Tarone, 1977; Váradi, 1980). These processes can be seen as "problem solving" in only a limited sense: Their application does not actually solve the original problem but rather helps the speaker get over the problem situation and thus avoid a complete communication breakdown.

The second option available to the speaker when experiencing difficulties in encoding the message due to lexical deficits is to keep the macroplan of the intended message unaltered and reformulate only the preverbal plan by means of lexical problem-solving mechanisms to compensate for the L2 deficiency. Poulisse (1993) asserted that three main psycholinguistic processes could underlie lexical compensatory strategies (her term for lexical problem-solving mechanisms). First, in the search of a new lemma, one or more conceptual specifications set in the preverbal message might be changed or omitted, and thus the original lexical item can be substituted by an alternative one; this Poulisse called a *substitution strategy*. Second, in addition to the modification of the conceptual specifications of the lemma, the speaker may also apply L1 or L2 morphological and/or phonological encoding processes, resulting in a *substitution plus strategy*. The third process is termed *reconceptualization strategy* because it involves the alteration of more than one chunk of the preverbal message.

Although the three types of compensatory strategies postulated by Poulisse (1993) are associated with three distinct psycholinguistic processes, Kellerman and Bialystok (1997) pointed out that it was not always easy to

TABLE 7.2
Lexical Problem-Solving Mechanisms (PSM)

Class and Type of PSM	Description	Examples and Retrospective Comments
Content reduction		
Message abandonment	Leaving a message unfinished because of some language difficulty.	that is a flat … in a house … [Retrospective comment:] Speaker: First I wanted to explain "housing estate" … and in the end I couldn't explain it. Interviewer: Why? S: The words were missing.
Message reduction	Reducing the message by avoiding certain language structures or topics problematic languagewise or by leaving out some intended elements for a lack of linguistic resources.	he is responsible … for the … cleanness of the house and er … he locks the door … at night and opens it … in the morning [Retrospective comment:] I couldn't say what I wanted in English, that he was responsible for the running of the house so that things would go smoothly and so on.
Message replacement	Substituting the original message with a new one because of not feeling capable of executing it.	you can … stay here until … midnight or … how do you want. [Retrospective comment:] Here I wanted to say that until "dawn" or "morning" and I found the word but I did not like it, and I had to say something so I said this.
Substitution		
Code-Switching	Including L1 or L3 words with L1 or L3 pronunciation in L2 speech; this may involve stretches of discourse ranging from single words to whole chunks and even complete turns.	[Retrospective comment after saying "ferrum":] I immediately remembered chemistry classes. I knew we used the sign "Fe" which is "ferrum" in Latin and that an English speaker uses a word like that too. He might understand something of it. But I couldn't remember "iron" at all.
Approximation	Using a single alternative lexical item, such as a superordinate or a related term, that shares semantic features with the target word or structure.	and er … takes the apple in its mouth. [Retrospective comment:] Here I couldn't remember "beak."
Use of all-purpose words	Extending a general "empty" lexical item to contexts where specific words are lacking.	The overuse of thing, stuff, make, do, as well as words like thingie, what-do-you-call-it; e.g., I can't can't work until you repair my … thing.

Complete omission	Leaving a gap when not knowing a word and carrying on as if it had been said.	then ... er ... the sun is is ... hm sun is ... and the Mickey Mouse ... [Retrospective comment:] I didn't know what "shine" was.
Substitution plus		
Foreignizing	Using an L1 or L3 word by adjusting it to L2 phonology (i.e., with an L2 pronunciation) or morphology.	my guest from the ... ministerium [ministry] [with an English pronunciation].
Grammatical word coinage	Creating a nonexisting L2 word by applying a supposed L2 rule to an existing L2 word.	[Retrospective comment after using dejunktion and unjunktion for "street clearing": I think I approached it in a very scientific way: From "junk" I formed a noun and I tried to add the negative prefix "de-"; to "unjunk" is to "clear the junk" and "unjunktion" is "street clearing."
Literal translation	Translating literally a lexical item, an idiom, a compound word, or a structure from L1 to L3 to L2.	[Retrospective comment after saying "snowman": I don't really know the English expression, so this is actually the literal translation of the Hungarian word, and the hesitation must be due to the fact that I am not sure that this is how to say it but there isn't anything better.
Macroreconceptualization		
Restructuring	Abandoning the execution of a verbal plan because of language difficulties, leaving the utterance unfinished, and communicating the intended message according to an alternative plan.	She has to care about the house, to care about the garbage, and to care about the ... or to clean the house. [Retrospective comment:] Here I wanted to say "cleanness" but I couldn't remember it.
Microreconceptualization		
Circumlocution	Exemplifying, illustrating, or describing the properties of the target object or action.	[Retrospective comment:] Well, here for instance, if I had known how to say "melt," then I would have said that. But I didn't know this and that's why I said "it becomes water."
Semantic word coinage	Creating a nonexisting L2 word by compounding words.	snowsculpture for "snowman"

Note. From Dörnyei and Kormos (1998). Copyright 1998 by Cambridge University Press.

143

classify the overt manifestations of these strategies according to Poulisse's categories. Therefore, in order to establish more straightforward correspondences between verbalized problem-solving devices and the underlying psycholinguistic processes, Dörnyei and Kormos (1998) suggested that Poulisse's tripartite model and some definitions of the components should slightly be modified.

Poulisse (1993) cited code-switching and approximation as the two primary examples of substitution strategies. With regard to code-switching, she argued that the intentional use of an L1 lexical item in L2 speech involved merely resetting the parameter of the language tag attached to the lexical concept specified in the preverbal message. Thus, instead of the specification [+ L2], the speaker will choose the parameter [+ L1] (see also the section titled The Influence of L1 on Lexical Encoding in chap. 4). This process is similar to the one underlying approximation, where one or more features of the concept are either deleted (e.g., if the speaker cannot retrieve the word corresponding to the concept CARNATION, he or she will choose to remove certain specifications and reduce the notion to FLOWER) or substituted (as in cohyponyms); in some rare cases, even extra features might be added to the lexical chunk (resulting in a subordinate term, such as "pines" instead of "conifers"). Some researchers in the past have indeed kept various types of approximation separate (e.g., Yarmohamhadi & Seif, 1992), but from a psycholinguistic point of view Poulisse's substitution category subsumes these variations.

Besides approximation and code-switching, substitution processes underlie a third problem-solving device as well, the use of *all-purpose-words*. In these, so many features of the concept are removed that only a general specification such as [OBJECT] (e.g., "thing," "thingie") or [CAUSE TO HAPPEN] (e.g., "make," "do") remains, and the interlocutor uses contextual clues to reconstruct the intended meaning.

Among substitution plus strategies, which involve modifying one or more features of the lexical concept plus employing L1 or L2 morphological/phonological encoding procedures, Poulisse (1993) listed *foreignizing* and *grammatical word coinage*. An interesting question is whether *literal translation* can be subsumed under this category. Literal translation is a process in which the speaker first substitutes the [+ L2] language tag of the concept to be encoded by [+ L1], and when the L1 lexical entry (which is usually a compound word, or an idiomatic collocation) has become available, considers its components separately and retrieves the corresponding L2 lemmas one by one, thereby creating a new (often incorrect) L2 lexical entry not previously stored in the mental lexicon. Thus, in applying literal translation, a substitution process is followed not so much by morphological or phonological encoding but rather by lexical encoding. Although literal translation, foreignizing, and word coinage are obviously not produced by exactly the same psycholinguistic processes, because all three involve an initial substitution process and subsequent construction process leading to the creation of a new lexical entry, at this stage literal translation can be categorized under substitution plus strategies by extending the "plus" component to also include lexical encoding.

In Poulisse's (1993) framework, reconceptualization strategies involve the modification of more than one single chunk of the preverbal message. Poulisse listed *circumlocution, semantic word coinage,* and *mime* as examples of reconceptualization. In the case of circumlocution, the speaker encodes the conceptual features of the intended lexical item separately, thus changing the whole of the preverbal chunk. In the case of semantic word coinage, two lexical items are selected and combined into one word (e.g., a "suit carrier" for "suitbag"). The third device, mime, posits a problematic case and is discussed in the Phonological Problem-Solving Mechanisms section.[1]

Kellerman and Bialystok (1997) argued that Poulisse's (1993a) tripartite model "does not seem to be able to draw a clear distinction between substitution and reconceptualization strategies" (p. 45), for example, in cases of definition-like structures (e.g., "Stuff to kill flies") and strategy tokens that exemplify superordinate categories by lists of category members (e.g., "tables, beds, chairs, and cupboards for FURNITURE"). It is indeed questionable how many lexical concepts are involved in the verbalization of these examples. One solution to the conceptual ambiguity may be to tie reconceptualizing strategies more closely to the original concept of "reconceptualization" rather than to the number of changes involved. The two problematic examples quoted by Kellerman and Bialystok are clearly distinct from substitution strategies in that they involve more than the mere retrieval of lexical items of less conceptual accuracy (which is what happens during substitution-based processes), as

---

[1]The analysis of mime as an independent mechanism is problematic. It is not a substitution-based mechanism: It involves more than just substituting a set of gestures for a word, in that it requires the analysis of the concept to be expressed in order for the speaker to be able to select the most appropriate gestures for encoding it. Yet, mime is not a reconceptualization strategy either because only one preverbal chunk is involved at a time and there does not seem to be any decomposition and recombination processes involved. In fact, the question of mime raises the more general issue of how body language or other nonverbal, gestural codes (e.g., sign language) can be made compatible with a system specifying the production of verbal messages. Without attempting a detailed analysis, these diverse types of production processes can be considered similar to speech production up to the point of conceptualizing the preverbal message but are then processed by different formulators depending on the type of the communication code involved. If this is the case, however, then mime cannot be comprehensively discussed within a speech production framework.

they entail the *analysis* and *decomposition* of the preverbal chunk in order to be able to express it through a *combination* of lexical items. This series of analysis, decomposition, and recombination can be summarized by the concept of reconceptualization, which then makes up the core feature of the corresponding strategy type.

If we accept that the process of reconceptualization (analysis-decomposition-recombination) is the primary defining criterion for reconceptualization strategies, we can logically distinguish *microreconceptualization*, which involves reconceptualizing one preverbal chunk (as is the case in circumlocution and semantic word coinage), and *macroreconceptualization*, which involves the modification of more than one single chunk in the preverbal message. The advantage of this would be that *restructuring*, a CS often mentioned in the literature (e.g., Færch & Kasper, 1983), could be placed in the framework as an example of macroreconceptualization because by resorting to it the speaker seeks an alternative manner of expressing the intended message. In "On Mickey's face we can see the ... so he's he's wondering," for example, the speaker cannot retrieve the lemma for "surprise" or "bewilderment" in the L2 and thus decides to completely reformulate the preverbal plan for the utterance in order to be able to express his or her message with the available resources.

In sum, lexical problem-solving mechanisms are considered to be attempts by the speaker to overcome problems in lemma retrieval. Following Poulisse (1993), they can be classified as substitution strategies, which involve changing one or more features of the concept; substitution plus strategies, which entail a combination of a substitution strategy and further phonological, morphological, or lexical encoding; microreconceptualization strategies, which involve the decomposition of the concept specified by the preverbal message into components, which will then be retrieved separately; and macroreconceptualization strategies, where more than one single concept in the preverbal message is modified.

GRAMMATICAL PROBLEM-SOLVING MECHANISMS

Grammatical encoding is a continuation of the lexical retrieval process, as this is the point when the grammatical form of the lemma (information about the diacritic parameters of the lemma such as person, number, tense, gender, etc.) and the argument structure (determining what place the lemma can occupy in the sentence and what obligatory and optional complements it can take) are accessed and encoded, and when the lemmas are ordered in a phrase. Problems in grammatical encoding can arise at three different points of the encoding process: (a) when the lemmas activated by the preverbal message are inspected for optional and obligatory complements, specifiers, and diacritic values, (b) when the complements, specifiers, and diacritic parameters are handled, and (c) when phrases and clauses are assembled. Insufficient knowledge of the grammatical form and the argument structure of the lemmas can prevent the message from being encoded in the way it was originally planned, and in such cases the speaker needs to resort to certain problem-solving mechanisms.

Problem-solving mechanisms triggered by deficiencies in grammatical knowledge can be of several types. Because, according to Levelt (1989), grammatical information is stored by the lemmas, one way of getting around grammatical problems is by simply not activating the lemma associated with the problem issue but calling into action some lexical problem-solving mechanism instead. There are, however, two grammatical problem-solving mechanisms specifically related to grammatically motivated communication difficulties (see Table 7.3). First, we can conceive of *grammatical substitution mechanisms,* which involve changing certain features of the lemma in terms of either its grammatical form or argument structure. Such processes can draw on two main sources, the syntactic information of the corresponding L1 or L3 lemma (transfer) and the syntactic information of a similar or synonymous L2 lemma (overgeneralization). These processes can be employed when the L2 speaker lacks the syntactic knowledge to process the complements, specifiers, diacritic values, or phrase and clause structure. In this case, the speaker can resort to the subroutines or rules that the corresponding L1 or L3 lemmas point to, or overgeneralize L2 rules. These cases are very similar to "subsidiary transfer" described by Færch and Kasper (1986) and can be in either subsidiary or focal attention.

The second mechanism frequently applied is *grammatical reduction,* whereby the speaker uses intentionally simplified grammar hoping that the interlocutor will be able to reconstruct the grammatical meaning from the context. Anecdotal evidence and our own experience suggests that a variety of this strategy is very common in languages such as Russian or German, where speakers often mumble or completely omit the inflections of adjectives, verbs, or nouns.

PHONOLOGICAL PROBLEM-SOLVING MECHANISMS

Once the L2 speaker has succeeded in retrieving the appropriate lemma and has completed the grammatical processing phase, the surface structure needs to be encoded phonologically and then articulated; as Tarone, Cohen, and Dumas (1976) pointed out, these processing phases might also posit potential problems to the L2 speakers, for example, when the retrieval of the lexeme (i.e., the morpho-phonological form) of a particular lexical entry is hampered

TABLE 7.3

Grammatical and Phonological Lexical Problem-Solving
Mechanisms (PSM)

Class and Type of PSM	Description	Examples and Retrospective Comments
Grammatical PSM		
Grammatical substitution	Changing certain grammatical specifications of the lemma through transfer or overgeneralization.	and this mouse put a bowl to the table.
Grammatical reduction	Using simplified grammar in the belief that the interlocutor will be able to reconstruct the grammatical meaning from the context.	When she er come back again [Retrospective comment:] I'm always in doubt what tense to use and then I decided that I'd stick to the present tense because that's the easiest.
Phonological and Articulatory PSM		
Phonological retrieval		
Tip-of-the-tongue phenomenon	In an attempt to retrieve and articulate a lexical item, saying a series of incomplete or wrong forms or structures before reaching the optimal form.	it's some kind of er ... co ... cop ... copper
Phonological and articulatory substitution		
Use of similar-sounding words	Compensating for a lexical item whose form the speaker is unsure of with a word (either existing or nonexisting) that sounds more or less like the target item.	[In the following example, the question intonation indicates that the speaker was aware that she said only the approximate form:] Speaker: ... snowman smelt? or ... Interlocutor: Melt.
Phonological and articulatory reduction		
Mumbling	Swallowing or muttering inaudibly a word (or part of a word) whose correct form the speaker is uncertain about.	And uh well Mickey Mouse looks surprise or sort of XXX [the "sort of" marker indicates that the unintelligible part is not just a mere recording failure but a strategy].

Note. From Dörnyei and Kormos (1998). Copyright 1998 by Cambridge University Press.

for some reason. L2 speakers might experience problems in all the three major phases of phonological encoding (see Levelt, 1989, 1993; Roelofs, 1997b): (a) They might encounter difficulties upon generating the metrical frames, which consist of phonological words; (b) adding the segmental information, the specifications of the phonemes, and inserting them into the frames can also pose a problem, if the L2 speaker has not acquired the lexeme of the given word appropriately; and (c) problems can arise when the speaker maps "the syllabified and metrically specified phonological strings onto phonetic or articulatory programs" (Levelt, 1993, p. 5).

Similarly to grammatical problems, when phonological difficulties occur, speakers can resort to lexical problem-solving mechanisms to avoid using the word(s) they cannot verbalize. Additionally, although very little research has been done on this aspect of L2 problem management, one can also conceive of certain phonological problem-solving mechanisms (see Table 7.3). One mechanism often documented in the literature is *phonological retrieval,* whereby the speaker attempts to retrieve a lexeme for which only incomplete phonological information (e.g., some phonemes, usually the initial ones) is available; in this case, the speaker experiences a "tip of the tongue" phenomenon, and articulates several versions of the item so that by running the alternatives through the audition and speech comprehension modules he or she can test them and select the best version.

As an analogy to lexical and grammatical substitution, we may conceptualize *phonological substitution,* which allows the speaker to encode and articulate the problematic lexical item by substituting certain phonological features (via inter/intralingual transfer). It is an interesting question whether the use of *similar-sounding words* is a subtype of this mechanism: This device is applied when the speaker finds a lemma that matches the preverbal chunk but cannot retrieve the accompanying lexeme fully, and therefore utters a string of sounds that bears some resemblance to the original item, which is hoped to help the listener make the association with the target word. In this case, therefore, the word is substituted by an underspecified phonological representation. Levelt (1995) argued that a lexeme's phonological information was of two kinds—the word's meter (or accent pattern) and the word's segments of morphemes—and as has found that "phonological segments are not fixated in their position, but have to be inserted in the right metrical slot as we speak" (p. 19). Similar-sounding words, then, can be seen as metrically similar versions of the original lexeme in which one or more phonological segments have been replaced.

Finally, we can also identify two *phonological reduction* mechanisms. A more extreme version of the use of a similar-sounding word is a mechanism

Dörnyei and Scott (1997) labeled as *mumbling,* whereby a deliberately nonunderstandable word is uttered in the slot of the problematic lexical item within the utterance, and the listener is expected to guess the missing item from the context. Mumbling is also a metrically similar-sounding version of the originally intended lexeme, but it differs from similar-sounding words in that the problematic phonetic segments are not properly substituted but rather are swallowed.

TIME PRESSURE–RELATED PROBLEM-SOLVING MECHANISMS

Because speech production for L2 speakers is less automatic than speech processing in the L1, at certain phases of language production the encoding processes can only proceed serially. This results in delayed production and, as a consequence, retrieval may take "more time than the production system will allow" (de Bot, 1992, p. 14). In addition, L2 speakers are usually aware that in order to be able to remain in the conversation, they need to observe certain temporal organizational principles, particularly (in the case of English, for example) the need to avoid lengthy silences, which can terminate the conversation or deter the interlocutor; in Hatch's (1978) words, learners must do their best to use "whatever fillers they can to show the native speaker that they really are trying" (p. 434). Instances of needing more processing time than would be naturally available in conversation occur in two phases of speech processing: (a) during macro- and microplanning when the content and the form of the message are generated, and (b) while the preverbal plan is processed to generate the articulated message.

When speakers perceive that language production (i.e., conceptualization, formulation, and articulation) will take more time than what the production system or the communicative situation allows, they have three options: (a) They may resort to message reduction or message abandonment to avoid extreme hesitations caused by planning and processing; (b) they may employ other resource deficit–related strategies, because the application of an alternative encoding mechanism may prove to be faster than the encoding of the original preverbal plan; (c) in order to keep the communication channel open and provide more time and attentional resources, speakers can apply various *stalling mechanisms* (see Table 7.4). The three options are not mutually exclusive; the first two options also require some cognitive attendance, although less than the encoding of the original difficult preverbal plan, and can therefore also be accompanied by stalling mechanisms.

TABLE 7.4

Time Pressure–Related Problem-Solving Mechanisms

Class and Type of PSM	Description	Examples and Retrospective Comments
Nonlexicalized pauses		
Unfilled pauses	Remaining silent while thinking.	
Umming and erring	Using nonlexicalized filled pauses (er, uh, mhm).	[Retrospective comment:] Interviewer: Why were you "erring" here? Speaker: I didn't know what to say ... I was thinking about how to phrase it.
Sound length-ening (drawling)	Lengthening a sound in hesitation.	[Retrospective comment:] when I said "I'm" I lengthened the "m" to gain said "uh." And the same participant later: Interviewer: When you said "look," you stressed the "k" at the end. Speaker: Unfortunately, I didn't have an "m" here and I couldn't lengthen it, that was how I gained time. I: And what were you thinking about? S: What to put after it.
Lexicalized pauses		
Fillers	Using filling words or gambits to fill pauses, to stall, and to gain time in order to keep the commu-nication channel open and maintain discourse at times of difficulty.	Filling words or short phrases such as well; you know; actually; okay; how can I say that; this is rather difficult to ex-plain; E.g., Uhm, it's interesting be cause the hall ... is er ... forty person. [Retrospective comment:] Here I was still thinking over what I was going to say and I said "it's interesting." I have no idea why I said it, it did not mean anything in this context.
Repetitions		
Self-repetition	Repeating a word or a string of words immediately after they were said.	[Retrospective comment:] Interviewer: [Why did you say] if you ... if you ... ? Speaker: I probably wanted to gain some time because I couldn't continue immediately.
Other-repetition	Repeating some-thing interlocutor said to gain time.	Interviewer: Do you know whether you have rubber washer at home? Speaker: Rubber, rubber washer ... er [Retrospective comment:] I: Why did you repeat "rubber washer"? S: What can "rubber" mean ... I was thinking hard about it.

Note. From Döornyei and Kormos (1998). Copyright 1998 by Cambridge University Press.

Time-gaining mechanisms can surface in two major types of realization: *pauses* (cf. van Hest, 1996) and *repetitions*. Pauses may involve (a) *unfilled* or *nonlexicalized filled pauses* (e.g., silence or "umming and erring"), which require no additional processing but are inadequate in maintaining the appearance of fluency as they result in hesitant and disjointed speech; (b) *lengthening a sound* or *drawling* while thinking ahead, which is a more elaborate variation of nonlexicalized filled pauses, effective in holding the floor; and (c) *lexicalized pauses*, which involve the use of various filling words or more complex prefabricated chunks (cf. Pawley & Syder, 1983; Raupach, 1984; Towel et al., 1996). Based on Newell and Rosenbloom's (Newell, 1990; Newell & Rosenbloom, 1981; Rosenbloom & Newell, 1987) general chunking theory, prefabricated chunks are assumed to be stored as one unit in the lexicon and retrieved as a block. In order for them to serve as time-gaining devices, they need to be fully automatized so that their encoding does not require attention and thus their use frees the speaker's attentional resources (cf. Schmidt, 1992).

The second main type of stalling mechanisms, repetitions, can involve (a) *own repetition*, which have the same function as lexicalized pauses, because by retrieving a recently processed string of words as one unit from short-term memory, the speaker does not use any attentional resources; and (b) *other repetition*, whereby part of the interlocutor's utterance is repeated by retrieving it from the speech comprehension system as one unit, which again does not require much conscious encoding capacity.

Finally, I would like to note that stalling mechanisms are not L2-specific but are also used by L1 speakers for both problematic and unproblematic processing. Their role, however, may be more prominent in L2 use as the encoding processes of L2 speakers are less automatized and therefore require more time than L1 speech processing.

COMMUNICATION STRATEGIES AND LANGUAGE LEARNING

The role of communication strategies in language learning has been rather controversial. For a long time, communication strategies have been seen as devices used to compensate for lack of knowledge and as such being the signals of lack of competence (e.g., Bialystok & Kellerman, 1987). A number of researchers claimed that L2 learners can freely transfer the strategies they use in L1 to L2, and therefore there is no need to develop students' strategic competence by means of explicit teaching (e.g., Bongaerts & Poulisse, 1989; Kellerman, 1991). On the other hand, Dörnyei (1995) argued that communication strategies are teachable; moreover, they should be taught in L2 courses in order to help learners express their intended message. The experimental study he conducted in

Hungary demonstrated that the teaching of certain types of CSs was successful as students used these strategies more frequently after instruction, and the participants' fluency also increased. Dörnyei's study shows that CSs play an important role in language learning for a number of reasons. First of all, they contribute to increased fluency with which learners can express their message. In addition, they help L2 speakers stay in communication, which contributes to producing more output. The production of increased amount of output has been found to promote second language acquisition as it serves to test hypotheses about the L2, trigger creative solutions to problems, and expand the learners' existing resources (Swain, 1995; Swain & Lapkin, 1995).

How the use of CSs changes as a result of the development of L2 competence has also been researched. Poulisse and Schils (1989) investigated the differences in three groups of learners' use of communication in different types of tasks. They found that more-proficient learners applied fewer CSs than their less-competent peers, which is the result of the fact that advanced students have fewer gaps in their knowledge. Their results also indicated that competent L2 speakers tended to use more approximations, whereas intermediate students often resorted to L1-based strategies such as transfer. Poulisse and Schils explained these differences by pointing out that proficient L2 speakers have a large enough vocabulary in L2, which aids them in finding words that have similar meaning to the intended one

SUMMARY

In this chapter, I made an attempt to bring together the different mechanisms L2 speakers can employ when running into communication difficulty into an integrative model that enables us to establish links between different processes of L2 production that have so far been handled by different conceptual frameworks. I related the problem-solving devices used in the case of lack of linguistic knowledge and under time pressure to encode one's message to the various stages of speech production. As regards CSs used to cope with resource deficit, lexical, grammatical, and phonological problem-solving mechanisms were analyzed in detail. The psycholinguistic mechanisms involved in coping with time pressure were also discussed in the light of theories of automaticity. Finally, the role of CSs in promoting second language acquisition was considered.

ACKNOWLEDGMENTS

This chapter is a revised version of the following article: Dörnyei, Z., Kormos, J. (1998). Problem-solving mechanisms in L2 communication: A psycholinguistic perspective. *Studies in Second Language Acquisition, 20*, 349–385.

8   Fluency and Automaticity in L2 Speech Production

Besides accent, one of the most easily noticeable differences between L1 and L2 speakers is the speed with which they talk. Whereas L1 speech is generally produced without any considerable effort, producing utterances in L2 requires attention on the part of the speaker, which slows down the speed of delivery to a considerable extent. Several studies have shown that speech rate and the mean length of runs is considerably lower in L2 than in L1 (Deschamps, 1980; Raupach, 1984; Wiese, 1984). This difference might be caused by a number of factors such as the deficient knowledge of L2 lexis, syntax, morphology, and phonology, attentional resources needed for suppressing L1 production procedures, and greater demands on self-monitoring, which have all been discussed in previous chapters of this book. Here we focus on one of the most important reasons why L2 speech is slower than L1 speech, which is the degree of automaticity with which L1 and L2 speech is produced. In L1 production, only speech planning and monitoring require attention; the rest of the speech production mechanisms can run automatically and in parallel without the speakers' conscious supervision. In L2 speech, however, syntactic and phonological encoding might not be automatized at all in the case of beginners, or might only be partially automatic even in the case of advanced learners (de Bot, 1992; Rehbein, 1987; Sajavaara, 1987). Due to the lack of automaticity, processes of L2 production cannot run in parallel as in L1, which slows speech down to a considerable extent. In chapter 3, we saw how the development of automaticity can be related to monolingual models of speech processing. In this chapter, an attempt is made to explain L2 speech production fluency in the light of models of automatization. I first discuss the definitions of fluency in second language speech production. Next, I relate theories of automaticity and learning to the development of L2 fluency. Finally, studies conducted on the measurement and perceptions of fluency in L2 speech production are reviewed.

DEFINITIONS OF FLUENCY

The term fluency is usually used in two senses (Lennon, 1990, 2000). In the so-called broad sense, fluency seems to equal global oral proficiency; in other words, it means that a fluent speaker has generally high command of the foreign or second language. In its narrower sense, fluency is usually considered to be only one component of oral proficiency, which is often used as one of the scores in assessing candidates' oral language skills in an exam situation. Fillmore's (1979) conceptualization is one of the examples of what fluency means in the broad sense. He argued that the term fluency can have four different interpretations. First, he defined fluency as the ability to talk at length with few pauses and to be able to fill the time with talk. Second, a fluent speaker is capable not only of talking without hesitations but of expressing his or her message in a coherent, reasoned, and "semantically dense" manner. Third, a person is considered to be fluent if he or she knows what to say in a wide of range of contexts. Finally, Fillmore argued that fluent speakers are creative and imaginative in their language use and a maximally fluent speaker has all of the aforementioned abilities. Fillmore's definition of fluency is very extensive, but it is unclear how this conceptualization differs from the definition of global oral proficiency. The definition proposed by Sajavaara (1987) can also be regarded as a broad conceptualization of fluency. He defined fluency as "the communicative acceptability of the speech act, or 'communicative fit'" (p. 62). He also pointed out that expectations concerning what is appropriate in a communicative context vary according to the situation; therefore, his definition seems to be very difficult to operationalize. This conceptualization of fluency bears resemblance to the third aspect of fluency described by Fillmore.

As regards the narrow interpretation of fluency, Lennon (1990) claimed that fluency differs from the other scores in oral language exams (e.g., accuracy, appropriacy) in that it is purely a performance phenomenon, and consequently defined fluency as "an impression on the listener's part that the psycholinguistic processes of speech planning and speech production are functioning easily and efficiently" (p. 391). Thus, he argued, "Fluency reflects the speaker's ability to focus the listener's attention on his or her message by presenting a finished product, rather than inviting the listener to focus on the working of the production mechanisms" (pp. 391–392). Rehbein (1987) provided a similar definition, claiming that "fluency means that the activities of planning and uttering can be executed nearly simultaneously by the speaker of the language" (p. 104). He also added that fluency depends on the context, namely on the "speaker's evaluation of the hearer's expectations" (p. 104). Schmidt (1992) refined Lennon's definition by adding that fluency in speech production is an "automatic procedural skill" (based on Carlson, Sullivan, & Schneider, 1989) and that fluent speech "is automatic, not requiring much attention or effort" (p. 358). In a more recent study, Lennon (2000) synthesized earlier definitions and proposed that "a working definition of fluency might be the rapid, smooth, accurate, lucid, and efficient translation of thought or communicative intention into language under the temporal constraints of on-line processing" (p. 26).

THEORIES OF AUTOMATICITY AND THE DEVELOPMENT OF L2 FLUENCY

As mentioned previously, one of the most comprehensive definitions of fluency is that fluency means "the rapid, smooth, accurate, lucid, and efficient translation of thought or communicative intention into language under the temporal constraints of on-line processing" (Lennon, 2000, p. 26). If one considers the theories of automaticity described in chapter 3, it becomes apparent that two interrelated processes are responsible for the development of fluency in L2: automatization of encoding processes and the use of prefabricated language units called formulaic language. Automatization and learning might take place in three different ways: (a) Consciously learned rules of language might become automatic in the sense that their application does not require attention on the part of the speaker; (b) phrases and clauses first assembled with the help of syntactic and phonological rules might later be stored as one unit in memory and retrieved as a whole; and (c) learners might start out using memorized chunks of language without being aware of the syntactic and phonological rules applying to those chunks and might deduce the rules from these units of language at later stages of the learning process. In what follows, I discuss these three possible ways of learning, relate them to theories of automaticity, and review empirical studies in the field of SLA research that attempted to test these theories.

One of the most comprehensive accounts of how the application of rules becomes automatic was provided by Anderson's (1983) ACT* (adaptive control of thought) and his (1995) ACT–R theory (adaptive control of thought–revised). As described in chapter 3, in this model it is assumed that the development of automatic processes not only involves the faster application of rules and the withdrawal of attention from rule-based processing, but also qualitative changes such as the creation of macroproductions, that is, chunks from smaller units, generalization (widening the scope of the application of rules to all the appropriate contexts), and discrimination (using the rules only in the appropriate contexts). Anderson's ACT* and ACT–R model have exerted significant influence on cognitive theories of language learning, but as Raupach (1987) and Schmidt (1992) pointed out, little research has been carried out to adapt this theory for the development of fluency despite the fact that it has a lot to offer for the field of SLA. In an exploratory study, Towell et al. (1996) made an attempt to relate Anderson's theory to Levelt's (1989) model of speech production. They argued that the only logical place where proceduralization can take place is the formulator module of Levelt's model, the role of which is to give linguistic shape to messages and forward these encoded messages to the articulator. They hypothesized that proceduralization can be assumed to have taken place if in the course of learning, the mean length of fluent runs increases, the mean length of pauses does not change or decreases, and the phonation time ratio remains either unchanged or increases; in other words, if more time is spent speaking than pausing and if learners are able to produce longer stretches of words without pausing. The quantitative analysis of 12 learners' speech before and after a year spent in the target language environment showed that major improvement took place in the length of fluent runs. The detailed qualitative analysis of two participants' output revealed that this change is mainly caused by the fact that these learners succeeded in proceduralizing syntactic knowledge. Towell et al. argued that their participants converted "linguistic knowledge already acquired into rapidly-usable on-line 'productions'" (p. 113). Poulisse (1999), who investigated the slips of the tongue found in the speech of Dutch learners of English at three different levels of proficiency, also made an attempt to relate her findings to Anderson's ACT* theory. In accordance with the assumptions of ACT*-theory (but also any other theory of learning), she found that less-proficient learners made more slips, that is, displayed more variable performance, than advanced speakers. The comparison of the different types of slips at the different stages of language development showed that proceduralization took place mainly in the processes of lexical access, morphological encoding of verbs, and phonological encoding. Raupach acknowledged the potentials of ACT* theory, but he warned against adapting it for the investigation of L2 learning without reservation. He assumed that in SLA not every instance of procedural knowledge is encoded via conversion from declarative knowledge; that is, it is possible that learners acquire certain types of procedural knowledge directly or through the transfer of L1 procedural knowledge. Moreover, his investigation of the temporal variables in the speech of German learners of French before and after a study abroad program showed that some learners acquired certain L2 structures by imitation, in other words, as unanalyzed linguistic units.

McLaughlin's (1990) theory of L2 learning also drew on the ACT* model and Cheng's (1985) theory of restructuring. In McLaughlin's theory, it is assumed that first the automatization of speech production processes takes place, which is followed by restructuring. This order of psychological mechanisms can explain the U-shaped behavior in the course of L2 learning (e.g., Kellerman, 1983), namely, that after a period of correct use (automatization), L2 speakers implement qualitative changes in the application of a rule. Initially this might result in incorrect productions, and certain time is needed before the correct form reappears. In his article, McLaughlin did not discuss whether this U-shaped development also applies to the attainment of fluency, but theoretically it is possible that beginning learners rely on a limited repertoire of memorized units in order to keep communication going at an acceptable speed. When they start analyzing these units and applying the rules deduced from these chunks consciously, their speech might become slower. Finally, these rules might be used automatically and efficiently combined with memorized units, which results in increased fluency. Unfortunately, the scarcity of longitudinal studies of fluency development do not allow for testing this assumption empirically.

Anderson's (1983, 1995) theory of learning has great relevance and high applicability in L2 production research. L2 speech production has two important processes where rule-based knowledge plays an important role: syntactic and phonological encoding. Studies investigating the development of speech production processes have shown that it is indeed in these two steps of encoding where major changes contributing to fluency development take place. Towell et al. (1996) found that the increased length of fluent runs was caused by the proceduralization of syntactic knowledge, whereas Poulisse's (1999) research indicated that with the development of language proficiency, performance becomes more stable and less error-prone in the field of morphological and phonological encoding (she also found that lexical access was automatized, to which we return later). The few experimental studies that have investigated the acquisition of syntactic rules in laboratory settings to date (DeKeyser, 1997; Robinson & Ha, 1993) also suggest that it is primarily Anderson's theory of proceduralization that can explain the patterns of learning emerging from this type of research.

Logan's (1988) instance theory is radically different from Anderson's ACT* (1983) and ACT–R (1995) model and addresses the issue raised by Raupach (1987), namely that not all learning involves the conversion from declarative to procedural learning. As mentioned in chapter 3, Logan assumed that automatic processing equals memory retrieval; that is, the use of an algorithm is substituted by a single-step retrieval of the solution from memory. In one of the first studies that explored the relevance of instance theory in SLA, Robinson and Ha (1993) investigated whether learners use algorithm-based mechanisms or memory retrieval in making grammaticality judgments. The findings of their study suggested that these two processes are not either/or options, but there seems to be an interface between them and both might contribute to the development of automaticity. DeKeyser (2001), in his discussion of Robinson and Ha's (1993) and Robinson's (1997) research, pointed out that perhaps the recently revised memory-based learning theories such as Palmeri's (1997) exemplar-based random walk model that allows for memory retrieval in the case of similar (and not necessarily the same) stimuli can account for the findings of these studies better than traditional instance theory.

Despite the fact that the role of memory-based theories of learning is often questioned in SLA research (e.g., DeKeyser, 2001; N. Segalowitz, 2003), certain aspects of L1 and L2 fluency can be explained with reference to these models. Pawley and Syder (1983) argued that nativelike fluency is determined by the availability of prefabricated patterns and formulaic expressions, which are retrieved from the memory as a whole. In other words, these authors claimed that fluency involves not only the automatic application of rules but also the memory retrieval of the appropriate expressions. In chapter 3, we saw that the memorization of chunks of language plays an important role in L1 acquisition as many children (but not all of them) memorize formulaic expressions used to express manipulative functions and apply them as unanalyzed units. Wray (2002) in her review of research concerned with formulas in L2 learning concluded that this process is also typical of children learning the L2 in naturalistic settings (e.g., Bohn, 1986; Wong Fillmore, 1976). Several studies have shown that adult learners acquiring the language both in natural settings (e.g., Rehbein, 1987; Schmidt, 1983; Yorio, 1989) and in instructed classroom environment (e.g., Myles, Hooper, & Mitchell, 1998; R. Ellis, 1984) memorize certain formulaic expressions without analysis and use them to achieve particular communicative functions. Research evidence also suggests that at later stages of learning, L2 speakers, especially instructed ones, start analyzing these units, deduce rules from them, and apply these rules and formulaic expressions in a creative manner (Bolander, 1989; Myles et al., 1998; Myles, Mitchell, & Hooper, 1999). Studies on formulaic language indicate that there is empirical support for the assumptions of theories of chunking that cognitive skills such as speaking are learned by creating macroproductions from smaller units and that it is possible to abstract rules of the language from chunks memorized as a whole (N. Ellis, 2001, 2003). The question is whether the opposite process is possible, that is, whether with practice word sequences that are first produced based on rule-based processing can become stored as one unit in memory and be retrieved as a whole. Wray's

(2002) model of how vocabulary is acquired in L2 implies that this route of acquisition is also possible. She claimed that:

> Whereas the first language learner starts with large and complex strings, and never breaks them down any more than necessary, the post-childhood second language learner is starting with small units and trying to build them up. Phrases and clauses may be what learners encounter in their input material, but what they notice and deal with are words and how they can be glued together. The result is that the classroom learner homes in on individual words, and throws away all the really important information, namely, what they occurred with. (p. 206)

Strength theories of automatization (e.g., MacKay, 1982) also have relevance for the development of fluency and the automaticity of lexical encoding in L2 production. In order to efficiently retrieve words, strong links between concepts and words need to be established, and search mechanisms need to be replaced by direct one-step retrieval. In strength theories, it is assumed that practice strengthens the links between nodes in hierarchical networks such as language, in this case, between concepts and lexical items. As described in chapter 3, lexical retrieval can be considered automatized if the concept that is activated by visual or other types of input passes on the highest level of activation to the corresponding lexical node. In sum, the major process of automatization in lexical encoding involves the strengthening of links between concepts and L2 lexical items. Strength theory can also account for how formulaic sequences are learned. At the beginning of the acquisition process, links between words that form a particular phrase are weak; therefore, learners create variable phrases. In the course of learning, strong connections between words are established, and words constituting a formulaic sequence are retrieved as a unit. Oppenheim (2000) investigated recurrent sequences in the speech of six nonnative speakers of English when giving the same speech twice. She found that rather than using exact repetitions of phrases, students tended to use partially overlapping sequences that they often varied by adding new elements, by reordering, and by combining them into larger units. She argued that instance theory would predict that participants would use exactly the same recurrent sequences when delivering their talk for the second time, and because this was not the case, this theory does not seem to be a viable account of how L2 speech production processes are learned. She claimed that strength theory and theories of chunking can explain that participants applied the recurrent phrases in a variable manner. Strength theory would allow for variability through the different levels of connections that can exist between words, whereas theories of chunking can explain that students create larger units from smaller ones or that they break down longer phrases into shorter sequences (Table 8.1 contains an overview of the applicability of psychological models of learning to speech production processes).

T. Ullman (2001) investigated automatization from a neurolinguistic perspective by a meta-analysis of research on what brain areas are activated in lexical and syntactic processing in native and nonnative speakers, in early and late language learners, as well as in proficient and nonproficient L2 learners. The starting point of his analysis was his declarative/procedural model, which assumes that:

> The memorization, storage, and processing of the stored sound-meaning pairings of lexical memory are subserved by declarative memory, a brain system rooted in temporal lobe structures, and implicated in the learning and use of knowledge about facts and events. In contrast, the learning, representation, and processing of aspects of grammar depend largely upon procedural memory, a distinct brain system rooted in left frontal/basal-ganglia structures, and implicated in the learning and expression of motor and cognitive skills and habits. (p. 117)

He argued that L2 speakers who started to acquire the language after puberty, especially if they did not have enough practice using the language, tended to rely on declarative memory for processing grammar, which might mean that instead of

TABLE 8.1

An Overview of the Applicability of Psychological Theories of Skill Learning to Processes in Speech Production

	ACT Theory	Instance Theory/ Exemplar-Based Random Walk Model	Strength Theories	Chunking Theories
Syntactic and phonological encoding	Fast and efficient application of rules without attentional supervision	Competition of rule-based processing and memory retrieval	—	Deduction of rules from the analysis of chunks
Lexical retrieval	—	—	Strengthening of links between concepts and lexical items	—
Use of formulaic language	Macroproductions are created from smaller units of language	Formulas are retrieved in a single step from memory	Strengthening of links between words that form formulas	Formulas are first learned as unanalyzed units

using automatic computational mechanisms in procedural memory (e.g., encoding past tense by adding the suffix -ed to verbs), they memorize linguistic forms as one unit (e.g., walked), apply rules consciously in declarative memory, and exploit "the ability of the associative lexical memory to generalize patterns to new forms" (p. 118). From the review of neuroimaging and electrophysiological research as well as studies of aphasics, Ullman concluded that the predictions of his model are largely borne out. Ullman's model is similar to Anderson's (1983, 1995) ACT theory in that it claims that learning takes place via conversion from declarative to procedural knowledge, but it also allows for memory-based exemplar learning. It is, however, clearly different from connectionist theories, which do not posit different computational systems for lexical and grammatical learning and argue that this system has broad anatomic distribution (e.g., Bates & MacWhinney, 1989).

MEASURES OF L2 FLUENCY

Just as defining fluency is rather problematic, the establishment of the components of fluency is not without difficulty, either. Four different approaches to delineating the measures of fluency exist in the investigation of L2 learner's speech. The first trend of research is concerned with the temporal aspects of speech production (e.g., Lennon, 1990; Möhle, 1984), the second combines the investigation of these variables with the study of interactive features such as turn-taking mechanisms (e.g., Riggenbach, 1991), and the third approach explores the phonological aspects of fluency (e.g., Hieke, 1984; Wennerstrom, 2000). Finally, recent studies have included the analysis of formulaic speech in studying fluency in second language speech (e.g., Ejzenberg, 2000; Towell et al., 1996). The empirical studies in this field used three different approaches: Either they investigated the development of fluency longitudinally (Freed, 1995, 2000; Lennon, 1990; Towell et al., 1996), or compared fluent and nonfluent speakers (Ejzenberg, 2000; Riggenbach, 1991; Tonkyn, 2001), or correlated fluency scores with temporal variables (Fulcher, 1996; Rekart & Dunkel, 1992). We have to note that the number of participants investigated was very small in most of these research projects, and in many of them no statistical analyses and computer technology for identifying pauses reliably were used. Table 8.2 contains the most frequently used temporal variables in these studies and their definitions.

Nevertheless most of the studies conclude that the best predictors of fluency are *speech rate,* that is, the number of syllables articulated per minute, and the *mean length of runs,* that is, the average number of syllables produced in utter-

TABLE 8.2
An Overview of Measures of Fluency

Measure	Definition
Speech rate	The total number of syllables produced in a given speech sample divided by the amount of total time required to produce the sample (including pause time), expressed in seconds. This figure is then multiplied by sixty to give a figure expressed in syllables per minute. Riggenbach (1991) suggested that unfilled pauses under 3 seconds should not be included in the calculation of speech rate.
Articulation rate	The total number of syllables produced in a given speech sample divided by the amount of time taken to produce them in seconds, which is then multiplied by sixty. Unlike in the calculation of speech rate, pause time is excluded. Articulation rate is expressed as the mean number of syllables produced per minute over the total amount of time spent speaking when producing the speech sample.
Phonation-time ratio	The percentage of time spent speaking as a percentage proportion of the time taken to produce the speech sample (Towell, Hawkins, & Bazergui, 1996).
Mean length of runs	An average number of syllables produced in utterances between pauses of 0.25 seconds and above.
The number of silent pauses per minute	The total number of pauses over 0.2 sec divided by the total amount of time spent speaking expressed in seconds and is multiplied by 60.
The mean length of pauses	The total length of pauses above 0.2 seconds divided by the total number of pauses above 0.2 seconds.
The number of filled pauses per minute	The total number of filled pauses such as uhm, er, mm divided by the total amount of time expressed in seconds and multiplied by 60.
The number of disfluencies per minute	The total number of disfluencies such as repetitions, restarts and repairs are divided by the total amount of time expressed in seconds and multiplied by 60.
Pace	The number of stressed words per minute (Vanderplank, 1993).
Space	The proportion of stressed words to the total number of words (Vanderplank, 1993).

ances between pauses of 0.25 seconds and above (e.g., Ejzenberg, 2000; Freed, 1995, 2000; Lennon, 1990; Riggenbach, 1991; Towell et al., 1996). *Phonation-time ratio,* that is, the percentage of time spent speaking as a percentage proportion of the time taken to produce the speech sample, was also found to be a good predictor of fluency (Lennon, 1990; Towell et al., 1996; van Gelderen, 1994). Research findings are equivocal concerning the frequency of filled and unfilled pauses as well as disfluencies such as repetitions, restarts, and repairs. The studies with small numbers of participants found that the frequency of silent and filled pauses distinguished between fluent and nonfluent speakers (e.g., Freed, 1995, 2000; Lennon, 1990; Riggenbach, 1991). On the other hand, in research projects in which a higher number of students participated, the number of filled and unfilled pauses and ratings of fluency did not correlate (Rekart & Dunkel, 1992; van Gelderen, 1994). Most researchers agree that disfluencies tend to occur in clusters in the speech of nonfluent L2 learners (e.g., Freed, 1995, 2000; Riggenbach, 1991), whereas fluent students tend to pause at grammatical junctures (Lennon, 1990; Towell et al., 1996).

Based on the assumption that fluency is context-dependent (e.g., Lennon, 1990; Rehbein, 1987; Sajavaara, 1987), Riggenbach (1991) complemented the analysis of temporal variables underlying second language fluency with the investigation of interactive features. Her results revealed that topic initiations, back channels, substantive comments, latching, and overlapping as well as the amount of speech produced also contributed to fluency judgments, though to a limited extent.

In the field of phonological research, Hieke (1985) established additional measures of fluency on the basis of the assumption that fluent speech equals connected speech, in which certain phonological procedures, such as *consonant attraction* are at work. Consonant attraction "occurs where final consonants are drawn to the following syllable if that begins with a vowel" (p. 140). In an earlier study, Hieke (1984) found that consonant attraction can be a reliable indicator of the fluency of nonnative speech in informal English style. Wennerstrom (2000) in her research investigated in what ways intonation influences the perception of fluency by means of analyzing dialogues between speakers of English as a second language and native English speakers. Her study suggests that it is the ability to speak in phrases instead of speaking word-by-word that can lead to the perception of fluent speech, rather than longer utterances or shorter pauses. In another study, Vanderplank (1993) suggested that pacing (the number of stressed words per minute) and spacing (the proportion of stressed words to the total number of words) are better indicators of difficulty in listening materials than standard speech rate measures such as syllable per minute. Indirectly, this would mean that these variables are also useful in predicting fluency scores.

In a recent study, Kormos and Dénes (2004) explored which variables predict native and nonnative speaking teachers' perception of fluency and distinguish fluent from nonfluent L2 learners. In addition to traditional measures of the quality of students' output such as accuracy and lexical diversity, they investigated speech samples collected from 16 Hungarian L2 learners at two distinct levels of proficiency with the help of computer analysis of pauses. The two groups of students were compared and their temporal and linguistic measures were correlated with the fluency scores they were awarded by three experienced native and three nonnative speaker teacher judges. The teachers' written comments concerning the students' performance were also taken into consideration. For all the native and nonnative teachers, speech rate, the mean length of utterance, phonation time ratio, and the number of stressed words produced per minute were the best predictors of fluency scores. However, the raters differed as regards how much importance they attributed to accuracy, lexical diversity, and the mean length of pauses. The number of filled and unfilled pauses and other disfluency phenomena were not found to influence perceptions of fluency in this study.

SUMMARY

This chapter discussed how fluency can be defined and measured, how it can be related to theories of automatization and learning, and what the results of empirical studies reveal about the perceptions and development of fluency. In reviewing various definitions of fluency, I pointed out that the term "fluency" is generally used in two senses: meaning global oral proficiency and the ability to produce talk smoothly within the time constraints of real-life communication. In this chapter, we were concerned with this second sense of fluency and have adopted Lennon's (2000) definition, which characterized fluency as the "rapid, smooth, accurate, lucid, and efficient translation of thought or communicative intention under the temporal constraints of on-line processing" (p. 26). An attempt was also made to explain the development of fluency with reference to various theories of automatization and learning. I argued that in order to account for how L2 learners' speech becomes fluent, three processes need to be considered: the automatization of syntactic, morphological, and phonological encoding processes, the creation of formulaic sequences from smaller units of language, and the deduction of rules from memorized chunks acquired as an unanalyzed unit. Anderson's (1983, 1995) ACT* and ACT–R theory were found to be appropriate for explaining how linguistic rules become automatized, whereas strength theory and theories of chunking could provide a viable explanation for the acquisition of formulaic language. Theories of chunking could also account for how various rules of language are inferred from memorized units. The overview of research on the measurement of fluency showed that the temporal variables that can predict fluency scores the most accurately are speech rate and the mean length of fluent runs.

9   Conclusion: Toward an Integrated Model of L2 Speech Production

In this concluding chapter, I draw up a comprehensive model of L2 speech production, which is both in line with current theories of speech processing and accommodates the research findings that I described in the previous chapters. The model uses Levelt's (1999a) blueprint for the speaker as a starting point, but some of its theoretical underpinnings are modified in order to account for the results of recent studies that suggest the possibility of cascading of activation. In this bilingual speech production model, I not only incorporate L2 knowledge stores and processing systems but also make an attempt to explain how formulae are encoded and how speech production mechanisms are acquired. I first outline the general theoretical considerations that underlie the model, which are then followed by the presentation of the model. Finally, I also describe how transfer, code-switching, communication strategies, and the development of proficiency can be accommodated in this new bilingual speech production framework.

THE GENERAL CHARACTERISTICS OF THE BILINGUAL SPEECH PRODUCTION MODEL

The bilingual speech production model I propose is based on Levelt's (1989, 1999a) theory of speech production because, as I argued in the Summary section of chapter 2, this model is the empirically best supported theory of monolingual speech processing. Consequently, I assume that bilingual speech production is modular in the sense that it consists of separate encoding modules: the conceptualizer, the formulator, and the articulator, which work with their own characteristic input. It is postulated that similarly to L1 speech processing, L2 speech production can also work incrementally; that is, a fragment of a module's characteristic input can trigger encoding procedures in this module. For example, once the first syllable of a word is phonologically encoded, its articulation can start in the articulator. This also entails that for learners above a certain level of proficiency, parallel processing is theoretically possible. However, as long as an encoding process requires conscious attentional control, encoding can only work serially. Nonetheless, this bilingual speech production model is not a strictly serial model in the sense that the cascading of activation is allowed from the lexical to the phonological level. In other words, activated but not selected word nodes can pass on activation to lower level phonological nodes. On the other hand, the model does not permit the backward flow of activation between levels, and monitoring is done with the help of the speech comprehension system.

In Levelt's (1999a) model, there are three knowledge stores: the store for the knowledge of external and internal world, the mental lexicon, and the syllabary. Based on major theories of memory research (e.g., Tulving, 1972), I propose that the new model contains one large memory store, called long-term memory, which consists of several subcomponents: episodic memory, semantic memory including the mental lexicon, the syllabary, and a store for declarative knowledge of L2 rules (see Fig. 9.1). Semantic memory contains linguistic and nonlinguistic concepts as well as meaning-related memory traces associated with these concepts, whereas episodic memory is the store of temporally organized events or episodes experienced in one's life. In order to account for findings of speech production research, semantic memory is assumed to have a hierarchical structure and consists of three levels: conceptual, lemma, and lexeme level. The lemma level contains syntactic information and the lexeme level morpho-phonological information related to lexical items. The syllabary stores the automatized gestural scores used to produce syllables. Based on empirical findings discussed in the earlier chapters of this book, it is hypothesized that all the knowledge stores described so far are shared between L1 and L2; in other words, there is a common episodic and semantic memory for L1 and L2, a shared store for L1 and L2 lemmas and lexemes, and for L1 and L2 articulatory scores. In L2 production, however, we need to postulate the existence of a fourth and L2 specific knowledge store: a declarative memory of syntactic and phonological rules in L2. In L1 production, rules are assumed to be automatized and to be part of the encoding systems (Levelt, 1989). On the other hand, for bilingual speakers many of the phrase- and clause-building as well as lexical and postlexical phonological rules are not automatic and are stored in the form of declarative knowledge. T. Ullman (2001) cited several pieces of evidence from neuroimaging research (for details, see the Theories of Automaticity and the Development of L2 Fluency section in chap. 8) that declarative knowledge concerning grammar is stored in a brain region distinct from the area that is responsible for the processing of automatized rules of grammar. Therefore, it seems to be justified that for L2 speakers a fourth knowledge store for not yet automatized syntactic and phonological rules is included in the model (see Fig. 9.1).

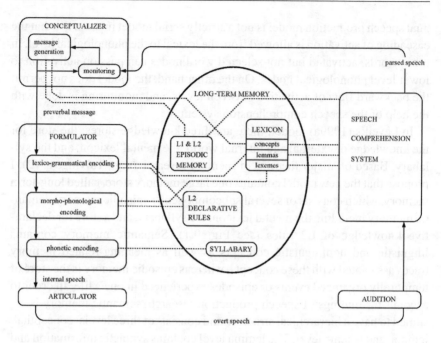

FIG. 9.1. The model of bilingual speech production.

Episodic and semantic memory are closely related, which is indicated by adjacent circles in the figure. This means that episodic memories can activate concepts and vice versa. The hierarchical nature of the semantic memory entails that in speech production activation flows from the conceptual to the lemma and finally to the lexeme level, whereas in speech comprehension activation flows in the opposite direction.

The model aims to follow the principle of ecology and simplicity, which is prevalent in human cognition. Therefore, except for the addition of a new knowledge store for the declarative knowledge of production rules and the incorporation of L2 concepts, lemmas, lexemes, and syllable programs (gestural scores), the bilingual production model proposed here is not significantly different from a model constructed for monolingual speakers. Abutelebi et al.'s (2001, 2005) reviews of neuroimaging studies of L2 production seem to provide support for the essentially similar nature of L1 and L2 speech processing. Abutelabi et al.'s meta-analyses of existing research in this field suggest that neither the extent of brain activation nor the regions involved in processing in L1 and L2 are different for bilinguals who learned the L2 early in their lives and for highly proficient speakers with extensive L2 exposure. However, late bilinguals, especially those who are not proficient in the L2 and have had low exposure to the target language, were found to activate larger and slightly different cerebral areas when speaking in L2 than in L1. The model accounts for this finding because proficient bilinguals do not rely on the separate knowledge store of declarative rules, whereas for learners at lower stages of proficiency grammatical and phonological rules are stored in a separate region of the brain.

ENCODING MECHANISMS AND THE STRUCTURE OF KNOWLEDGE STORES IN L2 SPEECH PRODUCTION

The processing of L2 speech starts with conceptualizing the message, which involves the activation of the relevant concepts to be encoded and deciding on the language in which the message will be spoken. As already mentioned in the preceding section, L1 and L2 concepts are assumed to be stored together in the semantic memory (see also Francis, 2005). In this model, a concept is seen to be a conglomerate of interrelated memory traces consisting of information concerning word meaning (see de Groot, 2000; Hintzman, 1986). When a concept is called on, not all the memory traces are activated; only the contextually relevant pieces of information become active (Hintzman, 1986). The assumption that concepts consist of a network of memory traces allows that L1 and L2 concepts can be identical, shared, or rarely completely separate. The extent to which L1 and L2 concepts are shared depends on the concept (e.g., concepts expressed by concrete nouns tend to be shared, whereas those expressed by abstract nouns show partial overlap), the situation in which the L2 was acquired (e.g., if the two languages were learned and are used in different environments, concepts might be separate), and the speaker's level of proficiency (e.g., at the beginning level L2 concepts are completely mapped on L1 concepts, whereas at advanced levels the L2 conceptual representation is greatly enriched) (see de Groot's, 1992, conceptual feature model in the Models of the Organization of the Bilingual Lexicon section in chap. 4).

The language of the message also needs to be set in the conceptualization phase. Language choice is largely dependent on sociolinguistic factors such as the nature of the communicative situation, relationship of the interlocutors, prestige of the languages involved, and so on. In this model, we opt for the most simple and economical solution, namely that language choice is indicated in the form of a language cue, which is added to the activated conceptual information. We have to emphasize that the language cue is added to each concept separately, and therefore it is possible that in the case of encoding a sentence, a preverbal plan consists of a string of activated concepts to which different language cues are added. For example, upon encoding the sentence,

"The policeman fined the motorist," a German-English bilingual speaker might add a language cue + English to the concepts of POLICEMAN and MOTORIST, whereas the concept of FINE might receive a tag + German.

In line with Levelt's (1989, 1999a) and Levelt et al.'s (1999) theory as well as with the spreading activation accounts of speech production (Dell, 1986; Dell & Juliano, 1996), this model also assumes that in semantic memory not only the concept that the speaker wants to encode is activated, but semantically related concepts also receive activation. For example, in the case of the concept of MOTHER, related concepts such as FATHER, CHILD, LOVE, and so on, also become active. This also entails that if separate concepts exist for the same notion in L1 and L2, which is a rare case, when the bilingual speaker uses one of his languages, the concept in the other language will also be activated. If conceptual representations are identical or partly overlap, the cohort of the conceptual features will be activated. The bilingual speech production model assumes that only the intended concept in the selected language is chosen for further processing (e.g., Bloem et al., 2004; Levelt, 1989). The selected concept activates not only the matching lexical item but also semantically related lemmas including lemmas in the nonselected language.

Remaining still at the phase of conceptualization, we also need to consider the problem that not every instance of language is creatively constructed. In fact, the majority of our utterances are combinations of memorized phrases, clauses, and sentences, which together are called formulaic language (Pawley & Syder, 1983). In order to account for the use of formulas, we need to assume that chunking, that is, the creation of larger production units, is done at the level of the conceptualizer. In other words, it is postulated that for expressing various communicative functions such as requesting, apologizing, expressing surprise, and so forth, native speakers have conceptual chunks consisting of a group of concepts, which they activate as one unit when routinely expressing certain communicative intentions. These conceptual chunks spread activation to the corresponding linguistic chunks, which are also stored and retrieved as one unit (i.e., one lemma).

In this bilingual speech production model, lexical encoding means the matching of the conceptual specifications and the language cue with the appropriate lexical entry in the mental lexicon. Based on empirical evidence summarized in the Lexical Activation and Selection in L2 section in chapter 4, the conceptual specifications send activation to both L1 and L2 lemmas (Costa et al., 2000; Hermans et al., 1998), and they both compete for selection (Costa, Colomé, et al., 2003; Hermans et al., 1998; Lee & Williams, 2001). The winner of the competition is the lemma whose features match all the conceptual specifications including the language cue (La Heij, 2005; Poulisse, 1999; Poulisse & Bongaerts, 1994). Neither inhibitory nor additional checking mechanisms are believed to be necessary to control bilingual lexical encoding.

The mental lexicon contains L1 and L2 lemmas and lexemes; in other words, it is a depository of a speaker's knowledge of word forms (lexemes) and their syntactic and morphological features (lemmas). The bilingual lexicon is assumed to consist of single L1 and L2 words as well as longer word sequences in L1 and L2 that correspond to conceptual chunks. These longer sequences can be idioms, conventionalized expressions, and phrases, which form a single entry and have their own syntactic information. Like the conceptual system, the lexicon is conceived of as a network in which entries have connections with each other. Connections might exist between L1 and L2 lemmas and lexemes, and between items within languages. Well-known and frequently used L2 entries occupy a central position in the network and have a high number of links with other items, whereas words not known very well by L2 speakers can be found at the periphery of the network (Wilks & Meara, 2002; Wolter, 2001). The strength of connections might also vary; at the beginning of the learning process links between L1 and L2 items might be stronger than links among L2 lexical entries (Kroll & Stewart, 1990, 1994). Moreover, connections might also be asymmetrical, which means that in certain cases it is possible that there is only a one-way link pointing for example from an L2 entry to an L1 item (passive vocabulary that one is able to recognize) (Meara, 1997).

Syntactic encoding in L1 production entails two important procedures: the activation of syntactic information related to a lexical item such as gender, countability status, and optional and obligatory complements, and the use of syntactic encoding mechanisms to assemble phrases and clauses using the activated words and their syntactic features. In the first phase, the L1 speaker relies on declarative knowledge, whereas the second stage involves applying procedural knowledge. We have rather limited knowledge of syntactic encoding in L2; therefore, some of the claims made in the bilingual speech production model are going to be speculative. In this model, I assume that as regards the general process of syntactic encoding there is no fundamental difference between L1 and L2 production, and that syntactic processing follows the steps of Kempen and Hoenkamp's (1987) Incremental Procedural Grammar (see the Syntactic Processing section in chap. 2 and the General Overview section in chap. 5). This means that syntactic encoding is lexically driven and consists of distinct stages that follow each other.

The first major stage of the process is the activation of the syntactic properties of the lemma that corresponds to the first conceptual chunk of the message. It is hypothesized that for balanced bilinguals L2 lemmas point to syntactic information that is specific for the given L2 entry, whereas for lower level learners L2 lemmas might point to the syntactic information of the corresponding L1 item. This is supported by the frequent occurrence of transfer errors, when syntactic information concerning particular words is transferred from L1 (e.g., Hungarian speakers of English frequently say "enter into a room" because they transfer the VP + PP structure that the Hungarian equivalent of "enter" points to). This processing stage draws on declarative knowledge stored in the mental lexicon. The next major phase involves phrase and clause structure building and arranging phrases in the appropriate order. At this stage, L1 speakers and balanced bilinguals use procedural knowledge of syntactic and morphological rules of the language, which are automatically applied. L2 learners at a lower level of proficiency might proceed in several ways. First of all, some of the rules might be acquired already in the form of procedural knowledge, whereas other rules might be stored in declarative memory and used consciously. It is also possible that some rules are not acquired at all. In this case, some kind of communication strategy is used, which might be the conscious transfer of the rule from L1 or simply juxtaposing the lexically encoded concepts after each other to express the intended message (for a discussion of communication strategies and the use of transfer see the next section).

The next phase of processing is phonological encoding, which involves the activation of the phonological form of the word to be encoded, syllabification, and setting the parameters for the loudness, pitch, and duration of intonational phrases consisting of several words. At this stage again, I propose that basic mechanisms of phonological encoding are not different in L1 and L2 production. As far as the activation of phonological word forms in L2 processing is concerned, it is assumed that the phonological form of nonselected lemmas can also be activated, which means that both L1 and L2 lexemes compete for selection in bilingual phonological encoding (Colomé, 2001; Costa et al., 2000; Hermans, 2000; Kroll et al., 2000). This implies that activation can cascade from the lemma in the language not in use to its phonological form and that cascading of activation is possible between lemma and lexeme level in this model. As a next step, phonological word forms activate the phonemes of the word in serial fashion, starting from the first phoneme and ending with the last one (Roelofs, 1997b, 1999, 2003b). Phonemes are assumed to be stored and retrieved as one unit such as [b] and not as a list of features such as [+ voiced] [+ labial] [− nasal] (Roelofs, 1999, 2003b). L1 and L2 phonemes are stored in a single network (Poulisse, 1999) within the lexicon at the lexeme level, and memory representations for phonemes that are identical in L1 and L2 are shared (Roelofs, 2003b). Once acquired, phonemes that are different in L1 and L2 are stored as separate representations. At the beginning of the acquisition process, however, L2-specific phonemes are frequently equated with an L1 phoneme that is similar to the target phoneme (Flege, 1987). In the case of balanced bilinguals, syllabification and metrical encoding proceeds in the same way. Similarly to the processes of syntactic encoding, L2 learners at lower levels might need to resort to the declarative knowledge of lexical and postlexical phonological rules or in the lack of it, transfer these rules from their L1.

In phonetic encoding, articulatory gestures for syllables are retrieved. In this model, it is assumed that syllable programs for L1 and L2 are stored together in the syllabary. In accordance with de Bot's (1992) view, it is hypothesized that beginning L2 speakers mostly rely on L1 syllable programs, whereas advanced L2 speakers usually succeed in creating separate chunks for L2 syllables.

The final process of speech production to be discussed is monitoring, which proceeds in a similar way in both L1 and L2 production. Similarly to Levelt's (1989) model, three monitor loops are assumed to be responsible for inspecting the outcome of the production processes. The first loop involves the comparison of the preverbal plan with the original intentions of the speaker. The second loop concerns the monitoring of the phonetic plan (i.e., "internal speech") before articulation, which is also called "covert monitoring" (see also Postma & Kolk, 1992, 1993; Postma, Kolk, & Povel, 1990; Wheeldon & Levelt, 1995). Finally, the generated utterance is also checked after articulation, which constitutes the final, external loop of monitoring, involving the acoustic-phonetic processor. Upon perceiving an error or inappropriacy in the output in any of these three loops of control, the monitor issues an alarm signal, which, in turn, triggers the production mechanism for a second time starting from the phase of conceptualization (Kormos, 2002). Monitoring is assumed to involve the same mechanisms as speech comprehension.

The most important difference between monitoring in L1 and L2 is caused by the fact that monitoring requires attention. Attentional resources are limited, and because L2 speech processing frequently needs attention at the level of lexical, syntactic, and phonological processing (unlike in L1), L2 speakers have little attention available for monitoring. Therefore, they often have to make conscious decisions what they pay attention to when monitoring, and these decisions most frequently involve prioritizing content over form, lexis over grammar, or vice versa (Kormos, 1999).

TRANSFER, CODE-SWITCHING, AND COMMUNICATION
STRATEGIES IN THE BILINGUAL SPEECH PRODUCTION MODEL

There are three important differences between L1 and L2 speech production, the first of which is the influence of L1 on L2 processing, which can manifest itself in the transfer of L1 knowledge and encoding procedures as well as in code-switching. The second difference is the frequently incomplete knowledge of the L2 for the compensation of which speakers resort to communication strategies, and the third is the speed with which utterances are constructed (de Bot, 1992). This third difference is caused by the competition between L1 and L2 items, the frequently incomplete knowledge of the L2, and the conscious controlled nature of processing in the case of learners for whom syntactic and phonological encoding procedures are not or only partially automatized. In this section, we test whether the previously outlined model is viable by making an attempt to account for transfer, code-switching, and the use of communication strategies in L2 speech.

There are two possible causes of L1 influence in the case of both transfer and code-switching. One possibility is that the L2 item (declarative knowledge) or procedural rule has been acquired, but instead of the target word or structure the L1 item or procedure is used erroneously, which can be regarded as a lapse in performance. This happens because the knowledge stores are shared, which means that L1 and L2 concepts, lemmas, lexemes, syllable programs, and proceduralized rules are stored together, and therefore they compete for selection. In the case of L2 learners who are not balanced bilinguals, L1 items and rules are more frequently used; therefore, they have a higher resting level of activation than L2 items and procedures. This can result in an erroneous selection of the L1 item or encoding process, which explains unconscious code-switching at the lexical level (L1 lexeme is accidentally selected instead of the L2 one; see La Heij, 2005; Poulisse, 1999; Poulisse & Bongaerts, 1994), certain cases of the transfer of automatized rules of grammar and phonology, and phonological slips of the tongue. The other possible cause of transfer and code-switching is the lack of L2 competence, which forces L2 speakers to rely on the knowledge of their mother tongue. Speakers might be aware of their limited resources, in which case they use a communication strategy (Dörnyei & Scott, 1997), or might believe that the L2 works in the same way as the L1. L2 learners might assume that certain features of L2 items might be associated with the features of their translation equivalents. In conceptual memory, meanings of L2 words might be associated with that of the corresponding L1 concept, which accounts for semantic transfer. In the mental lexicon, L2 lemmas might point to the syntactic information belonging to that of the L1 translation equivalent, which might explain a number of cases of syntactic transfer. Syntactic transfer and some cases of phonological rule transfer can also be the result of the application of the procedural knowledge of L1 rules for encoding an L2 phrase or sentence. Because the model is based on Kempen and Hoenkamp's (1987) Incremental Procedural Grammar, it is assumed that in the case of lack of L2 competence not every syntactic rule of L1 is transferable at any level of proficiency. In line with Pienemann's (1998) processability theory, transfer is constrained by the acquisition hierarchy. In other words, L2 learners need to acquire lower order grammatical encoding procedures before being able to transfer L1 syntactic structures at the superordinate levels of the hierarchy.

Intentional lexical code-switching can also be accommodated in the bilingual speech production model. It is assumed that intentional lexical switches are produced when speakers intentionally replace the L2 specification for a particular concept in the preverbal plan with an L1 specification (La Heij, 2005; Poulisse, 1999; Poulisse & Bongaerts, 1994). This can happen for several reasons: the lack of knowledge of the appropriate L2 lexical item or because the L1 lexical item meets the conceptual (semantic and/or lexical) specifications better than the L2 word (see Myers-Scotton & Jake, 1995). What is more difficult to explain is how the syntactic structure for code-switched utterances is established. In line with Myers-Scotton's (1993) matrix language frame model (see the Code-Switching and Syntactic Encoding section of chap. 5), I assume that one language is always the more dominant mode of communication, and the conceptual structure of the utterance is going to be assembled based on this language. The conceptual structure of the utterance is going to determine the order in which words are retrieved and how the sentence is constructed. Within the utterance, however, it is possible to reset the language cue for certain concepts for the other, less dominant language (embedded language). In this case, the lemma corresponding to the concept in the embedded language will be retrieved, but the syntactic procedures related to the matrix language and activated by the lemmas in the matrix language will be used to encode the sentence.

Communication strategies can also be explained with reference to the bilingual speech production model proposed here. L2 speakers might need to apply communication strategies in order to solve four different types of problems: (a) resource deficits, (b) processing time pressure, (c) perceived deficiencies in one's own language output, and (d) perceived deficiencies in decoding the interlocutor's message (this fourth problem source was not discussed in this book as this concerns speech comprehension rather than production) (Dörnyei & Scott, 1997). Resource deficit might mean lack of lexical, syntactic, and phonological knowledge of the L2. Lexical communication strategies can involve three different processes: (a) the modification of one or more features of the lexical concept for which the L2 speaker is unable to retrieve the appropriate L2 lemma, which is called a substitution strategy, (b) the use of a substitution strategy in combination with further phonological and grammatical processes, and (c) the modification of more than one lexical concept specified by the preverbal plan (Dörnyei & Kormos, 1998; Poulisse, 1993). Grammatical problem-solving mechanisms most frequently mean that L2 speakers consciously change certain syntactic features of the lemma in terms of its grammatical form and argument structure by relying on transfer from L1 or L3 or by overgeneralizing L2 rules (Dörnyei & Kormos, 1998). It is also hypothesized that phonological problem-solving mechanisms generally involve the encoding and articulation of the problematic lexical item by substituting one or more of the item's phonological features (Dörnyei & Kormos, 1998).

In addition to the lack of knowledge of L2 lexis, syntax, and phonology, L2 speakers often have to face the problem that due to limited attentional resources they cannot process their message within the time constraints of real-life communication. Based on Dörnyei and Kormos' (1998) study, it is proposed that in this case L2 learners might reduce or abandon their message, might employ resource deficit–related strategies, or might resort to stalling mechanisms such as filled, unfilled, and lexicalized pauses as well as to repeating what they or their interlocutors have just said. Lexicalized pauses and own- and other-repetition help learners free their attentional resources as these chunks are retrieved as one unit from memory and do not require conscious encoding.

L2 speakers might also experience problems deciding on whether their message has been accurate, appropriate, and understandable to the interlocutor, which problems arise in the phase of monitoring. This might occur if certain encoding processes are not yet fully automatized or appropriately encoded in memory, and as a result, the learner cannot decide whether what he or she has said contains an error (Kormos, 1999).

DEVELOPMENT OF L2 COMPETENCE IN THE BILINGUAL MODEL

When discussing the development of L2 competence in speech production, we need to consider three important aspects of what learning means in general: the acquisition of declarative knowledge, the development of automatic encoding procedures, and the memorization of responses to frequent stimuli. In L2 speech production, two basic types of knowledge are acquired as factual knowledge: words including their semantic, syntactic, morphological, phonological, stylistic, pragmatic, and idiomatic characteristics; and with a few exceptions, rules of grammatical and phonological encoding (in early childhood, L2 acquisition rules are not learned consciously in the form of declarative knowledge). Once rules are learned in the declarative form, their proceduralization can begin, which means that conscious controlled knowledge will become automatic. Not only can production rules be automatized but so too can retrieval processes of factual information such as words. At the beginning of the learning process, the word form corresponding to the intended concept and the syntactic and phonological information related to a particular word are generally retrieved by a search mechanism, whereas with the development of proficiency these pieces of information become available automatically. The third important aspect of language learning involves the memorization of larger production units used to express a wide range of communicative intentions.

Now, let us see how these learning mechanisms can be accommodated in the bilingual speech production model. The acquisition of words in L2 production involves the creation of memory traces for word forms (lemmas), and establishing the semantic referent of the lemma in the conceptual system (Truscott & Sharwood-Smith, 2004). As mentioned earlier, at the beginning of the acquisition process L2 word forms are usually associated with the semantic features of the corresponding L1 concept, and new L2 specific semantic, stylistic, and pragmatic characteristics are created slowly in the acquisition process (Jiang, 2004; N. Schmitt, 1998; N. Schmitt & Meara, 1997). The acquisition of syntactic, phonological, and morphological information stored in the mental lexicon also involves the creation of new memory traces. In certain cases, it is also possible that L2 learners first connect the L2 lemma with the syntactic and rarely the phonological information of the corresponding L1 lemma, and only later do they develop L2 specific representations.

Knowledge of rules of grammar and phonology can be acquired through the memorization of the rule that is presented explicitly to the learner, in which case students create a memory trace for the production rule in the store of declarative knowledge for grammar and phonology. Rules can also be learned deductively from the analysis of input, which most frequently leads to memorizing the rule in the form of declarative knowledge and then converting it to an automatic procedure. In naturalistic and early L2 acquisition, the automatic application of rules can also take place directly through the input.

Grammatical and phonological rules become proceduralized in the formulator (Poulisse, 1999; Towell et. al, 1996), which means that through qualitative and quantitative changes the declarative knowledge of rules is converted into automatic procedures (for how this conversion can happen, see the section Encoding Mechanisms and the Structure of Knowledge Stores). Lexical retrieval and the access of syntactic and phonological information can be considered automatized if the input item passes on the highest level of activation to the corresponding lexical, syntactic, or phonological node (e.g., not to a node in the nonintended language). The major process of automatization in factual-information retrieval involves the strengthening of links between the input and the relevant piece of information (MacKay, 1982).

The acquisition of larger memorized production units is assumed to take place in both the conceptualizer and the lexicon. Learners first establish conceptual units for various communicative functions in L2 such as opening a conversation, leave taking, requesting, apologizing, and advising by means of creating chunks from concepts. The next steps are chunking and the strengthening of links between items. In the course of learning, strong connections between lemmas are established, and lemmas constituting a formulaic sequence are retrieved as a unit.

SUMMARY

In this chapter, I outlined a bilingual speech production model that incorporates our recent knowledge of L1 and L2 speech processing. With some modifications, the model is based on Levelt's (1999a) blueprint of the speaker. The bilingual speech production model I presented follows the principle of modularity as it consists of processing modules that are specialists in their particular functions, but it is not strictly serial because cascading of activation is allowed between the lexical and phonological level of encoding. The model assumes that production mechanisms are essentially the same in both L1 and L2 and that most knowledge stores are shared between L1 and L2 items. The only additional knowledge store that I postulated for L2 production is the store of declarative knowledge of syntactic and phonological rules. The knowledge stores of Levelt's model were also slightly restructured in order to accord with theories of memory research. In this model, all the knowledge stores are located within the long-term memory, and they include four main memory systems: episodic memory, semantic memory, the syllabary, and the store for declarative knowledge of L2 rules. Semantic memory is further subdivided into a conceptual/semantic, syntactic, and phonological level.

In various phases of speech processing, the model assumes that the major difference between L1 and L2 processing involves the competition of L1 and L2 items and encoding procedures and the need for compensatory mechanisms in order to make up for missing knowledge in L2 production. Separation of the two languages is hypothesized to be controlled by the language cue added to concepts in the conceptualization phase; that is, the encoding of language-specific information is believed to take place by matching the language cue with the appropriate items in the knowledge store.

The model is also able to account for the use of communication strategies, code-switching, and transfer, and can accommodate formulaic language use as well as the development of encoding procedures. However, the model is quite sketchy in a number of respects, especially in the field of syntactic and phonological encoding, and the syntactic processing of mixed-language utterances. Further studies on the psycholinguistic processes of the acquisition of L2 speech could also help refining our knowledge of the development of memory traces of declarative knowledge about language, the automatization of rule-based mechanisms, and the creation of memorized formulas.

RECOMMENDED READINGS

1. de Bot, K. (1992). A bilingual production model: Levelt's "speaking" model adapted. *Applied Linguistics, 13,* 1–24. De Bot's article is the first attempt in the field of SLA to relate L2 speech production processes to Levelt's (1989) model of speech processing. De Bot claims that there are three major differences between L1 and L2 speech: L2 speakers tend to speak more slowly and hesitantly than L1 speakers do, L2 learners' knowledge of the target language is rarely complete, and L1 often affects the L2 verbalization process either by means of transfer or by intentional code-switches. He argues that in order to explain the first two of the differences no qualitative changes need to be implemented in Levelt's model. De Bot provides a detailed account of how the influence of L1 on L2 speech production can be accommodated in Levelt's theory with special focus on the bilingual lexicon and the interaction of L1 and L2 syntactic, morphological, and phonological encoding processes.

2. Kroll, J., & de Groot, A. M. B. (Eds.). (2005). *Handbook of bilingualism. Psycholinguistic approaches.* New York: Oxford University Press. This book is an invaluable resource for students and researchers interested in the psycholinguistic aspects of bilingualism. The chapters that are especially relevant for the study of L2 speech production are Costa's paper on the processes of lexical encoding, La Heij's chapter on control in lexical access, Pienemann and

his colleagues' article on the transferability of syntactic encoding processes, Kroll and Tokowitz's writing on the bilingual lexicon, Myers-Scotton's work on code-switching, and Segalowitz and Hulstijn's chapter on automaticity. The book also contains excellent reviews on theories of language acquisition and recent neurolinguistic research.

3. Costa, A. (2004). Bilingual speech production. In T. K. Bathia (Ed.), *Handbook of bilingualism* (pp. 201–223). Oxford, England: Blackwell. Costa's chapter in the Handbook of second language acquisition is an easily accessible and up-to-date overview of the field of second language speech production. The author primarily concentrates on issues of lexical encoding, such as lexical access and selection and control in lexical encoding, but brief summaries of recent psycholinguistic work on syntactic and phonological encoding can also be found in the chapter. The paper contains a good overview of empirical studies in the field of lexical encoding.

4. Poulisse, N. (1999). *Slips of the tongue: Speech errors in first and second language production.* Amsterdam and Philadelphia: John Benjamins. This book describes Poulisse's extensive research on slips of the tongue in L1 and L2 speech production. The book starts with a detailed review of monolingual and bilingual models of speech production, cognitive theories of language learning, and previous research on slips of the tongue in L1 and L2 production. This is followed by the meticulous description of the research and the results of the project. The findings are discussed in the light of the theories of speech production and learning presented in the first part of the book. The book is an excellent example of how research using naturally elicited speech production data can be conducted and what it can contribute to our understanding of L2 processing.

5. Meijer, P. J. A., & Fox Tee, J. E. (2003). Building syntactic structures in speaking: A bilingual exploration. *Experimental Psychology, 50,* 184–195. This study is one of the few research papers written on syntactic encoding in L2 speech production. The authors investigated what happens if L1 and L2 syntactic procedures for specific structures are the same in both languages by means of syntactic priming. The main question of the study was whether seeing a different structure in the Spanish or English prime sentence induces participants to use this structure in the sentence to be recalled in the other language. They found that speakers in both L1 and L2 switched from one structure to the other possible syntactic structure if they saw it in the prime sentence, with the exception of double negative, which turned out to be a semantically marked structure in Spanish. On the basis of this result, they argued that syntactic rules necessary for both languages are centrally stored and that they are not labeled with respect to language.

6. Roelofs, A. (2003). Shared phonological encoding processes and representations of languages in bilingual speakers. *Language and Cognitive Processes, 18,* 175–204. Roelofs' study investigated to what extent memory representations of phonological segments that are common in L1 and L2 are shared and whether phonological encoding in advanced bilinguals proceeds in the same rightward incremental fashion as described by his WEAVER model for monolingual speakers. Roelofs was also interested in whether phonological segments common to both languages are stored and accessed as one unit or as a combination of phonological features. In the experiments, which aimed to give insight into these questions, he used the form preparation paradigm (also called implicit priming) developed by Meyer (1990, 1991) with Dutch speakers of English. Roelofs concluded that the predictions of the WEAVER model for L2 phonological encoding are right as far as rightward incrementality is concerned and that L2 phonological segments are also stored as one unit and not as a set of features.

7. Leather, J. (1999). Second language speech research: An introduction. *Language Learning, 49,* 1–56. This article provides an excellent summary of phonological processes in L2 speech production. Although the primary focus of the article is not the psycholinguistic processes involved in phonological encoding, one can gain a good insight into what is known today about various aspects of the acquisition of phonological knowledge such as phonemes, phonological rules, stress, and intonation. Leather also discusses the different theories of how L2 phonology is learned including connectionist and nativist theories of learning.

8. Schmidt, R. (1992.) Psychological mechanisms underlying second language fluency. *Studies in Second Language Acquisition, 14,* 357–385. In this article, Schmidt discusses the most important cognitive theories of learning such as Anderson's ACT theory, instance theory, strength theory, theories of competitive chunking and connectionism, and their relevance to second language fluency. The article starts with the definition of fluency and in the subsequent sections, models of general skill learning are described and related to the field of second language acquisition. In the conclusion of the paper, Schmidt evaluates the models from the perspective of L2 learning and suggests further directions of research, which were indeed taken up by a number of researchers following the publication of the article.

Glossary

Activation spreading: the exchange of simple signals called activations via the connections between items in a network or in a hierarchical system.

Appropriacy repair: correction of the message that involves the encoding of the originally intended information in a modified way.

Cascading of activation: the flow of activation from the nonselected but to some extent activated lexical item to its phonological form.

Code-switching: the use of two or more languages in the same discourse.

Cognates: orthographically and or phonologically similar words, which have similar meanings in the two languages.

Communication strategy: intentional and conscious attempt made to solve any kind of language-related problem in the course of communication.

Compound lexical representation: process wherein conceptual representations for a given word are shared in L1 and L2.

Conceptualization: the planning of one's message.

Coordinate lexical representation: process wherein separate conceptual representations exist for a given L1 lexical item and its L2 translation equivalent.

Covert monitoring: checking the correctness and appropriacy of one's message before it is articulated.

Covert repair: correction of the erroneous part of the message before it is articulated.

Declarative knowledge: the knowledge of facts and figures stored in long-term memory.

Different-information repair: correction of the message that involves the encoding of new and different information from the originally intended one.

Error repair: correction of a lapse of performance (syntactic, lexical, and phonological mistakes).

Formulaic language (formulas): strings of words (phrases, idioms, expression, clauses, or even sentences) retrieved from the mental lexicon as one unit. Formulas usually have a particular pragmatic function such as requesting, apologizing, and so on.

Formulation: the lexical, grammatical, and phonological encoding of one's message.

Gestural scores: chunks of automatized movements used to produce the syllables of a given language.

Grammatical problem-solving mechanism: conscious attempt to solve a problem caused by the insufficient knowledge of the grammatical form and argument structure of the lemma and the phrase and clause structure rules of the L2.

Incremental processing: the ability of a processing component to work with a fragment of its characteristic input.

Lemma: item in the mental lexicon that contains syntactic information about the lexical entry.

Lexeme: item in the mental lexicon that contains morpho-phonological information about the lexical entry.

Lexical problem-solving mechanism: conscious attempt to solve a problem arising from the inability to retrieve the appropriate L2 lemma that corresponds to the intended concept.

Mean length of runs: a frequently used measure of fluency expressed as the average number of syllables produced in utterances between pauses of 0.25 seconds and above.

Output hypothesis: Swain's (1985, 1995) theory that claims that output in general as well as pushed output, that is, output that is slightly above the learner's level of competence, promotes second language acquisition.

Parser: the speech comprehension system.

Phonation-time ratio: a good predictor of fluency measured as the percentage of time spent speaking as a percentage proportion of the time taken to produce the speech sample.

Phonological problem-solving mechanism: conscious attempt to overcome difficulties caused by the lack of phonological knowledge of a word or phonological rules used in producing L2 speech.

Prearticulatory monitoring: see covert monitoring.

Preverbal plan: in modular models of speech production, the end product of the conceptualization phase. It contains all the necessary information to convert meaning into language.

Procedural knowledge: the knowledge of production rules such as "if an action happens in the past, insert the suffix '-ed' after the stem of the verb."

Rephrasing repairs: correction of parts of the message about the accuracy of which the speaker is uncertain.

Reconceptualization strategy: lexical problem-solving mechanism that involves the modification of more than one concept in the preverbal plan.

Self-monitoring: the checking of the correctness and appropriateness of the produced verbal output.

Self-repair: a self-initiated and self-completed correction of one's message.

Speech rate: one of the most frequently used measures of fluency, calculated by dividing the total number of syllables produced in a given speech sample by the amount of total time required to produce the sample.

Subordinate lexical representation: the process wherein the concept for a given lexical item is directly linked to the L1 word, therefore the concept cannot be directly retrieved by the L2 word, only via the L1 translation equivalent.

Substitution strategy: lexical problem-solving mechanism that involves the modification of the conceptual specifications of an L2 lemma.

Substitution plus strategy: lexical problem-solving mechanism that, in addition to the modification of the conceptual specifications of an L2 lemma, involves the application of L1 or L2 morphological and/or phonological encoding processes.

Syllabary: the store of chunks of automatized movements used to produce syllables.

Transfer: the influence of L1 on acquisition, language use, and comprehension.

References

Abrahamsson, N. (2003). Development and recoverability of L2 codas. A longitudinal study of Chinese-Swedish interphonology. *Studies in Second Language Acquisition, 25,* 313–349.

Abutalebi, J., Cappa, S. F., & Perani, D. (2001). The bilingual brain as a function of functional neuroimaging. *Bilingualism: Language and Cognition, 4,* 179–190.

Abutalebi, J., Cappa, S. F., & Perani, D. (2005). What can functional neuroimaging tell us about the bilingual brain. In J. Kroll, & A. M. B. de Groot (Eds.), *Handbook of bilingualism: Psycholinguistic perspectives* (pp. 497–515). New York: Oxford University Press.

Aitchison, J. (1987). *Words in the mind.* Oxford, England: Basil Blackwell.

Altenberg, B. (1998). On the phraseology of spoken English: The evidence of recurrent word-combinations. In A. P. Cowie (Ed.), *Phraseology: Theory, analysis, and applications* (pp. 101–122). Oxford, England: Oxford University Press.

Anderson, J. R. (1983). *The architecture of cognition.* Cambridge, MA: Harvard University Press.

Anderson, J. R. (1995). *Learning and memory. An integrated approach.* New York: Wiley.

Anderson, J. R., Fincham, J. M., & Douglass, S. (1997). The role of examples and rules in the acquisition of a cognitive skill. *Journal of Experimental Psychology: Learning, Memory, and Cognition, 23,* 932–945.

Archibald, J. (1997). The acquisition of English stress by speakers of tone languages. Lexical storage versus computation. *Linguistics, 35,* 167–181.

Archibald, J. (1998a). *Second language phonology.* Amsterdam: John Benjamins.

Archibald, J. (1998b). Second language phonology, phonetics and typology. *Studies in Second Language Acquisition, 20,* 189–213.

Austin, J. (1962). *How to do things with words.* Oxford, England: Clarendon.

Baars, B. J., Motley, M. T., & MacKay, D. G. (1975). Output editing for lexical status in artificially elicited slips of the tongue. *Journal of Verbal Learning and Verbal Behaviour, 14,* 382–391.

Baddeley, A. D. (1978). The trouble with levels: A re-examination of Craik and Lockhart's framework for memory research. *Psychological Review, 85,* 139–152.

Bates, E., & MacWhinney, B. (1989). Functionalism and the competition model. In B. MacWhinney & E. Bates (Eds.), *The crosslinguistic study of sentence processing* (pp. 3–73). Cambridge, England: Cambridge University Press.

Beattie, G. (1984). "Are there cognitive rhythms in speech?"—A reply to Power (1983). *Language and Speech, 27,* 193–195.

Belazi, H., Rubin, E., & Toribio, A. J. (1994). Code-switching and X'-bar theory: The functional head constraint. *Linguistic Inquiry, 25,* 221–237.

Berg, T. (1986). The problem of language control: Editing, monitoring and feedback. *Psychological Research, 48,* 133–144.

Berg, T. (1992). Production and perceptual constraints on speech-error correction. *Psychological Research, 54,* 114–126.

Bialystok, E. (1990). *Communication strategies.* Oxford, England: Blackwell.

Bialystok, E., & Kellerman, E. (1987). Language strategies in the classroom. In B. K. Das (Ed.), *Communication and learning in the classroom community* (pp. 160–175). Singapore: Seameo Regional Language Center.

Bierwisch, M., & Schreuder, R. (1992). From concepts to lexical items. *Cognition, 42,* 23–60.

Blackmer, E. R., & Mitton, J. L. (1991). Theories of monitoring and the timing of repairs in spontaneous speech. *Cognition, 39,* 173–194.

Bloem, I., van den Boogaard, S., & La Heij, W. (2004). Semantic facilitation and semantic interference in language production: Further evidence for the conceptual selection model of lexical access. *Journal of Memory and Language, 51,* 307–323.

Bock, K. (1986). Syntactic persistence in language production. *Cognitive Psychology, 18,* 355–387.

Bock, K. (1996). Language production: Methods and methodologies. *Psychonomic Bulletin and Review, 3,* 395–421.

Bock, K., & Levelt, W. J. M. (1994). Language production: grammatical encoding. In M. A. Gernsbacher (Ed.), *Handbook of psycholinguistics* (pp. 945–984). San Diego: Academic Press.

Bohn, O. S. (1986) Formulas, frame structures and stereotypes in early syntactic development. *Linguistics, 24,* 185–202.

Bolander, M. (1989). Prefabs, patterns and rules in interaction? Formulaic speech in adult learners' L2 Swedish. In K. Hyltenstam & L. Obler (Eds.), *Bilingualism across the lifespan: Aspects of acquisition, maturity and loss* (pp. 73–86). Cambridge, England: Cambridge University Press.

Bongaerts, T., & Poulisse, N. (1989). Communication strategies in L1 and L2: same or different? *Applied Linguistics, 10,* 253–268.

Brédart, S. (1991). Word interruption in self-repairing. *Journal of Psycholinguistic Research, 20,* 123–137.

Bresnan, J. (1982). *The mental representation of grammatical relations.* Cambridge, MA: MIT Press.

Broadbent, D. E. (1958). *Perception and communication.* Oxford, England: Pergamon.

Broselow, E. (1984). An investigation of transfer in second language phonology. *International Review of Applied Linguistics, 22,* 253–269.

Broselow, E. (1987). An investigation of transfer in second language phonology. In G. Ioup & S. Weinberger (Eds.), *Interlanguage phonology: The acquisition of second language sound system* (pp. 261–278). Rowley, MA: Newbury House.

Broselow, E., Chen, S.-I., & Wang, C. (1998). The emergence of the unmarked in second language phonology. *Studies in Second Language Acquisition, 20,* 261–280.

Brown, C. (1998). The role of the L1 grammar in the acquisition of L2 segmental structure. *Second Language Research, 14,* 136–193.

Bygate, M. (1996). Effects of task repetition: Appraising the developing language of learners. In. D. Willis & J. Willis (Eds.), *Challenge: Change in language teaching* (pp. 136–146). London: Heinemann.

Bygate, M. (1999). Task as a context for the framing, reframing and unframing of language. *System, 27,* 33–48.

Caramazza, A. (1997). How many levels of processing are there in lexical access? *Cognitive Neuropsychology, 14,* 177–208.

Caramazza., A., & Miozzo, M. (1997). The relationship between syntactic and phonological knowledge in lexical access: Evidence from the "tip of the tongue" phenomenon. *Cognition, 64,* 309–343.

Caramazza., A., Miozzo, M., Costa., Schiller, N., & Alario, F. X. (2001). Lexical selection. A cross-language investigation of determiner production. In E. Dupoux (Ed.), *Language, brain, and cognitive development: Essays in honor of Jacques Mehler* (pp. 209–226). Cambridge, MA: MIT Press.

Carlson, R. A., Sullivan, M., & Schneider, W. (1989). Practice and working memory effects in building procedural skill. *Journal of Experimental Psychology: Learning, Memory, and Cognition, 15,* 517–526.

Chen, H.-C., & Lueng, Y.-S. (1989). Patterns of lexical processing in a non-native language. *Journal of Experimental Psychology: Learning, Memory, and Cognition, 15,* 316–325.

Cheng, P. W. (1985). Restructuring versus automaticity: Alternative accounts of skill acquisition. *Psychological Review, 92,* 414–423.

Chomsky, N. (1965). *Aspects of the theory of syntax.* Cambridge, MA: MIT Press.

Chomsky, N. (1995). *The minimalist program.* Cambridge, MA: MIT Press.

Clahsen, H. (1980). Psycholinguistic aspects of L2 acquisition. In S. W. Felis (Ed.), *Second language development: Trends and issues* (pp. 57–79). Tübingen, Germany: Narr.

Clahsen, H., Meisel, J., & Pienemann, M. (1983). *Deutsch als Zweitsprache: Der Spracherwerb ausländischer Arbeiter* [German as a second language: The language acquisition of guest workers]. Tübingen, Germany: Narr.

Clahsen, H., & Muysken, P. (1989). The UG paradox and L2 acquisition. *Second Language Research, 2,* 93–119.

Clark, E. V. (1993). *The lexicon in acquisition.* Cambridge, England: Cambridge University Press.

Clark, H. H. (1994). Managing problems in speaking. *Speech Communications, 15,* 243–250.

Colomé, A. (2001). Lexical activation in bilinguals' speech production: Language specific or language-independent? *Journal of Memory and Language, 45,* 721–736.

Costa, A. (2005). Lexical access in bilingual production. In J. Kroll & A. M. B. DeGroot (Eds.), *Handbook of bilingualism: Psycholinguistic perspectives* (pp. 308–325). New York: Oxford University Press.

Costa, A., & Caramazza, A. (1999). Is lexical selection in bilingual speech production language-specific? Further evidence from Spanish-English and English-Spanish bilinguals. *Bilingualism: Language and Cognition, 2,* 231–244.

Costa, A., Caramazza, A., & Sebastian-Gallés, N. (2000). The cognate facilitation effect: Implications for models of lexical access. *Journal of Experimental Psychology: Learning, Memory, and Cognition, 26,* 1283–1296.

Costa, A., Colomé, A., Gomez, O., & Sebastian-Gallés, N. (2003). Another look at cross-language competition in bilingual speech production: Lexical and phonological factors. *Bilingualism: Language and Cognition, 6,* 167–179.

Costa, A., Kovacic, D., Franck, J., & Caramazza, A. (2003). On the autonomy of the grammatical gender systems of the two languages of a bilingual. *Bilingualism: Language and Cognition, 6,* 181–200.

Costa, A., Miozzo, M., & Caramazza, A. (1999). Lexical selection in bilinguals: Do words in the bilinguals' two lexicons compete for selection? *Journal of Memory and Language, 41,* 78–104.

Craik, F. I. M., & Lockhart, R. S. (1972). Levels of processing: A framework for memory research. *Journal of Verbal Learning and Verbal Behavior, 11,* 671–684.

Crystal, D. (1987). *The Cambridge encyclopedia of language.* Cambridge, England: Cambridge University Press.

Cutillas Espinosa, J. A. (2002). Sonority and constraint interaction: The acquisition of complex onsets by Spanish learners of English. *Anglogermanica Online.* http://www.uv.es/anglogermanica/2002-1/home.htm

de Bot, K. (1992). A bilingual production model: Levelt's "speaking" model adapted. *Applied Linguistics, 13,* 1–24.

de Bot, K. (1996). The psycholinguistics of the output hypothesis. *Language Learning, 46,* 529–555.

de Bot, K. (1998). Does the formulator know its LFG? *Bilingualism: Language and Cognition, 1,* 25–26.

de Bot, K. (2002). Cognitive processing in bilinguals: Language choice and code-switching. In R. B. Kaplan (Ed), *The Oxford handbook of applied linguistics* (pp. 286–300). Oxford, England: Oxford University Press.

de Bot, K., & Schreuder, R. (1993). Word production and the bilingual lexicon. In R. Schreuder & B. Weltens. (Eds.), *The bilingual lexicon* (pp.191–214). Amsterdam: Benjamins.

de Groot, A. M. B. (1992). Determinants of word translation. *Journal of Experimental Psychology: Learning, Memory, and Cognition, 18,* 1001–1018.

de Groot, A. M. B. (2000). On the source and nature of semantic and conceptual knowledge. *Bilingualism: Language and Cognition, 3,* 7–9.

de Groot, A. M. B., & Poot, R. (1997). Word translation at three levels of proficiency in a second language. The ubiquitous involvement of conceptual memory. *Language Learning, 47,* 215–264.

de Groot, A. M. B., & van Hell, R. (2005). Learning foreign language vocabulary. In J. Kroll & A. M. B. de Groot (Eds.), *Handbook of bilingualism: Psycholinguistic perspectives* (pp. 9–29). New York: Oxford University Press.

de Smedt, K., & Kempen, G. (1987). Incremental sentence production, self-correction, and coordination. In G. Kempen (Ed.), *Natural language generation: Recent advances in artificial intelligence, psychology and linguistics* (pp. 365–376). Dordrecht, Netherlands: Kluwer.

DeKeyser, R. M. (1997). Beyond explicit rule learning: Automatizing second language. *Studies in Second Language Acquisition, 19*, 195–221.

DeKeyser, R. M. (2001). Automaticity and automatization. In P. Robinson (Ed.), *Cognition and second language instruction* (pp. 125–151). Cambridge, England: Cambridge University Press.

Dell, G. S. (1986). A spreading activation theory of retrieval in sentence production. *Psychological Review, 93*, 283–321.

Dell, G. S., & Juliano, C. (1996). Computational models of phonological encoding. In T. Dijstra & K. de Smedt (Eds.), *Computational psycholinguistics: AI and connectionists models of human language processing* (pp. 328–359). London: Taylor & Francis.

Dell, G. S., Juliano, C., & Govindjee, A. (1993). Structure and content in language production: A theory of frame constrains in phonological speech errors. *Cognitive Science, 14*, 179–211.

Dell, G. S., & O'Seaghda, G. P. (1991). Mediated and convergent lexical priming in language production: A comment on Levelt et al. (1991). *Psychological Review, 98*, 604–614.

Deschamps, A. (1980). The syntactic distribution of pauses in English spoken as a foreign language by French students. In H. W. Dechert & M. Raupach (Eds.), *Temporal variables in speech* (pp. 255–266). The Hague, Netherlands: Mouton.

Di Biase, B., & Kawaguchi, S. (2002). Exploring the typological plausibility of processability theory: Language development in Italian second language and Japanese second language. *Second Language Research, 18*, 274–302.

Dijsktra, A., Van Heuven, W. J. B., & Grainger, J. (1998). Simulating competitior effects with the bilingual interactive activation model. *Psychologica Belgica, 38*, 177–196.

Döpke, S. (2001). Generation of and retraction from cross-linguistically motivated structures in bilingual first language acquisition. *Bilingualism: Language and Cognition, 3*, 209–226.

Dörnyei, Z. (1995). On the teachability of communication strategies. *TESOL Quarterly, 29*, 55–85.

Dörnyei, Z., & Kormos, J. (1998). Problem-solving mechanisms in L2 communication: A psycholinguistic perspective. *Studies in Second Language Acquisition, 20*, 349–385.

Dörnyei, Z., & Scott, M. L. (1997). Communication strategies in a second language: Definitions and taxonomies. *Language Learning, 47*, 173–210.

Dufour, R., Kroll, J. F., & Sholl, A. (1996). *Bilingual naming and translation. Accessing lexical and conceptual knowledge in two languages.* Unpublished manuscript.

Dulay, H., & Burt, M. (1974). Natural sequences in child language acquisition. *Language Learning, 24*, 37–53.

Eeg-Olofsson, M., & Altenberg, B. (1994). Discontinous recurrent work combinations in the London–Lund corpus. In U. Fries, G. Tottie, & P. Schneider (Eds.), *Creating and using English language corpora* (pp. 63–77). Amsterdam: Rodopi.

Eckman, F. (1977). Markedness and the contrastive analysis hypothesis. *Language Learning, 27*, 195–216.

Eckman, F., & Iverson, G. (1995). *Second language pronunciation: A new look at an old problem* (Occasional Paper No. 95-02). University of Wisconsin–Milwaukee, Center for International Studies, Marquette University.

Ejzenberg, R. (2000). The juggling act of oral fluency: A psycho-sociolinguistic metaphor. In H. Riggenbach (Ed.), *Perspectives on fluency* (pp. 287–314). Ann Arbor: University of Michigan Press.

Ellis, N. (1997). Vocabulary acquisition: Word structure, collocation, word-class, and meaning. In N. Schmitt & M. McCarthy (Eds.), *Vocabulary: Description, acquisition and pedagogy* (pp. 122–139). Cambridge, England: Cambridge University Press.

Ellis, N. (1998). Emergentism, connectionism and language learning. *Language Learning, 48,* 631–664.

Ellis, N. (2001). Memory for language. In P. Robinson (Ed.), *Cognition and second language instruction* (pp. 33–68). Cambridge, England: Cambridge University Press.

Ellis, N. (2003). Constructions, chunking and connectionism: The emergence of second language structure. In C. J. Doughty & M. H. Long (Eds.), *Handbook of second language acquisition* (pp. 63–103). Malden, MA: Blackwell.

Ellis, N., & Schmidt, R. (1998). Rules or associations in the acquisition of morphology. The frequency by regularity interaction in human and PDP learning of morphosyntax. *Language and Cognitive Processes, 13,* 307–336.

Ellis, R. (1984). Formulaic speech in early classroom second language development. In J. Handscombe, R. A. Orem, & B. Taylor (Eds.), *On TESOL '83* (pp. 53–65). Washington, DC: TESOL.

Ervin, S., & Osgood, C. E. (1954). Second language learning and bilingualism. *Journal of Abnormal and Social Psychology, 49,* 139–146.

Eubank, L. (1993). On the transfer of parametric values in L2 development. *Language Acquisition, 3,* 183–208

Evans, M. (1985). Self-initiated speech repairs: A reflection of communicative monitoring in young children. *Developmental Psychology, 21,* 365–371.

Færch, C., & Kasper, G. (1983). Plans and strategies in foreign language communication. In C. Færch & G. Kasper (Eds.), *Strategies in interlanguage communication* (pp. 20–60). London: Longman.

Færch, C., & Kasper, G. (1986). Cognitive dimensions of language transfer. In E. Kellerman & M. Sharwood Smith (Eds.), *Crosslinguistic influence in second language acquisition* (pp. 49–65). New York: Pergamon.

Fathman, A. K. (1980). Repetition and correction as an indication of speech planning and execution processes among second language learners. In H. W. Dechert & M. Raupach (Eds.), *Towards a crosslinguistic assessment of speech production* (pp. 77–85). Frankfurt, Germany: Peter D. Lang.

Felix, S. (1985). More evidence on competing cognitive systems. *Second Language Research, 7,* 47–72.

Fiez, J. A. (2001). Neuroimaging studies of speech: An overview of techniques and methodological approaches. *Journal of Communication Disorders, 34,* 445–454.

Fillmore, C. J. (1979). On fluency. In D. Kempler & W. S. Y. Wang (Eds.), *Individual differences in language ability and language behavior* (pp. 85–102). New York: Academic Press.

Flege, J. E. (1987). The production of "new" and "similar" phones in a foreign language: Evidence for the effect of equivalence classification. *Journal of Phonetics, 15,* 47–65.

Flege, J. E. (1995). Second-language speech learning. Theory, findings and problems. In W. Strange (Ed.), *Speech perception and linguistic experience: Theoretical and methodological issues* (pp. 233–272). Timonium, MD: York Press.

Flege, J. E., Frieda, E. M., Walley, A. C., & Randazza, L. A. (1998). Lexical factors and segmental accuracy in second language speech production. *Studies in Second Language Acquisition, 20,* 155–187.

Foster, P., & Skehan, P. (1996). The influence of planning and task type on second language performance. *Studies in Second Language Acquisition, 18,* 293–323.

Francis. W. S. (2005). Bilingual semantic and conceptual representation. In J. Kroll & A. M. B. de Groot (Eds.), *Handbook of bilingualism: Psycholinguistic perspectives* (pp. 251–267). New York: Oxford University Press.

Freed, B. (1995). What makes us think that students who study abroad become fluent? In B. Freed (Ed.), *Second language acquisition in a study abroad context* (pp. 123–48). Amsterdam: Benjamins.

Freed, B. F. (2000). Is fluency, like beauty, in the eyes (and ears) of the beholder? In H. Riggenbach (Ed.), *Perspectives on fluency* (pp. 243–265). Ann Arbor: University of Michigan Press.

Friedman, L. A., & O'Connell, D. C. (1991). Pause reports for spontaneous dialogic speech. *Bulletin of the Psychonomic Society, 29,* 223–225.

Fry, D. (1969). The linguistic evidence of speech errors. *BRNO Studies of English, 8,* 69–74.

Fulcher, G. (1996). Does thick description lead to smart tests? A data-based approach to rating scale construction. *Language Testing, 13,* 208–238.

Garnsey, S. M., & Dell, S. G. (1984). Some neurolinguistic implications of prearticulatory editing in production. *Brain and Language, 23,* 64–73.

Garrett, M. F. (1976). Syntactic processes in sentence production. In R. J. Wales & E. Walker (Eds.), *New approaches to language mechanisms* (pp. 274–293). Amsterdam: North Holland.

Garrett, M. F. (1980). The limits of accommodation: Arguments for independent processing levels in sentence production. In V. A. Fromkin (Ed.), *Errors in linguistic performance. Slips of the tongue, ear, pen, and hand.* (pp. 114–128). New York: Academic Press.

Gass, S. M., & Selinker, L. (1994). *Second language acquisition: An introductory course.* Hillsdale, NJ: Lawrence Erlbaum Associates.

Gass, S. M., & Varonis, E. M. (1991). Miscommunication in nonnative discourse. In N. Coupland, H. Giles, & J. M. Wiemann (Eds.), *"Miscommunication" and problematic talk* (pp. 121–145). Thousand Oaks, CA: Sage.

Gathercole, S. E., & Baddeley, A. (1994). *Working memory and language.* Hillsdale NJ: Lawrence Erlbaum Associates.

Gollan, T. H., & Silverberg, N. B. (2001). Tip-of-the-tongue states in Hebrew-English bilinguals. *Bilingualism: Language and Cognition, 4,* 63–83.

Green, D. W. (1998). Mental control of the bilingual lexico-semantic system. *Bilingualism: Language and Cognition, 1,* 67–81.

Green, P. S., & Hecht, K. (1993). Pupil self-correction in oral communication in English as a foreign language. *System, 21,* 151–163.

Greene, J. (1984). Speech preparation processes and verbal fluency. *Human Communication Research, 11,* 61–84.

Greene, J., & Cappella, J. (1986). Cognition and talk: The relationship of semantic units to temporal patters of fluency in spontaneous speech. *Language and Speech, 29,* 141–157.

Grosjean, F. (1998). Studying bilinguals: Methodological and conceptual issues. *Bilingualism: Language and Cognition, 1,* 131–149.

Haberzettl, S. (2000). *Der Erwerb der Verbstellung in der Zweitsprache Deutsch durch Kinder mit typologisch verschiedenen Muttersprachen. Eine Auseinandersetzung mit Theorien zum Syntaxerwerb anhand von vier Fallstudien* [The acquisition of verbs in German as a second language by children from typologically different language backgrounds: An evaluation of the theories of syntax acquisition based on four case studies]. Unpublished doctoral dissertation, University of Potsdam, Germany.

Håkansson, G., Pienemann, M., & Sayehli, S. (2002). Transfer and typological proximity in the context of L2 processing. *Second Language Research, 18,* 250–273.

Hancin-Bhatt, B. (1994). Segment transfer: A consequence of dynamic system. *Second Language Research, 10,* 241–269.

Hancin-Bhatt, B., & Bhatt, R. (1992). On the nature of L1 filter and cross-language transfer effects. In J. Leather & A. James (Eds.), *New Sounds 92: Proceedings of the 1992 Amsterdam symposium on the acquisition of second language speech* (pp. 124–134). Klagenfurt, Austria: University of Klagenfurt.

Hancin-Bhatt, B., & Bhatt, R. (1997). Optimal L2 syllables: Interactions of transfer and developmental effects. *Studies in Second Language Acquisition, 19,* 331–378.

Hancin-Bhatt, B., & Govindjee, A. , R. (1999). A computational model of feature competition in L2 transfer. In P. Broeder & J. Murre (Eds.), *Language and thought in development: Cross-linguistic studies* (pp. 145–161). Tübingen, Germany: Günter Narr.

Hansen, J. G. (2004). Developmental sequences in the acquisition of English L2 syllable codas. A preliminary study. *Studies in Second Language Acquisition, 26,* 85–124.

Harrington, M. (2001). Sentence processing. In: P. J. Robinson (Ed.), *Cognition and second language instruction* (pp. 91–124). Cambridge, England: Cambridge University Press.

Hartsuiker, R. J., & Kolk, H. H. J. (2001). Error monitoring in speech production: A computational test of the perceptual loop theory. *Cognitive Psychology, 42,* 113–157.

Hatch, E. M. (1978). Discourse analysis and second language acquisition. In E. M. Hatch (Ed.), *Second language acquisition* (pp. 401–435). Rowley, MA: Newbury House.

Hawkins, R., & Chan, Y.-H. C. (1997). The partial availability of Universal Grammar in second language acquisition: The "failed functional features hypothesis." *Second Language Research, 13,* 187–226.

Henderson, A., Goldman-Eisler, F., & Skarbek, A. (1966). Sequential temporal patterns in spontaneous speech. *Language and Speech, 8,* 236–242.

Hermans, D. (2000). *Word production in a foreign language.* Unpublished doctoral dissertation, University of Nijmegen, the Netherlands.

Hermans, D., Bongaerts, T., de Bot. K., & Schreuder, R. (1998). Producing words in a foreign language: Can speakers prevent interference from their first language. *Bilingualism: Language and Cognition, 3,* 213–229.

Hieke, A. E. (1984). Linking as a marker of fluent speech. *Language and Speech, 27,* 343–354.

Hieke, A. E. (1985). A componential approach to oral fluency evaluation. *Modern Language Journal, 69,* 135–142.

Hintzman, D. (1986). "Schema abstraction" in a multiple-trace memory model. *Psychological Review, 93,* 411–428.

Holden, K., & Hogan, J. (1993). The emotive impact of foreign intonation. An experiment in switching English and Russian intonation. *Language and Speech, 36,* 67–88.

Hulstijn, J. H., & Laufer, B. (2001). Some empirical evidence for the involvement load hypothesis in vocabulary acquisition. *Language Learning, 51,* 539–558.

Indefrey, P., & Levelt, W. J. M. (2000). The neural correlates of language production. In M. Gazzaniga (Ed.), *The new cognitive neurosciences* (pp. 845–865). Cambridge, MA: MIT Press.

Indefrey, P., & Levelt, W. J. M. (2004). The spatial and temporal signatures of word production components. *Cognition, 92,* 101–144.

Izumi, S. (2003). Comprehension and production processes in second language learning: In search of the psycholinguistic rationale for the output hypothesis. *Applied Linguistics, 24,* 168–196.

Jackendoff, R. (2002). *Foundations of language.* Oxford, England: Oxford University Press.

Jacoby, L. L. (1991). A process dissociation framework: Separating automatic from intentional uses of memory. *Journal of Memory and Language, 22,* 485–508.

Jaffe, J., Feldstein, S., & Gertsman, L. (1972). Random generation of apparent speech rhythms. *Language and Speech, 15,* 68–71.

Jarvis, S. (1998). *Conceptual transfer in the interlingual lexicon.* Bloomington: Indiana University Linguistics Club.

Jarvis, S. (2000). Semantic and conceptual transfer. *Bilingualism: Language and Cognition, 3,* 19–21.

Jescheniak, J., D., Hahne, A., & Schriefers, H. (2003). Information flow in the mental lexicon during speech planning: Evidence from event-related brain potentials. *Cognitive Brain Research, 15,* 261–276.

Jescheniak, J. D., & Schriefers, H. (1997). Lexical access in speech production: Serial or cascaded processing? *Language and Cognitive Processes, 12,* 847–852.

Jiang, N. (2004). Semantic transfer and development in L2 vocabulary acquisition. In P. Bogards & B. Laufer (Eds.), *Vocabulary in a second language* (pp. 101–126). Amsterdam: Benjamins.

Johnston, M. (1985). *Syntactic and morphological progressions in learner English.* Canberra, Australia: Commonwealth Department of Immigration and Ethnic Affairs.

Johnston, M. (1997). *Development and variation in learner language.* Unpublished doctoral dissertation, Australian National University, Canberra.

Kahnemann, D., & Treisman, A. (1984). Changing views of attention and automaticity. In R. Parasuraman & D. R. Davies (Eds.), *Varieties of attention* (pp. 29–61). New York: Academic Press.

Kasper, G. (1992). Pragmatic transfer. *Second Language Research, 8,* 203–231.

Kasper, G. (1995). Routine and indirection in interlanguage pragmatics. In L. Bouton & Y. Kachru (Eds.), *Pragmatics and language learning* (pp. 59–78). Urbana: University of Illinois at Urbana-Champaign.

Keating, P. A. (1984). Phonetic and phonological representation of stop consonant voicing. *Language, 25,* 29–50.

Keatley, C., Spinks, J., & de Gelder, B. (1994). Assymmetrical semantic facilitation between languages. *Memory & Cognition, 22,* 70–84.

Keidel, J. L., Zevin, J. D., Kluender, K. R., & Seidenberg, M. S. (2003). Modeling the role of native language knowledge in perceiving nonnative speech contrasts. In *Proceedings of the 15th International Congress of Phonetic Sciences* (pp. 2221–2224). Barcelona: Universitat Autonòma de Barcelona.

Kellerman, E. (1983). If at first you do succeed. In. S. Gass & C. Madden (Eds.), *Input in second language acquisition* (pp. 345–363). Rowley, MA: Newbury House.

Kellerman, E. (1991). Compensatory strategies in second language research: A critique, a revision, and some (non-)implications for the classroom. In R. Phillipson, E. Kellerman, L. Selinker, M. Sharwood Smith, & M. Swain (Eds.), *Foreign/second language pedagogy research: A commemorative volume for Claus Færch* (pp. 142–161). Clevedon, England: Multilingual Matters.

Kellerman, E., & Bialystok, E. (1997). On psychological plausibility in the study of communication strategies. In G. Kasper & E. Kellerman (Eds.), *Communication strategies: Psycholinguistic and sociolinguistic perspectives* (pp. 31–48). London: Longman.

Kempe, V., & MacWhinney, B. (1998). The acquisition of case-marking by adult learners of Russian and German. *Studies in Second Language Acquisition, 20,* 543–587.

Kempen, G., & Hoenkamp, E. (1987). An incremental procedural grammar for sentence formulation. *Cognitive Science, 11,* 201–258.

Kormos, J. (1999). Monitoring and self-repair in L2. *Language Learning, 49,* 303–342.

Kormos, J. (2000a). The role of attention in monitoring second language speech production. *Language Learning, 50,* 343–384.

Kormos, J. (2000b). The timing of self-repairs in second language speech production. *Studies in Second Language Acquisition, 22,* 145–169.

Kormos, J. (2002). *The structure of L2 self-repairs in the speech of Hungarian learners of English.* Unpublished manuscript.

Kormos, J. (2003). Attention and monitoring in a second language: A qualitative analysis. *Fremdsprachen Lehren und Lernen, 32,* 116–132.

Kormos, J., & Dénes, M. (2004). Exploring measures and perceptions of fluency in the speech of second language learners. *System, 32,* 146–164.

Kroll, J., & Curley, J. (1988). Lexical memory in novice bilinguals: Evidence from sentence priming. In M. Gruneberg , P. Morris, & R. Sykes (Eds.), *Practical aspects of memory* (Vol 2, pp. 389–395). London: Wiley.

Kroll, J., & de Groot, A. M. B. (1997). Lexical and conceptual memory in the bilingual. Mapping form to meaning in two languages. In A. de Groot & J. Kroll (Eds.), *Tutorials in bilingualism. Psycholinguistic perspectives* (pp. 169–199). Mahwah, NJ: Lawrence Erlbaum Associates.

Kroll, J. F., Dijkstra, A., Janssen, N., & Schriefers, H. (2000, November). *Selecting the language in which to speak: Experiments on lexical access in bilingual production.* Paper presented at the 41st annual meeting of the Psychonomic Society, New Orleans, LA.

Kroll, J. F., & Stewart, E. (1990). *Concept mediation in bilingual translation.* Paper presented at the 31st annual meeting of the Psychonomic Society. New Orleans, LA.

Kroll, J. F., & Stewart, E. (1994). Category interference in translation and picture naming: Evidence for asymmetric connections between bilingual memory representations. *Journal of Memory & Language, 33,* 149–174.

Kroll, J., & Tokowitz, N. (2005). Models of bilingual representation and processing: Looking back and to the future. In. J. Kroll & A. M. B. de Groot (Eds.), *Handbook of bilingualism: Psycholinguistic perspectives* (pp. 289–307). New York: Oxford University Press.

La Heij, W. (2005). Selection processes in monolingual and bilingual lexical access. In J. Kroll & A. M. B. de Groot (Eds.), *Handbook of bilingualism. Psycholinguistic approaches.* New York: Oxford University Press.

La Heij, W., Hooglander, A., Kerling, R., & van der Velden, E. (1996). Nonverbal context effects in forward and backward translation: Evidence for concept mediation. *Journal of Memory and Language, 35,* 648–665.

Laeufer, C. (1997). Towards a typology of bilingual phonological systems. In A. James & J. Leather (Eds.), *Second language speech* (pp. 324–342). Berlin: Mouton deGruyter.

Laufer, B., & Hulstijn, J. H. (2001). Incidental vocabulary acquisition in a second language: The construct of task induced involvement. *Applied Linguistics, 22,* 1–26.

Laver, J. (1980). Monitoring systems in the neurolinguistic control of speech production. In V. Fromkin (Ed.), *Errors in linguistic performance: Slips of the tongue, ear, pen and hand* (pp. 287–305). New York: Academic Press.

Leather, J. (1997). Interrelation of perceptual and productive learning in the initial acquisition of second-language tone. In A. James & J. Leather (Eds.), *Second language speech* (pp. 75–101). Berlin: Mouton deGruyter.

Leather, J. (1999). Second language speech research: An introduction. *Language Learning, 49,* 1–56.

Lee, M. W., & Williams, J. N. (2001). Lexical access in spoken word production by bilinguals: Evidence from the semantic competitor priming paradigm. *Bilingualism: Language and Cognition, 4,* 233–248.

Lennon, P. (1984). Retelling a story in English as a second language. In H. W. Dechert, D. Möhle, & M. Raupach (Eds.), *Second language productions* (pp. 50–68). Tübingen, Germany: Narr.

Lennon, P. (1990). Investigating fluency in EFL: A quantitative approach. *Language Learning, 40,* 387–417.

Lennon, P. (2000). The lexical element in spoken second language fluency. In H. Riggenbach (Ed.), *Perspectives on fluency* (pp. 25–42). Ann Arbor: University of Michigan Press.

Levelt, W. J. M. (1983). Monitoring and self-repair in speech. *Cognition, 33,* 41–103.

Levelt, W. J. M. (1989). *Speaking: From intention to articulation.* Cambridge, MA: MIT Press.

Levelt, W. J. M. (1992a). Accessing words in speech production: Stages, processes and representations. *Cognition, 42,* 1–22.

Levelt, W. J. M. (1993). Language use in normal speakers and its disorders. In G. Blanken, J. Dittmann, H. Grimm, J. C. Marshall & C-W. Wallesch (Eds.), *Linguistic disorders and pathologies* (pp. 1–15). Berlin: deGruyter.

Levelt, W. J. M. (1995). The ability to speak: From intentions to spoken words. *European Review, 3,* 13–23.

Levelt, W. J. M. (1999a). Language production: A blueprint of the speaker. In C. Brown & P. Hagoort (Eds.), *Neurocognition of language* (pp. 83–122). Oxford, England: Oxford University Press.

Levelt, W. J. M. (1999b). Models of word production. *Trends in Cognitive Sciences, 3,* 223–232.

Levelt, W. J. M., Roelofs, A., & Meyer, A. S. (1999). A theory of lexical access in speech production. *Behavioural and Brain Science, 22,* 1–38.

Levelt, W. J. M., Schriefers, H., Meyer, A. S., Pechmann, T., Vorberg, T., & Havinga, J. (1991a). Normal and deviant lexical processing: Reply to Dell and O'Seaghda. *Psychological Review, 98,* 615–618.

Levelt, W. J. M., Schriefers, H., Meyer, A. S., Pechmann T., Vorberg, T., & Havinga, J. (1991b). The time course of lexical access in speech production. A study of picture naming. *Psychological Review, 98,* 122–142.

Logan, G. D. (1988). Toward an instance theory of automatisation. *Psychological Review, 95,* 492–527.

MacKay, D. G. (1982). The problems of flexibility, fluency and speed-accuracy trade-off in skilled behaviour. *Psychological Review, 89,* 483–506.

MacKay, D. G. (1987). *The organization of perception and action: A theory for language and other cognitive skills.* New York: Springer.

MacKay, D. G. (1992). Awareness and error detection: New theories and research paradigms. *Consciousness and Cognition, 1,* 199–225.

MacLeod, C. M. (1991). Half a century of research on the Stroop effect: An integrative review. *Psychological Bulletin, 109,* 163–203.

MacSwan, J. (2000). The architecture of the bilingual language faculty: Evidence from intrasentential code-switching. *Bilingualism: Language and Cognition, 3,* 37–54.

MacSwan, J. (2003). Code switching and grammatical theory. In In C. J. Doughty & M. H. Long (Eds.), *Handbook of second language acquisition* (pp. 284–311). Malden, MA: Blackwell.

MacWhinney, B. (1997). Second language acquisition and the competition model. In A. de Groot & J. Kroll (Eds.), *Tutorials in bilingualism. Psycholinguistic perspectives* (pp. 113–142). Mahwah, NJ: Lawrence Erlbaum Associates.

MacWhinney, B. (2001). The competition model: the input, the context, and the brain. In P. Robinson (Ed.), *Cognition and second language instruction* (pp. 69–90). Cambridge, England: Cambridge University Press.

Major, R. (1987). A model for interlanguage phonology. In G. Ioup & S. Weinberger (Eds.), *Interlanguage phonology: The acquisition of a second language sound system* (pp. 101–124). New York: Newbury House.

Major, R., & Kim, E. (1999). The similarity differential rate hypothesis. *Language Learning, 49,* 275–302.

Mansouri, F. (2000). *Grammatical markedness and information processing in the acquisition of Arabic as second language.* München, Germany: Lincom.

Marslen-Wilson, W., & Tyler, L. (1980). The temporal structure of spoken language understanding. *Cognition, 8,* 1–71.

Matessa, M., & Anderson, J. R. (2000). Modelling focused learning in role assignment. *Language and Cognitive Processes, 15,* 263–292.

McLaughlin, B. (1990). Restructuring. *Applied Linguistics, 11,* 115–128.

McNamara, J. (1967): The bilingual's linguistic performance: A psychological overview. *Journal of Social Issues, 23,* 59–77.

McNamara, J., & Kushnir, S. L. (1972). Linguistic independence of bilinguals: The input switch. *Journal of Verbal Learning and Verbal Behaviour, 10,* 480–487.

Meara, P. (1984). The study of lexis in interlanguage. In A. Davies, A. Howart., & C. Criper (Eds.), *Interlanguage* (pp. 225–235). Edinburgh, Scotland: Edinburgh University.

Meara, P. (1997). Towards a new approach to modeling vocabulary acquisition. In N. Schmitt & M. McCarthy (Eds.), *Vocabulary: Description, acquisition and pedagogy* (pp. 109–121). Cambridge, England: Cambridge University Press.

Meara, P. (2004). Modelling vocabulary loss. *Applied Linguistics, 25,* 137–155.

Meijer, P. J. A., & Fox Tree, J. E. (2003). Building syntactic structures in speaking: A bilingual exploration. *Experimental Psychology, 50,* 184–195.

Meisel, J. (1991). Principles of Universal Grammar and strategies of language learning: Some similarities and differences between first and second language acquisition. In L. Eubank (Ed.), *Point counterpoint: Universal grammar in the second language* (pp. 231–276). Amsterdam: Benjamins.

Meisel, J. M., Clahsen, H., & Pienemann, M. (1981). On determining developmental stages in natural second language acquisition. *Studies in Second Language Acquisition, 3,* 109–135.

Meringer, R. (1908). *Aus dem Leben der Sprache* [About the life of language]. Berlin: Behr.

Meuter, R. F. I., & Allport, A. (1999). Bilingual language switching in naming: Asymmetrical costs of language selection. *Journal of Memory and Language, 40,* 25–40.

Meyer, A. S. (1990). The time course of phonological encoding in language production: The encoding of successive syllables of a word. *Journal of Memory and Language, 29,* 524–545.

Meyer, A. S. (1991). The time course of phonological encoding in language production: The phonological encoding inside a syllable. *Journal of Memory and Language, 30,* 69–89.

Mohanan, K. P. (1986). *The theory of lexical phonology.* Dordrecht, Netherlands: Reidel.

Möhle, D. (1984). A comparison of the second language speech production of different native speakers. In H. W. Dechert, D. Möhle, & M. Raupach (Eds.), *Second language productions* (pp. 50–68). Tübingen, Germany: Narr.

Moon, R. (1998). Frequencies and forms of phrasal lexemes in English. In In A. P. Cowie (Ed.), *Phraseology: Theory, analysis, and applications* (pp. 79–100). Oxford, England: Oxford University Press.

Morton, J. (1969). Interaction of information in word recognition. *Psychological Review, 76,* 165–178.

Motley, M. T., Camden, C. T., & Baars, B. J. (1982). Covert formulation and editing of anomalies in speech production: Evidence from experimentally elicited slips of the tongue. *Journal of Verbal Learning and Verbal Behaviour, 21,* 578–594.

Mowrey, R. A., & MacKay, I. R. A. (1990). Phonological primitives: Electromyographic speech error evidence. *Journal of the Acoustical Society of America, 88,* 1299–1312.

Murre, J. M. J. (2005). Models of monolingual and bilingual language acquisition. In J. Kroll & A. M. B. de Groot (Eds.), *Handbook of bilingualism: Psycholinguistic perspectives* (pp. 154–173). New York: Oxford University Press.

Myers-Scotton, C. (1993). *Duelling languages: Grammatical structure in code-switching.* Oxford, England: Clarendon.

Myers-Scotton, C. (2005). Supporting a differential access hypothesis: Code-switching and other contact data. In J. Kroll & A. M. B. de Groot (Eds.), *Handbook of bilingualism: Psycholinguistic perspectives* (pp. 326–348). New York: Oxford University Press.

Myers-Scotton, C., & Jake, J. (1995). Matching lemmas in a bilingual language production model: Evidence from intrasentential codeswitching. *Linguistics, 33,* 981–1024.

Myers-Scotton, C., & Jake, J. (2000). F-our types of morpheme: Evidence from aphasia, code-switching and second language acquisition. *Linguistics, 38,* 1053–1100.

Myles, F., Hooper, J., & Mitchell, R. (1998). Rote or rule? Exploring the role of formulaic language in classroom foreign language learning. *Language Learning, 48,* 323–63.

Myles, F., Mitchell, R., & Hooper, J. (1999). Interrogative chunks in French L2: A basis for creative construction? *Studies in Second Language Acquisition, 21,* 49–80.

Nation, I. S. P. (1990). *Teaching and learning vocabulary.* New York: Newbury House.

Neely, J. H. (1977). Semantic priming and retrieval from lexical memory: Roles of inhibitionless spreading activation and limited capacity attention. *Journal of Experimental Psychology: General, 106,* 226–254.

Newell, A. (1990). *Unified theories of cognition.* Cambridge, MA: Harvard University Press.

Newell, A., & Rosenbloom, P. S. (1981). Mechanisms of skill acquisition and the law of practice. In J. R. Anderson (Ed.), *Cognitive skills and their acquisition* (pp. 1–55). Hillsdale, NJ: Lawrence Erlbaum Associates.

Nooteboom, S. G. (1980). Speaking and unspeaking: Detection and correction of phonological and lexical errors in spontaneous speech. In V. A. Fromkin (Ed.), *Slips of the tongue, ear, pen and hand* (pp. 87–95). New York: Academic Press.

Norman, D. A. (1981). Categorization of action slips. *Psychological Review, 88,* 1–15.

Nosofsky, R. M., & Palmeri, T. J. (1997). An examplar-based random walk model of speeded classification. *Psychological Review, 104,* 266–300.

O'Connell, D. C. (1988). *Critical essays on language use and psychology.* New York: Springer.

O'Connor, N. (1988). Repairs as indicative of interlanguage variation and change. In T. J. Walsh (Ed.), *Georgetown University Round Table in Languages and Linguistics 1988: Synchronic and diachronic approaches to linguistic variation and change* (pp. 251–259). Washington, DC: Georgetown University Press.

Odlin, T. (1989). *Language transfer: Cross-linguistic influence in language learning.* Cambridge, England: Cambridge University Press.

Odlin, T. (2003). Cross-linguistic influence. In C. J. Doughty & M. H. Long (Eds.), *Handbook of second language acquisition* (pp. 436–486). Malden, MA: Blackwell.

Oomen, C. E., & Postma, A. (2001). Effects of time pressure on mechanisms of speech production and self-monitoring. *Journal of Psycholinguistic Research, 30,* 163–184.

Oppenheim, N. (2000). The importance of recurrent sequences for nonnative speaker fluency and cognition. In H. Riggenbach (Ed.), *Perspectives on fluency* (pp. 220–240). Ann Arbor: University of Michigan Press.

Palmeri, T. J. (1997). Examplar similarity and the development of automaticity. *Journal of Experimental Psychology: Learning, Memory, and Cognition, 23,* 324–354.

Paradis, M. (1994). Neurolinguistics aspects of implicit and explicit memory: Implications for bilingualism and SLA. In N. Ellis (Ed.), *Implicit and explicit learning of languages* (pp. 393–419). London: Academic Press.

Paradis, M. (1997). The cognitive neuropsychology of bilingualism. In A. de Groot & J. Kroll (Eds.), *Tutorials in bilingualism. Psycholinguistic perspectives* (pp. 331–354). Mahwah, NJ: Lawrence Erlbaum Associates.

Paradis, M. (2000). Cerebral representation of bilingual concepts. *Bilingualism: Language and Cognition, 3,* 22–24.

Pavlenko, A. (1997). *Bilingualism and cognition.* Unpublished doctoral dissertation, Cornell University, Ithaca, NY.

Pavlenko, A. (1999). New approaches to concepts in bilingual memory. *Bilingualism: Language and Cognition, 2,* 209–230.

Pawley, A., & Syder, F. H. (1983). Two puzzles for linguistic theory: Nativelike selection and nativelike fluency. In J. C. Richards & R. W. Schmidt (Eds.), *Language and communication* (pp. 317–331). London: Longman.

Peters, A. M. (1977). Language learning strategies: Does the whole equal the sum of the parts? *Language, 53,* 560–573.

Peterson, R. R., & Savoy, P. (1998). Lexical selection and phonological encoding during language production: evidence for cascaded processing. *Journal of Experimental Psychology: Learning, Memory, and Cognition, 24,* 539–557.

Phaf, R. H., van der Heijden, A. H. C., & Hudson. P. T. W. (1990). SLAM: A connectionist model for attention in visual selection tasks. *Cognitive Psychology, 22,* 273–341.

Pica, T. (1994). Research on negotiation: What does it reveal about second-language learning conditions, processes, and outcomes? *Language Learning, 44,* 493–527.

Pienemann, M. (1980). The second language acquisition of immigrant children. In S. W. Felix (Ed.), *Second language development: Trends and issues* (pp. 41–56). Tübingen, Germany: Narr.

Pienemann, M. (1998). Developmental dynamics in L1 and L2 acquisition: Processability theory and generative entrenchment. *Bilingualism: Language and Cognition, 1,* 1–20.

Pienemann, M. (in press). An introduction to processability theory. In M. Pienemann (Ed.), *Crosslinguistic aspects of L2 processability.* Amsterdam: Benjamins.

Pienemann, M., Di Biase, B., Kawaguchi, S., & Håkansson, G. (2005). Processing constraints on L1 transfer. In J. Kroll & A. M. B. de Groot (Eds.), *Handbook of bilingualism: Psycholinguistic perspectives* (pp. 128–153). New York: Oxford University Press.

Pienemann, M., & Håkansson, G. (1999). A unified approach towards the development of Swedish as L2: A processability account. *Studies in Second Language Acquisition, 21,* 383–420.

Pienemann, M., & Mackey, A. (1993). An empirical study of children's ESL development and rapid profile. In P. McKay (Ed.), *ESL development, language and literacy in schools* (Vol 2, pp. 115–259). Melbourne: Commonwealth of Australia and National Languages and Literacy Institute of Australia.

Poplack, S. (1979/1980). Sometimes I'll start a sentence in Spanish y termino en español. *Linguistics, 18,* 581–618.

Poplack, S. (1981). The syntactic structure and social function of code-switching. In R. Duran (Ed.), *Latino language and communicative behavior* (pp. 169–184). Norwood, NJ: Ablex.

Posner, M. I., & Boies, S. J. (1971). Components of attention. *Psychological Review, 78,* 391–408.

Postma, A. (2000). Detection of errors during speech production: A review of speech monitoring models. *Cognition, 77,* 97–131.

Postma, A., & Kolk, H. (1992). The effects of noise masking and required accuracy on speech errors disfluencies and self-repairs. *Journal of Speech and Hearing Research, 35,* 537–544.

Postma, A., & Kolk, H. (1993). The covert repair hypothesis: Prearticulatory repair processes in normal and stuttered disfluencies. *Journal of Speech and Hearing Research, 36,* 472–487.

Postma, A., Kolk, H., & Povel, D. J. (1990). On the relation among speech errors, disfluencies and self repairs. *Language and Speech, 33,* 19–29.

Postma, A., & Noordanus, C. (1996). Production and detection of speech errors in silent, mouthed, noise-masked and normal auditory feedback speech. *Language and Speech, 39,* 375–392.

Potter, M. C., & Lombardi, L. (1990). Regeneration in the short-term recall of sentences. *Journal of Memory and Language, 29,* 633–654.

Potter, M. C., So, K.-F., Von Eckardt, B., & Feldman, L. B. (1984). Lexical and conceptual representation in beginning and more proficient bilinguals. *Journal of Verbal Learning and Verbal Behaviour, 23,* 23–38.

Poulisse, N. (1993). A theoretical account of lexical communication strategies. In R. Schreuder & B. Weltens (Eds.), *The bilingual lexicon* (pp. 157–189). Amsterdam: Benjamins.

Poulisse, N. (1994). Communication strategies in a second language. In *The encyclopedia of language and linguistics* (Vol. 2, pp. 620–624). Oxford, England: Pergamon.

Poulisse, N. (1997a). Compensatory strategies and the principles of clarity and econ-
omy. In G. Kasper & E. Kellerman (Eds.), *Communication strategies:
Psycholinguistic and sociolinguistic perspectives* (pp. 49–64). London: Longman.

Poulisse, N. (1997b). Language production in bilinguals. In A. de Groot & J. Kroll
(Eds.), *Tutorials in bilingualism. Psycholinguistic perspectives* (pp. 201–224).
Mahwah, NJ: Lawrence Erlbaum Associates.

Poulisse, N. (1999). *Slips of the tongue: Speech errors in first and second language
production.* Amsterdam: Benjamins.

Poulisse, N., & Bongaerts, T. (1994). First language use in second language production. *Applied Linguistics, 15,* 36–57.

Poulisse, N., & Schils, E. (1989). The influence of task and proficiency related factors
on the use of communication strategies: A quantitative analysis. *Language Learning, 39,* 15–48.

Prince, A. S., & Smolensky, P. (1993). *Optimality theory: Constraint interaction in
generative grammar.* Unpublished manuscript, Rutgers University, New Bruns-
wick, NJ, and the University of Colorado at Boulder.

Rahman, R. A., & Sommer, W. (2003). Does phonological encoding in speech production always follow the retrieval of semantic knowledge? Electrophysiological evidence for parallel processing. *Cognitive Brain Research, 16,* 372–382.

Raupach, M. (1984). Formulae in second language production. In H. W. Dechert, D.
Möhle, & M. Raupach (Eds.), *Second language productions* (pp. 114–137).
Tübingen, Germany: Narr.

Raupach, M. (1987). Procedural learning in advanced learners of a foreign language.
In. J. A. Coleman & R. Towell (Eds.), *The advanced language learner* (pp.
123–155). London: CILT.

Rehbein, J. (1987). On fluency in second language speech. In H. W. Dechert & M.
Raupach (Eds.), *Psycholinguistic models of production* (pp. 97–105). Norwood,
NJ: Ablex.

Rekart, D., & Dunkel, P. (1992). The utility of objective (computer) measures of the
fluency of speakers of English as a second language. *Applied Language Learning,
3,* 65–85.

Rice, K. (1995, June). *What is a lateral?* Paper presented at the annual meeting of the
Canadian Linguistics Association, Alberta, Canada.

Rice, K., & Avery, P. (1995). Variability in a deterministic model of language acquisition: A theory of segmental elaboration. In J. Archibald (Ed.), *Phonological acquisition and phonological theory* (pp. 23–42). Hillsdale, NJ: Lawrence Erlbaum
Associates.

Riggenbach, H. (1991). Towards an understanding of fluency: A microanalysis of nonnative speaker conversation. *Discourse Processes, 14,* 423–441.

Roberts, B., & Kirsner, K. (2000). Temporal cycles in speech production. *Language
and Cognitive Processes, 15,* 129–157.

Robinson, P. (1995). Attention, memory and the "noticing" hypothesis. *Language
Learning, 45,* 283–331.

Robinson, P. (1997). Generalizability and automaticity of second language learning
under implicit, incidental, rule-enhanced, and instructed conditions. *Studies in Second Language Acquisition, 19,* 223–248.

Robinson, P. (2003). Attention and memory during SLA. In C. J. Doughty & M. H. Long (Eds.), *Handbook of second language acquisition* (pp. 631–671). Malden, MA: Blackwell.

Robinson, P., & Ha, M. A. (1993). Instance theory and second language rule learning under explicit conditions. *Studies in Second Language Acquisition, 15,* 413–438.

Roelofs, A. (1992). A spreading-activation theory of lemma retrieval in speaking. *Cognition, 42,* 107–142.

Roelofs, A. (1997a). A case for non-decomposition in conceptually driven word retrieval. *Journal of Psycholinguistic Research, 26,* 33–67.

Roelofs, A. (1997b). The WEAVER model of word-form encoding in speech production. *Cognition, 64,* 249–284.

Roelofs, A. (1998). Lemma selection without inhibition of languages in bilingual speakers. *Bilingualism: Language and Cognition, 1,* 94–95.

Roelofs, A. (1999). Phonological segments and features as planning units in speech production. *Language and Cognitive Processes, 14,* 173–200.

Roelofs, A. (2000). Word meanings and concepts: What do the findings from aphasia and language specificity really say? *Bilingualism: Language and Cognition, 3,* 19–21.

Roelofs, A. (2003a). Goal-referenced selection of verbal action: Modeling attentional control in the Stroop task. *Psychological Review, 110,* 88–125.

Roelofs, A. (2003b). Shared phonological encoding processes and representations of languages in bilingual speakers. *Language and Cognitive Processes, 18,* 175–204.

Roelofs, A., Meyer, A., & Levelt, W. J. M. (1998). A case for the lemma/lexeme distinction in models of speaking: comment on Caramazza and Miozzo (1997). *Cognition, 69,* 219–230.

Rogers, S. (1978). Self-initiated corrections in the speech of infant-school children. *Journal of Child Language, 5,* 365–371.

Rosenbloom, P., & Newell, A. (1987). Learning by chunking: A production system model of practice. In D. Klahr, P. Langley, & R. Neches (Eds.), *Production system models learning and development* (pp. 221–286). Cambridge, MA: MIT Press.

Rubach, J. (1984). Rule typology and phonological interference. In S. Eliasson (Ed.), *Theoretical issues in contrastive phonology* (pp. 37–50). Heidelberg, Germany: Groos.

Sajavaara, K. (1987). Second language speech production: Factors affecting fluency. In H. W. Dechert & M. Raupach (Eds.), *Psycholinguistic models of production* (pp. 45–65). Norwood, NJ: Ablex.

Schiller, N. O., & Caramazza, A. (2003). Grammatical feature selection in noun phrase production: Evidence from German and Dutch. *Journal of Memory and Language, 48,* 169–194

Schmidt, R. (1983). Interaction, acculturation, and acquisition of communicative competence. In N. Wolfson & E. Judd (Eds.), *Sociolinguistics and second language acquisition* (pp. 137–174). Rowley, MA: Newbury House.

Schmidt, R. (1990). The role of consciousness in second language learning. *Applied Linguistics, 11,* 129–158.

Schmidt, R. (1992). Psychological mechanisms underlying second language fluency. *Studies in Second Language Acquisition, 14,* 357–385.

Schmidt, R. (1993). Awareness and second language acquisition. *Annual Review of Applied Linguistics, 13*, 206–226.

Schmidt, R. (1994). Deconstructing consciousness in search of useful definitions for applied linguistics. *AILA Review, 11*, 11–26.

Schmidt, R., & Frota, S. (1986). Developing basic conversational ability in a second language: A case study of an adult learner. In R. Day (Ed.), *Talking to learn* (pp. 237–326). Rowley, MA: Newbury House.

Schmitt, B. M., Meyer, A. S., & Levelt, W. J. M. (1999). Lexical access in the production of pronouns. *Cognition, 69*, 313–335.

Schmitt, N. (1998). Tracking the incremental acquisition of second language vocabulary: A longitudinal study. *Language Learning, 48*, 281–317.

Schmitt, N., & Meara, P. (1997). Researching vocabulary through a word knowledge framework: Verbal associations and verbal suffixes. *Studies in Second Language Acquisition, 19*, 17–36.

Schneider, W., Dumas, S. T., & Shiffrin, R. M. (1984). Automatic and controlled processing and attention. In R. Parasuraman & D. R. Davies (Eds.), *Varieties of attention* (pp. 1–27). New York: Academic Press.

Schneider, W., & Shiffrin, R. M. (1977). Controlled and automatic human information processing: I. Detection, search and attention. *Psychological Review, 84*, 1–66.

Schriefers, H. (1993). Syntactic processes in the production of nounphrases. *Journal of Experimental Psychology: Learning, Memory, and Cognition, 19*, 841–850.

Schriefers, H., & Jescheniak, J. D. (1999). Representation and processing of grammatical gender in language production: A review. *Journal of Psycholinguistic Research, 28*, 575–600.

Schwanenflugel, P. J., Harnishfeger, K. K., & Stowe, R. W. (1988). Context availability and lexical decisions for abstract and concrete words. *Journal of Memory and Language, 27*, 499–520.

Schwartz, B., & Sprouse, R. (1996). L2 cognitive states and the full transfer/full access model. *Second Language Research, 12*, 40–72.

Searle, J. (1969). *Speech acts.* Cambridge, England: Cambridge University Press.

Segalowitz, N. (2003). Automaticity and second languages. In C. J. Doughty & M. H. Long (Eds.), *Handbook of second language acquisition* (pp. 383–408). Malden, MA: Blackwell.

Segalowitz, N., & Segalowitz, S. (1993). Skilled performance, practice, and the differentiation of speed-up from automatization effects: Evidence from second language word recognition. *Applied Psycholinguistics, 14*, 369–385.

Segalowitz, S., Segalowitz, N., & Wood, A. (1998). Assessing the development of automaticity in second language word recognition. *Applied Psycholinguistics, 19*, 53–67.

Selinker, L. (1972). Interlanguage. *International Review of Applied Linguistics, 10*, 209–230.

Servan-Schreiber, E., & Anderson, J. R. (1990). Learning artificial grammars with competitive chunking. *Journal of Experimental Psychology: Learning, Memory, and Cognition, 16*, 592–608.

Shattuck-Hufnagel, S. (1979). Speech errors as evidence for a serial order mechanism in sentence production. In W. E. Cooper, & E. C. T. Walker (Eds.), *Sentence pro-*

cessing: Psycholinguistic studies presented to Merrill Garrett (pp. 295–342). Hillsdale, NJ: Lawrence Erlbaum Associates.

Shiffrin, R. M., & Schneider, W. (1977). Controlled and automatic human information processing: II. Perceptual learning, automatic attending, and a general theory. *Psychological Review, 84,* 127–190.

Shiffrin, R. M., & Schneider, W. (1984). Automatic and controlled processing revisited. *Psychological Review, 91,* 269–276.

Sholl, A., Sankaranarayanan, A., & Kroll, J. F. (1995). Transfer between picture naming and translation: A test of asymmetries in bilingual memory. *Psychological Science, 6,* 45–49.

Skehan, P., & Foster, P. (1997). Task type and task processing conditions as influences on foreign language performance. *Language Teaching Research, 1,* 185–212.

Skehan, P., & Foster, P. (2001). Cognition and tasks. In P. Robinson (Ed.), *Cognition and second language instruction* (pp. 183–205). Cambridge, England: Cambridge University Press.

Starreveld, P. A., & La Heij, W. (1996). The locus of orthographic facilitation: Reply to Roelofs, Meyer, and Levelt (1996). *Journal of Experimental Psychology: Learning, Memory, and Cognition, 22,* 252–255.

Stemberger, J. P. (1985). An interactive activation model of language production. In A.W. Ellis (Ed.), *Progress in the psychology of language* (Vol. 1, pp.143–186). Hillsdale NJ: Lawrence Erlbaum Associates.

Swain, M. (1985). Communicative competence: Some roles of comprehensible input and comprehensible output in its development. In S. M. Gass & C. G. Madden (Eds.), *Input in second language acquisition* (pp. 235–253). Rowley, MA: Newbury House.

Swain, M. (1995). Three functions of output in second language learning. In G. Cook & B. Seidlhofer (Eds.), *Principle and practice in applied linguistics: Studies in honour of H. G. Widdowson.* Oxford, England: Oxford University Press.

Swain, M., & Lapkin, S. (1995). Problems in output and the cognitive process they generate: A step towards second language learning. *Applied Linguistics, 16,* 371–391.

Swan, M. (1997). The influence of the mother tongue on second language vocabulary acquisition and use. In N. Schmitt & M. McCarthy (Eds.), *Vocabulary: Description, acquisition and pedagogy* (pp. 156–180). Cambridge, England: Cambridge University Press.

Talamas, A., Kroll, J. F., & Dufour, R. (1995). *Form-related errors in second language learning: A preliminary stage in the acquisition of L2 vocabulary.* Unpublished manuscript, Pennsylvania State University, University Park.

Tarone, E. (1977). Conscious communication strategies in interlanguage: A progress report. In H. D. Brown, C. A. Yorio, & R. C. Crymes (Eds.), *On TESOL '77* (pp. 194–203). Washington, DC: TESOL.

Tarone, E. (1980). Communication strategies, foreigner talk, and repair in interlanguage. *Language Learning, 30,* 417–431.

Tarone, E. (1983). On the variability of the interlanguage system. *Applied Linguistics, 4,* 143–63.

Tarone, E. (1985). Variability in interlanguage use: A study of style-shifting in morphology and syntax. *Language Learning, 35,* 373–403.

Tarone, E., Cohen, A. D., & Dumas, G. (1976). A closer look at some interlanguage terminology: A framework for communication strategies. *Working Papers on Bilingualism, 9,* 76–90.

Tarone, E., & Parrish, B. (1988). Task-related variation in interlanguage. The case of articles. *Language Learning, 38,* 21–44.

Tonkyn, A. (2001, September). *The many voices of fluency.* Paper presented at the annual meeting of the BAAL, Reading, England.

Towell, R., Hawkins, R., & Bazergui, N. (1996). The development of fluency in advanced learners of French. *Applied Linguistics, 17,* 84–119.

Trammell, R. L. (1993). English ambisyllabic consonants and half-closed syllables in language teaching. *Language Learning, 43,* 195–238.

Tree, J .E. F., & Mejer, P. A. J. B. (1999). Building syntactic structure in speaking. *Journal of Psycholinguistic Research, 28,* 71–92.

Truscott, J., & Sharwood-Smith, M. (2004). Acquisition by processing: A modular perspective on language development. *Bilingualism: Language and Cognition, 7,* 1–20.

Tulving, E. (1972). Episodic and semantic memory. In E. Tulving & W. Donaldson (Eds.), *Organization of memory* (pp. 381–403). New York: Academic Press.

Ullman, T. (2001). The neural basis of lexicon and grammar in first and second language: The declarative/procedural model. *Bilingualism: Language and Cognition, 4,* 105–112.

Vainikka, A., & Young-Scholten, M. (1994). Direct access to X' theory: Evidence from Korean and Turkish adults learning German. In T. Hoekstra & B. Schwartz (Eds.), *Language acquisition studies in generative grammar* (pp. 265–316). Amsterdam: Benjamins.

van Gelderen, A. (1994). Prediction of global ratings of fluency and delivery in narrative discourse by linguistic and phonetic measures—oral performances of students aged 11–12 years. *Language Testing, 11,* 291–319.

van Hell, J. G., & de Groot, A. M. B. (1998). Conceptual representation in bilinguals memory: Effects of concreteness and cognate status in word association. *Bilingualism: Language and Cognition, 1,* 193–211.

van Hest, E. (1996). *Self-repair in L1 and L2 production.* Tilburg, Netherlands: Tilburg University Press.

Vanderplank, R. (1993). Pacing and spacing as predictors of difficulty in speaking and understanding English. *English Language Teaching Journal, 47,* 117–125.

van Turennout, M., & Hagoort, P., & Brown, C. M. (1997). Electrophysiological evidence on the time course of semantic and phonological processes in speech production. *Experimental Psychology: Learning, Memory, and Cognition, 23,* 787–806.

van Turennout, M., Hagoort, P., & Brown, C. (1999). The time course of grammatical and phonological processing during speaking: Evidence from event-related brain potentials. *Journal of Psycholinguistic Research, 28,* 649–676.

VanPatten, B. (1990). Attending to form and content in the input. *Studies in Second Language Acquisition, 12,* 287–301.

VanPatten, B. (1994). Evaluating the role of consciousness in SLA: Terms, linguistic features, and research methodology. *AILA Review, 11,* 27–36.

VanPatten, B. (1996). *Input processing and grammar instruction.* New York: Ablex.

VanPatten, B., & Cadiorno, T. (1993). Explicit instruction and input processing. *Studies in Second Language Acquisition, 15,* 225–243.

Váradi, T. (1980). Strategies of target language learner communication: Message adjustment. *IRAL, 18,* 59–71.

Verhoeven, L. T. (1989). Monitoring in children's second language speech. *Second Language Research, 5,* 141–155.

Vigliocco, G., & Lauer, M., Damian, M. F., & Levelt, W. J. M. (2002). Semantic and syntactic forces in noun phrase production. *Journal of Experimental Psychology: Learning, Memory, and Cognition, 28,* 46–58.

Vigliocco, G., Vinson, D. P., Indefrey, P., Levelt, W. J. M., & Hellwig, F. (2004). Role of grammatical gender and semantics in German word production. *Journal of Experimental Psychology: Learning Memory, and Cognition, 30,* 483–497.

Vosse, T., & Kempen, G. (2000). Syntactic structure assembly in human parsing: a computational model based on inhibition and lexicalist grammar. *Cognition, 75,* 105–143.

Warner, R. M. (1979). Periodic rhythms in conversational speech. *Language and Speech, 22,* 381–396.

Wennerstrom, A. (2000). The role of intonation in second language fluency. In H. Riggenbach (Ed.), *Perspectives on fluency* (pp. 102–127). Ann Arbor: University of Michigan Press.

Wei, L. (2000). Unequal election of morphemes in adult second language acquisition. *Applied Linguistics, 21,* 106–140.

Weinreich, U. (1953). *Languages in contact.* New York: Linguistic Circle of New York.

Widdowson, H. (1978). *Teaching language as communication.* Oxford, England: Oxford University Press.

Wiese, R. (1984). Language production in foreign and native languages: Same or different? In H. Dechert, D. Möhle, & M. Raupach (Eds.), *Second language productions* (pp. 11–25). Tübingen, Germany: Narr.

Wheeldon, L. R., & Levelt, W. J. M. (1995). Monitoring the time course of phonological encoding. *Journal of Memory and Language, 34,* 311–334.

White, L. (1996). Universal grammar and second language acquisition: current trends and new directions. In W. Ritchie & T. Bhatia (Eds.), *Handbook of second language acquisition* (pp. 85–120). New York: Academic Press.

White, L. (2003). *Second language acquisition and Universal Grammar.* Cambridge, England: Cambridge University Press.

Wilks, C., & Meara, P. (2002). Untangling word webs: Graph theory and the notion of density in second language word association networks. *Second Language Research, 18,* 303–324.

Wolter, B. (2001). Comparing the L1 and L2 mental lexicon: A depth of individual word knowledge model. *Studies in Second Language Acquisition, 23,* 41–69.

Wong Fillmore, L. (1976). Individual differences in second language acquisition. In C. J. Fillmore, D. Kempler, & W. S.-Y. Wang (Eds.), *Individual differences in language ability and language behaviour* (pp. 203–228). London: Academic Press.

Woolford, E. (1983). Bilingual code-switching and syntactic theory. *Linguistic Inquiry, 14,* 520–536.

Wray, A. (2002). *Formulaic language and the lexicon.* Cambridge, England: Cambridge University Press.

Yarmohammadi, L., & Seif, S. (1992). More on communication strategies: Classification, resources, frequency and underlying processes. *IRAL, 30,* 223–232.

Yorio, C. A. (1989). Idiomaticity as an indicator of second language proficiency. In K. Hyltenstam & L. K. Obler (Eds.), *Bilingualism across the lifespan: Aspects of acquisition, maturity, and loss* (pp. 55–72). Cambridge, England: Cambridge University Press.

Young-Scholten, M. (1997). Interlanguage and post-lexical transfer. In A. James & J. Leather (Eds.), *Second language speech* (pp. 351–360). Berlin: Mouton deGruyter.

Yule, G. (1997). *Referential communication tasks.* Mahwah, NJ: Lawrence Erlbaum Associates.

Yule, G., & Tarone, E. (1991). The other side of the page: Integrating the study of communication strategies and negotiated input in SLA. In R. Phillipson, E. Kellerman, L. Selinker, M. Sharwood Smith, & M. Swain (Eds.), *Foreign/second language pedagogy research: A commemorative volume for Claus Færch* (pp. 162–171). Clevedon, England: Multilingual Matters.

Zhang, Y. (in press). Processability: Acquisition of L2 Chinese grammatical morphemes. In M. Pienemann (Ed.), *Cross-linguistic perspectives in second language processing.* Amsterdam: Benjamins.

Author Index

A

Abrahamsson, N., 120
Abutalebi, J., 35
Aitchison, J., 81
Alario, F. X., 95
Allport, A., 66
Altenberg, B., xx
Anderson, J. R., 42, 44, 47, 48, 135, 156, 157, 158, 162, 165, 181
Archibald, J., 117, 118, 120
Austin, J., 9
Avery, P., 117

B

Baars, B. J., 30, 122, 136
Baddeley, A. D., 89, 130
Bates, E., 102, 118, 126, 162
Bazergui, N., 162, 163, 164, 178
Beattie, G., 16
Belazi, H., 108
Berg, T., 24, 31, 120
Bhatt, R., 110, 117
Bialystok, E., 136, 141, 145, 152, 165
Bierwisch, M., 17
Blackmer, E. R., 31, 33, 127
Bloem I., 56, 63, 170
Bock, K., 13, 14, 25, 26, 99
Bohn, O. S., 159
Boies, S. J., 40
Bolander, M., 159
Bongaerts, T., xxi, xxv, 3, 57, 58, 59, 60, 62, 65, 67, 83, 84, 90, 110, 131, 152, 170, 171, 174, 175
Brédart, S., 125
Bresnan, J., 10
Broadbent, D. E., 130
Broselow, E., 116, 118

Brown, C., 117
Brown, C. M., 22, 27, 51, 111
Burt, M., 101
Bygate, M., 130

C

Cadiorno, T., 130
Cappa, S. F., 35
Cappella, J., 16
Caramazza, A., xxi, xxii, xxiii, 3, 26, 59, 60, 61, 62, 63, 64, 78, 93, 94, 95, 96, 108, 110, 111, 170, 172
Carlson, R. A., 155
Chan, Y.-H. C., 102
Chen, H.-C., 175
Chen, S.-I., 116, 118
Cheng, P. W., 41, 157
Chomsky, N., 4, 91, 101, 103
Clahsen, H., 101, 102, 104, 105
Clark, E. V., 85
Clark, H. H., 136
Cohen, A. D., 147
Colomé, A., xxi, xxiii, 3, 58 59, 60, 62, 66, 110, 111, 170, 172
Costa, A., xxi, xxii, xxiii, 59, 60, 61, 62, 63, 64, 66, 67, 78, 93, 94, 95, 96, 108, 110, 111, 170, 172
Craik, F. I. M., 89
Crystal, D., xvii
Curley, J., 75
Cutillas Espinosa, J. A., 120

D

Damian, M. F., 24, 95
de Bot, K., xx, xxi, xxiv, 3, 57, 58, 59, 60, 62, 65, 83, 110, 170
de Gelder, B., 76

de Groot, A. M. B., xxii, 3, 68, 69, 70,
        73, 75, 76, 78, 79, 80, 85, 87,
        169, 179
de Smedt, K., 129
DeKeyser, R. M., 39, 43, 133, 158, 159
Dell, G. S., xix, 3, 4, 5, 6, 24, 27, 30, 49,
        122, 136, 170
Dénes, M., 164
Deschamps, A., 154
Di Biase, B., xxv, 99, 101, 104, 106,
        107, 109
Dijsktra, A., xxiii, 59, 77, 110, 111, 172
Döpke, S., 103
Dörnyei, Z., xxiv, 137, 138, 139, 143,
        144, 148, 152, 153, 174, 176
Dufour, R., 75, 78
Dulay, H., 101
Dumas, G., 147
Dumas, S. T., 39
Dunkel, P., 162, 164
Douglass, S., 44

E

Eckman, F., 116, 118
Eeg-Olofsson, M., xx
Ejzenberg, R., 162, 163
Ellis, N., 45, 46, 48, 55, 85, 102, 103,
        159
Ervin, S., 72
Eubank, L., 101
Evans, M., 132, 133

F

Færch, C., xxiv, 138, 141, 146, 147
Fathman, A. K., 130, 131
Feldman, L. B., 73, 74, 75, 77
Feldstein, S., 16
Felix, S., 101
Fiez, J. A., 15
Fillmore, C. J., 155
Fincham, J. M., 44
Flege, J. E., 110, 114, 117, 118, 119,
        121, 173
Foster, P., 130
Francis. W. S., 68, 169

Franck, J., xxii, 93, 94, 95, 96, 108, 110
Freed, B., 162, 163, 164
Frieda, E. M., 110, 17, 119, 121
Friedman, L. A., 13
Frota, S., 130, 135
Fry, D., xix, 3, 4
Fulcher, G., 162

G

Garnsey, S. M., 30, 122
Garrett, M. F., xix, 3, 4, 24
Gass, S. M., 137, 191
Gathercole, S. E., 130
Gertsman, L., 16
Goldman-Eisler, F., 16
Gollan, T. H., 111
Gomez, O., xxi, 62, 66, 170
Govindjee, A., 6, 117
Grainger, J., 77
Green, D. W., 65, 66
Green, P. S., 130
Greene, J., 16
Grosjean, F., 56, 83

H

Ha, M. A., 133, 158, 159
Haberzettl, S., 107
Hagoort, P., 22, 27, 51, 111
Hahne, A., 22, 111
Håkansson, G., xxv, 99, 101, 104, 106,
        107, 109
Hancin-Bhatt, B., 110, 117, 118
Hansen, J. G., 120
Harnishfeger, K. K., 79
Hartsuiker, R. J., 33, 127
Hatch, E. M., 150
Havinga, J., 6
Hawkins, R., 102, 44, 162, 163, 164, 178
Hecht, K., 130
Hellwig, F., 24
Henderson, A., 16
Hermans, D., xxi, xxiii, 57, 58, 59, 60,
        62, 63, 65, 110, 111, 170, 172
Hieke, A. E., 162, 164
Hintzman, D., 68, 79, 169

Hoenkamp, E., 8, 23, 104, 105, 140,
        171, 175
Hogan, J., 120
Holden, K., 120
Hooglander, A., 76, 77
Hooper, J., 80
Hudson, P. T. W., 21
Hulstijn, J. H., 87, 89, 90, 180

I

Indefrey, P., 24, 33, 34, 37
Iverson, G., 118
Izumi, S., 123, 134

J

Jackendoff, R., 103
Jacoby, L. L., 40
Jaffe, J., 16
Jake, J., 83, 84, 97, 98, 106, 108, 175
Janssen, N., xxiii, 59, 110, 111, 172
Jarvis, S., 70, 85
Jescheniak, J. D., 21, 22, 26, 111
Jiang, N., 55, 85, 177
Johnston, M., 105, 107
Juliano, C., 6, 27, 170

K

Kahnemann, D., 29
Kasper, G., xxiv, 45, 81, 138, 141, 146,
        147
Kawaguchi, S., xxv, 99, 101, 104, 106,
        107, 109
Keating, P. A., 113
Keatley, C., 76
Keidel, J. L., 117, 119
Kellermann, E., 140, 145, 152, 158, 165
Kempe, V., 103
Kempen, G., 8, 3, 91, 104, 105, 129,
        140, 171, 175
Kerling, R., 76, 77
Kim, E., 116
Kirsner, K., 16
Kluender, K. R., 117, 119

Kolk, H., 11, 31, 33, 50, 123, 127, 173
Kormos, J., xxiv, 123, 124, 125, 126,
        128, 129, 131, 132, 133, 134,
        136, 137, 143, 144, 148, 151,
        153, 164, 173, 176
Kovacic, D., xxii, 93, 94, 95, 96, 108,
        110
Kroll, J., xxii, xxiii, 59, 66, 72, 73, 75,
        76, 78, 79, 87, 88, 110, 111,
        171, 172, 179, 180
Kushnir, S. L., 57

L

La Heij, W., xxv, 18, 19, 20, 21, 35, 45,
        56, 63, 64, 67, 76, 77, 84, 90,
        128, 170, 171, 175, 179
Laeufer, C., 110, 113, 115
Lauer, M., 24, 95
Lapkin, S., 135, 184
Laufer, B., 87, 89, 90
Laver, J., xix, 3, 122, 128, 136
Leather, J., xxvi, 116, 120, 181
Lee, M. W., xxi, 61, 62, 66, 170
Lennon, P., 130, 131, 133, 154, 155,
        156, 162, 163, 164, 165
Levelt, W. J. M., xix, xx, xxi, xxiv, 3, 4,
        6, 7, 8, 9, 10, 11, 15, 16, 17,
        18, 20, 21, 24, 25, 26, 27, 28,
        30, 31, 32, 33, 34, 35, 36, 37,
        44, 45, 49, 51, 55, 56, 67, 68,
        80, 84, 91, 92, 93, 99, 108,
        122, 124, 125, 126, 127, 128,
        129, 134, 136, 139, 140, 141,
        147, 149, 157, 166, 167, 170,
        173, 178, 179
Lockhart, R. S., 89
Logan, G. D., 42, 43, 45, 46, 135, 158
Lombardi, L., 25, 99
Lueng, Y.-S., 175

M

MacKay, D. G., 27, 30, 32, 43, 47, 122,
        134, 135, 136, 160, 178
Mackey, A., 105
MacLeod, C. M., 57

MacSwan, J., xxv, 108
MacWhinney, B., 102, 103, 118, 126, 162,
Major, R., 116
Mansouri, F., 106
Marslen-Wilson, W., 127
Matessa, M., 47
McLaughlin, B., 157
McNamara, J., 57
Meara, P., xxii, 81, 82, 85, 86, 87, 88, 89, 171, 177
Meijer, P. J. A., 25, 50, 99, 109, 180
Meisel, J. 102, 104, 105
Meisel, J. M., 102
Meringer, R., 3
Meyer, A. S., xix, xxi, 3, 6, 7, 9, 18, 20, 21, 24, 26, 27, 28, 45, 55, 67, 68, 80, 84, 93, 112, 122, 124, 127, 129, 134, 136, 170, 181
Meuter, R. F. I., 66
Miozzo, M., xxi, 3, 26, 61, 62, 63, 64, 95
Mitchell, R., 80
Mitton, J. L., 31, 33, 127
Mohanan, K. P., 162
Möhle, D., 162
Moon, R., xx
Morton, J., 67
Motley, M. T., 30, 122, 136
Mowrey, R. A., 27
Murre, J. M. J., 103
Muysken, P., 101
Myers-Scotton, C., xxiii, 83, 84, 97, 98, 106, 108, 175
Myles, F., 80

N

Nation, I. S. P., 80
Neely, J. H., 40
Newell, A., 42, 152
Nooteboom, S. G., xix, 3, 31, 122, 128
Noordanus, C., 33
Norman, D. A., 31, 32
Nosofsky, R. M., 44, 46

O

O'Connell, D. C., 13

O'Connor, N., 132, 133, 134
Odlin, T., 55, 84
Ooemen, C. E., 33, 127
Oppenheim, N., 160
O'Seaghda, G. P., xix, 3, 6, 122, 136
Osgood, C. E., 72

P

Palmeri, T. J., 44, 46
Paradis, M., 68, 69, 70, 80, 91, 100
Parrish, B., 130
Pavlenko, A., xxi, 68, 69, 70, 71, 80, 85
Pawley, A., xx, 44, 152, 159, 170
Pechmann T., 6
Perani, D., 35
Peters, A. M., 46
Peterson, R. R., 21, 111
Phaf, R. H., 21
Pica, T., 137
Pienemann, M., xxv, 92, 98, 99, 101, 104, 105, 106, 107, 109, 175
Poot, R., 76
Poplack, S., 55, 107, 108
Posner, M. I., 40
Postma, A., 11, 31, 33, 50, 123, 127, 173
Potter, M. C., 25, 73, 74, 75, 77, 99
Poulisse, N., xxi, xxiii, xiv, xxv, 55, 60, 86, 110, 113, 121, 134, 137, 140, 141, 144, 145, 146, 153, 157, 172, 176, 178, 180
Prince, A. S., 91, 116

R

Rahman, R. A., 22
Randazza, L. A., 110, 117, 119, 121
Raupach, M., 152, 154, 156, 157, 158
Rehbein, J., 154, 155, 159, 164
Rekart, D., 162, 164
Rice, K., 117
Riggenbach, H., 162, 163, 164
Roberts, B., 16
Robinson, P., 130, 133, 135, 139, 158, 159
Roelofs, A., xix, xxi, xxiii, 3, 6, 7, 9, 14, 18, 20, 21, 24, 26, 27, 28, 29, 35, 36, 45, 49, 50, 55, 64, 67, 68, 69,

70, 80, 84, 93, 109, 110, 112,
113, 114, 121, 122, 124, 127,
129, 134, 136, 149, 170, 172,
173, 181
Rogers, S., 132
Rosenbloom, P., 42,152
Rubach, J., 118
Rubin, E., 108

S

Sajavaara, K., 154, 155, 164
Sankaranarayanan, A., 76
Savoy, P., 21, 111
Sayehli, S., 107
Schiller, N. O., 95
Schils, E., 153
Schmidt, R., 103, 130, 135, 152, 155, 156,
159, 181
Schmitt, B. M., 26, 93
Schmitt, N., 85, 87, 88, 177
Schneider, W., 39, 40, 155
Schreuder, R., xx, xxi, 3, 57, 58, 59, 60,
62, 65, 83, 110, 170
Schriefers, H., xxiii, 6, 21, 26, 59, 93, 95,
110, 111, 172
Schwanenflugel, P. J., 79
Schwartz, B., 102
Scott, M. L., xxiv, 137, 138, 139, 150, 174,
176
Searle, J., 9
Sebastian-Gallés, N., xxi, xxiii, 59, 60, 62,
66, 78, 111, 170, 172
Segalowitz, N., 40, 42, 159
Segalowitz, S., 42
Seidenberg, M. S., 117, 119
Seif, S., 144
Selinker, L., 100, 137, 138
Servan-Schreiber, E., 42
Sharwood-Smith, M., 87, 99, 103, 104,
177
Shattuck-Hufnagel, S., 27
Shiffrin, R. M., 39, 40
Sholl, A., 75, 76, 78
Silverberg, N. B., 111
Skarbek, A., 16
Skehan, P., 130
Smolensky, P., 91, 116

So, K.-F., 73, 74, 75, 77
Sommer, W., 22
Spinks, J., 76
Sprouse, R., 102
Starreveld, P. A., 20, 21
Stemberger, J. P., xix, 3, 4, 24, 122
Stewart, E., 75, 76, 79, 88, 171
Stowe, R. W., 79
Sullivan, M., 155
Swain, M., 134, 135, 153, 184
Syder, F. H., xx, 44, 152, 159, 170

T

Talamas, A., 75, 78
Tarone, E., xxiv, 130, 137, 138, 141, 147
Tokowitz, N., xxii, 66, 72, 76, 87, 180
Tonkyn, A., 162
Toribio, A. J., 108
Towell, R., 162, 163, 164, 178
Trammell, R. L., 120
Tree, J .E. F., 25, 50, 99, 100, 109, 180
Treisman, A., 29
Truscott, J., 87, 99, 103, 104, 177
Tyler, L., 127

U

Ullman, T., 91, 100, 161, 162, 167

V

Vainikka, A., 101
van den Boogaard, S., 56, 63, 170
Vanderplank, R., 163, 164
van der Heijden, A. H. C., 21
van der Velden, E., 76, 77
van Gelderen, A., 163, 164
van Hell, J. G., 79, 86
van Hest, E., xxiv, 123, 127, 128, 129, 130,
131, 132, 133, 134, 152, 160
van Heuven, W. J. B., 77
van Turennout, M., 22, 27, 51, 111
VanPatten, B., 130
Váradi, T., 141
Varonis, E. M., 191
Verhoeven, L. T., 132

Vigliocco, G., 24, 95
Vinson, D. P., 24
Von Eckardt, B., 73, 74, 75, 77
Vorberg, T., 6
Vosse, T., 91

W

Wang, C., 116, 118
Walley, A. C., 110, 117, 119, 121
Warner, R. M., 16
Wennerstorm, A., 162, 164
Wei, L., 106
Weinreich, U., 71, 72, 74, 113
Wheeldon, L. R., 32
White, L., 101, 102
Widdowson, H., 55
Wiese, R., 154
Wilks, C., 81, 171

Williams, J. N., xxi, 61, 62, 66, 170
Wolter, B., xx, 81, 82, 89, 171
Wong Fillmore, L., 159
Wood, A., 42
Woolford, E., xxv, 108
Wray, A., 45, 46, 159

Y

Yarmohammadi, L., 144
Yorio, C. A., 159
Young-Scholten, M., 101, 118
Yule, G., 140

Z

Zevin, J. D., 117, 119
Zhang, Y., 106

Subject Index

A

Adaptive Control of Thought Star (ACT*) model, 41–42, 47, 135, 156–159, 161–162, 165, 191
Acquisition by Processing Theory (APT), 87, 99, 103–104, 107, 109
Activation spreading, xix, 4, 12, 95–96, 122, 128, 130, 136, 207
  backward, xix, 6, 11–12, 30, 37, 122, 167
Activation flow
  from concepts to lexical items, 168
  from the lexical to the phonological level, xxiii, 21–23, 110–111, 167, 172
Activation level, xxii, 21, 24, 62, 65, 67, 77, 87, 95, 104, 109
Age of acquisition, 102, 114, 119
Aphasia, 69–70, 91, 97, 102
Articulator, xxvi, 157, 166
Attention, xviii, xxiv, xxv, xxvi, 16, 21, 30, 38–40, 43, 48, 66, 68, 78–79, 120, 130–134, 136, 140, 147, 152, 154–156, 173
Automatization, xxvi, 38–48, 128, 132, 133, 154, 156–165, 178–179
  of rules, 47–48, 157–159, 161–162
  of lexical access, 47–48, 160

B

Bilingual lexicon, xxii, 55, 68–82, 171
Bilingual mode, 83
Brain, 91, 100, 161, 167–169
Broca area, 34–35

C

Chomsky, Noam, 4, 91, 101, 103
Cascading
  of activation, xxiii, 21–23, 35–37, 110–111, 161, 167, 172, 178
Chunking, 41–42, 45–46, 152, 159–161, 165, 170, 178
Code switching, xxviii, xxv, 3, 55–56, 64, 92–84, 97, 107–109, 113, 142, 144, 174–175
  in syntactic encoding, 107–108, 175
  intentional, 55, 64, 67, 83–84, 175
  lexical, xxv, 64, 67, 82–84, 175
  unintentional, xxv, 3, 55, 83–84
Cognates, 59, 75, 78–79, 86, 111, 119
Communication strategies, xviii, xxiv–xxv, 79, 86, 105, 125–126, 137–153, 174–176
  characteristics of, 139
  definitions of, 138
  grammatical, 146–147, 176
  lexical, 140–146, 176
  phonological, 147–150, 176
Competition model, 102–103, 118, 126, 162
Complex access, simple selection, 67, 90
Compound lexical representation, *see* Lexical representation
Comprehension, 7–10, 31–33, 36–37, 42, 84, 91, 103, 109, 122, 127–128, 134, 136, 138, 149, 152, 167–168, 173
Concepts
  lexical, xxi, 64, 69–70, 144, 167, 176
  non-lexical, xxi, 69, 167
  representation of, 32, 64–65, 68–72, 75–77, 90, 92, 169
  selection of, 19–22, 34, 56–57, 63

Concept mediation model, 74–75, 78
Conceptual feature model, xxii, 79–80
Conceptual transfer, *see* Transfer
Conceptualizer, 7, 10, 17, 48, 53, 85,
         128, 140–141, 166, 170, 178
Complements, 10, 23, 86–87, 92,
         99–100, 105, 107, 146–147,
         171
Concreteness
         of words, 72, 79, 119, 169
Connectionist models, 48, 87, 102–103,
         107, 117, 119, 162
Content morphemes, *see* Morphemes
Control
         in L1 lexical encoding, xxi–xxii, 20–21
         in L2 lexical encoding, 65–67
Convergence problem, 16–17
Coordinate lexical representation, *see*
         Lexical representation

D

Declarative knowledge, 39–42, 44, 91,
         101, 133, 135, 157, 162,
         167–169, 171–174, 176–179
Declarative/procedural model, 91, 161,
         167
Determiners, 4, 23–24, 26, 97–98, 105,
         107–109, 146–147
Diacritic value, xxii, 23, 86, 92, 93–96,
         105, 107–109, 146–147
Discourse model, 7
Distributed feature model, 79–80, 85

E

Early system morphemes, *see* Mor-
         phemes
Editor, 122, 128, 136, *see also* Monitoring
Embedded language, 84, 108, 175
Episodic memory, *see* Memory stores
Event-related brain potential (ERP), 14,
         22
Exemplar-based random walk model,
         44, 46, 159, 161

F

Facilitation effect, 28, 57–60, 62–63, 75,
         78, 112–113
         cognate, 59–60, 75
         phonological, 57–59, 78
         translation, 62–63
Feature theory of word meaning, *see*
         Word meaning
Fluency
         definitions of, 154–156
         measurement of, 162–165
         development of, 156–162
Formulaic language, xx, 44–46, 48, 156,
         159–162, 165, 170, 178–179
Formulator, xxvi, 7, 10, 23, 44, 125,
         140–141, 157, 166, 178
Functional magnetic resonance imaging
         (fMRI), 15

G

Gender, xxii, 19, 21, 24, 26–27, 86,
         92–96, 108–109, 146, 171
Gestural scores, xxvi, 7, 29, 110, 114,
         118, 167–168
Go/no go task, 22

H

Hypernym problem, 17

I

Incremental processing, 7–8, 28, 50, 92,
         104, 110, 112, 166, 181
Incremental procedural grammar, 23,
         91–92, 98, 104, 171, 175,
In-depth processing, 89
Inhibitory control (IC) model, 65–66
Inhibitory processes, 65–67, 115, 171
Instance theory, 42–43, 45–46, 135,
         158
Intonation, 117, 120, 164, 172

J

James, William, 45

L

Language acquisition device, 101–102, 107
Language choice, 83, 169
Language cue, xxi, 67, 77, 83–84, 169–171, 179
Language tag, xx, 64–65, 67, 84, 115, 144
Late system morphemes, *see* Morphemes
Law of contiguity, 45
Lemma
    activation of , 9, 22, 84, 56–60
    selection of, 9, 22, 19–22, 56–66, 160, 170–171
    language specific, 60–66
    non-language specific, 60–66, 170–171
Lexeme, xxii–xxiii, 10, 21, 57, 80, 84, 86, 110–111, 148–150, 167–168, 171–172, 174
Lexical representation, *see also* Bilingual lexicon
    compound, 71–74
    co-ordinate, 71–74
    sub-ordinate, 71–74
Lexicon, *see* Bilingual lexicon
Linearization problem, 92
Linguistic input, 48, 101–103, 107, 117–118, 130, 160, 177

M

Markedness differential hypothesis, 116
Matrix language, 84, 108
Matrix language frame model, 107–108, 175
Mean length of runs, 154, 162–163
Memory stores, xix, xxiv, 23–24, 71–82, 92, 167
    episodic, 167–168, 178
    grammatical, 23–24, 92

semantic, 71–82,
Message abandonment, 141–142
Message replacement, 141–142
Minimalist program, 91, 103
Modularity, 21, 103, 178
Monitoring, xviii, xxiv–xxv, 6, 10–11, 29–33, 36–37, 108–110, 119, 121, 149
    editor theories of, 30, 32–33, 122–123, 135–136
    production theory of, 31–33, 122–123, 135–136
        and attention, xxiv, 130–132
        and proficiency, 130–132, 133–134
Morpheme order principle, 108
Morphemes, 4, 6, 10, 27–28, 49, 91, 97–98, 105–16, 108–110, 119, 121, 149
    bridge, 97–98
    content, 97–98, 106
    interphrasal, 97–98, 105–106
    lexical, 98, 105
    phrasal, 98, 105–106
    system, 97–98, 105–106, 108
        bridge late, 97–98, 106, 108
        outsider late, 97–98, 106, 108

N

Naming latency, 14
Neuroimaging, 3, 12, 14–15, 35–37, 162, 167–168
Node structure theory, 30, 32–33, 135–136

O

Ontogeny model, 116–117
Optimality theory, 91, 116
Output hypothesis, 134–135, 153

P

Parallel speech plan, xx, 83
Parser, 7, 10
Pauses, 13, 16, 133, 139, 151–153, 162–165, 176

filled, 13, 151–152, 163–165
  lexicalized, 151–152, 176
  unfilled, 151–152, 163, 165
Perceptual loop theory, 31–33, 122–123,
    135–136
Phonation time ratio, 157,163, 165
Phonemes, xxiii, xxv–xxvi, 4, 6, 16,
    22–28, 36, 49, 58–59, 61, 86,
    93, 110–121, 126, 149,
    172–173
  representation of, 110, 112–115, 173
Phonological features, 4, 6, 93, 111–113,
    117–118, 120, 149, 176
  competition of, 118
Phonological score, 10
Positron Emission Tomography (PET), 15
Power law of practice, 43
Preverbal plan, xx–xxii, 7, 9–11, 15, 18,
    32, 36, 48, 67, 83–84, 90, 97,
    108–109, 122, 124–126,
    140–141, 144–147, 149–150,
    169, 173, 175–176
Procedural knowledge, 40–41, 91,
    100–101, 157, 162, 171–172,
    175
Proceduralization, 41, 44, 47–48, 135,
    157–158, 177
Processability theory, 92, 98–99, 101,
    104–107, 109, 175

R

Reconceptualization, 141, 143
Repairs, 123–135
  appropriacy, 125–126, 128–129, 131
  covert, 123
  different information, 124–125,
      128–129
  error, 126, 128–129, 131
  pragmatic, 125, 131
  rephrasing, 126–127, 128–129
  syntactic structure of, 129–130
  timing of, 128–129
Resource deficit
  in lexical encoding, 140–146
  in grammatical encoding, 146–147
  in phonological encoding, 147–150
Restructuring, 143, 146
Revised hierarchical model, 75–76, 87

S

Self-correction, see Repair
Self-monitoring, see Monitoring
Semantic memory, see Memory
Semantic interference, 57–60, 62
Simple access, complex selection, 45,
    64–65
Slip of the tongue, xxi, 13, 57, 83, 110,
    113, 134, 157, 174
Specifier, 23, 92, 105, 107, 147
Speech learning model, 117–119
Speech rate, 133, 154, 162–165
Spreading activation theory, xix, xx,
    xxiv, xxvi, 3–7, 11–12, 15, 25,
    27, 31, 35–37, 49
Stalling mechanisms, 140, 150–151
Strength theory, 43, 47–48, 135,
    160–161
Stress, 10, 28, 117, 120
Stroop task, 13, 20, 66
Sub-ordinate lexical representation, see
    Lexical representation
Supervisory attentional system (SAS), 65
Switching cost, 66
Syllable, xxiv, xxvi, 4–7, 28–29, 32,
    49–50,110, 112–113, 116–117,
    119–121, 166–168, 173–174
Syllabary, xxiv, xxv, 7, 10, 29, 110, 167,
    173, 178
Syntactic frames, 4, 6, 11, 23–25, 36, 49,
    84, 108
Syntactic rules, 23, 44–48, 91–93,
    99–107, 158, 174–175, 133,
    167
System morphemes, see Morphemes

T

Task activation, 20
Temporal cycle, 15–16, 34
Tip-of-the-tongue phenomenon, 26, 148,
    150
Transfer, xxv, 84–86, 101–104,
    106–118, 120, 147–149,
    152–153, 157, 172–175
  conceptual, xxv, 84–85
  conscious, xxv, 86, 174

lexical, xxv, 84–86
syntactic, xxv, 86, 99, 101–104,
            106–107, 109, 147–148, 157,
            172, 175
phonological, xxv, 116–118, 120, 149,
            173, 175
unconscious, xxv
Translation-facilitation effect, *see* Facili-
            tation effect

U

Universal grammar, 87, 101–104, 116

V

Voice Onset Timing (VOT), 119

W

Wernicke area, 34
Word association model, 74–75, 78
Word form Encoding by Activation and
            VERification (WEAVER)
            model, 27–29, 109–110, 112
Word knowledge, 83, 86–90
    acquisition of, 86–90
    active, 89
    passive, 89
Word meaning, xxi, 4, 17–18, 68, 76,
            79–80, 85–86, 88, 169
    feature theory of, 17
Word order, 4, 24, 91, 93,101–102, 106
Word translation, 74, 76–78
Working memory, 39, 41, 46, 130, 135,
            152